NEO-FREUDIAN SOCIAL PHILOSOPHY

NEO-HEGELIAN SOCIAL PHILOSOPHY

Neo-Freudian
Social Philosophy

MARTIN BIRNBACH

———

STANFORD UNIVERSITY PRESS
STANFORD, CALIFORNIA
1961

Stanford University Press
Stanford, California
London: Oxford University Press

© 1961 by the Board of Trustees of the
Leland Stanford Junior University

Library of Congress Catalog Card Number: 61-12389
Printed in the United States of America

Published with the assistance of
the Ford Foundation

ACKNOWLEDGMENTS

RECOGNIZING the obligations I owe to others in connection with this book is more of a pleasure than falls to the lot of most authors, for those who contributed to making the volume possible did so as much by their personal qualities as by their professional or technical competence. Unhappily, the few words allowed me here by the conventions of authorship are insufficient for conveying the gratitude I feel toward them.

It was Dr. Harold Ehrlich, formerly of the Department of Economics of Rutgers University, who first pointed out to me the significance of Neo-Freudian thought and suggested its more than passing relevance to the social sciences generally and to political science in particular. And it was Professor Edward McNall Burns, Chairman of the Department of Political Science at Rutgers, who urged upon me the desirability of demonstrating such relevance with a work of this kind, and who supervised my research for it with the wisdom, foresight, and constructive criticism his students have one and all found to be among his leading attributes as a teacher. To both of these gentlemen I am indebted in the way that scholars are happy to be to their sources of intellectual stimulation.

If my translations from the German in the text below are correct, it is largely due to the invaluable aid rendered by my erstwhile colleague in the Department of Political Science at Rutgers, Mr. Charles R. Naef, in verifying them. It goes without saying, however, that I alone take full responsibility for their accuracy.

In carrying on research I have availed myself liberally of the facilities of the libraries at Rutgers University and the University of Puerto Rico, making especially heavy drafts upon the ingenuity of the research staff of the former. Miss Gini Lobaugh exhibited more patience and loyalty than any author has a right to expect from a typist. Proofreading chores were ungrudgingly shared by Misses María del Rosario Rodríguez Couto and Edna Droz Lube, and Mr. Germán A. González.

Acknowledgments for permission to quote from copyrighted material are rendered in the notes. It would be improper, however, to omit mention of my indebtedness to those who did not request special mention, for their unmeasured generosity is just as great a boon to scholarship. In particular, I wish to thank Professor Harold D. Lasswell for allowing me to employ extensive quotations from certain of his works, and Dr. Erich Fromm for similar largesse with respect to some of his earlier writings.

The confidence in my academic and personal capabilities displayed by Miss Winifred M. Darter and Mrs. Bernadette Potter (née McManus) has been an unfailing source of support over many years. But of this no one has given more amply than my wife Hilda, to whom a mere literary work would be an inadequate dedication.

M. B.

CONTENTS

1

THE
FREUDIAN SYSTEM:
ESSENTIALS

THIS BOOK is written from the standpoint of political science, and, more particularly, political philosophy. It is intended for the use of students and practitioners of all the social sciences. Even at this late date some may feel it still pertinent to ask, What has psychoanalysis to do with the social sciences? The answer is easy. Political science, like any of the social sciences, has to do with people. No matter how grandiose its concepts, how intricate its terminology, how subtle its analysis of social institutions or their historical development, sooner or later political science must come to grips with human beings. The problems it explores are at bottom the problems of men and women. To know more about these problems and ways of solving them it must know more, and more exactly, about people. Anything else is intellectual pyrotechnics at best, professional delinquency at worst. The same applies, *mutatis mutandis,* to the other social sciences.

The political scientist might assert some advantage over his colleagues in other fields. He can always turn to a great corpus of wisdom distilled over the centuries by Western political philosophers, dealing with such fundamental questions as what human nature is, how and to what extent (if at all) human beings are molded by their social environment, and how people can be expected to act in a political context. Yet any student who has acquainted himself with their writings must be puzzled at the various and sometimes contradictory answers they give. Aristotle's opinion of human nature is obviously different from Plato's, Jefferson's from Luther's, Hobbes's from Cicero's. Karl Marx's views on the effects of the environment on man could conceivably be shown to be similar to Rousseau's, but neither of them could be reconciled easily with those of St. Thomas Aquinas or Montesquieu. Lenin seems to have had little respect for the injunction of St. Paul about obeying the powers that be, yet he probably would not have felt a bond of kinship with another apologist for revolution, John Locke. The list is well-nigh inexhaustible. This legacy to political science is an embarrassment of riches that other social scientists perhaps need not envy.

If these and other basic issues have not been settled by now, it is not for want of application. A more legitimate question is whether they ever can be given a definitive treatment at all. After all, each generation solves its own problems in its own way. Aside from the fact that the social sciences are growing bodies of thought and practice and cannot remain fixed or complacent, the society in which they operate is ever changing and ever beset by new problems, though some of them no doubt are merely varieties of old ones. The Neo-Freudians make fresh proposals that accord with the needs of the present time, both socially and intellectually. Their writings contain a conception of man as he exists in our society, evidence of how he is formed by that society, and a social philosophy that does much to explain his behavior in a political or, if you like, a social context. Whether the truths they have uncovered will be valid for all eternity is not the issue. They may, however, be of guidance to social scientists in canvassing ideas in their respective fields of study. The present volume essays a synthesis and elucidation of their thoughts.

One of the faults of the term Neo-Freudian is that it means nothing to those unfamiliar with psychoanalytic literature. Who are the members of this oddly named group, and what doctrines do they mutually espouse to distinguish them from the more recognizable orthodox "Freudian" psychoanalysts? The first question is answered quickly enough. The names that are met with almost always include Karen Horney, Erich Fromm, Harry Stack Sullivan, and Abram Kardiner; sometimes Franz Alexander is mentioned too. If the term is used very loosely, Harold D. Lasswell is occasionally numbered among them, although we shall have cause to examine Lasswell's credentials with care.

It can be demonstrated that the people under study have sufficient in common to be called a school.* While none of them alone presents a fully developed social philosophy, a collation of their views on aspects of social life will, it is expected, be of value in reexamining some of the conventional categories of social philosophy. Such a reappraisal will not be attempted in any detail here; it is only urged that it will be well to do so in future forays into the field. What is of particular importance is the unique interpretation of "human nature" and its development that is afforded by their special technique, psychoanalysis. Political scientists in particular may well ruminate on the applicability of their discoveries to a more venerable discipline somewhat in need of resuscitation.

Another fault with the term Neo-Freudian is that it requires some explication of the term Freudian. For one thing, it is in large measure their differences from Freud that lend coherence to the Neo-Freudians as a school (Lasswell to a great extent being excepted). More important, the conclusions pointed to by the two trends of thought are much at variance. We shall therefore have to devote more than a few words to the Freudian system itself, less for its own sake than for what it portends for its successor.

The vagaries of psychoanalysis as a therapeutic science and as a source of philosophy are already notorious despite its mere six decades or so of existence. The system of its founder offers

* The late historian of three of the Neo-Freudians, Clara Thompson, mentions the obvious fact that Fromm, Horney, and Sullivan have exchanged mutually supplementary views over the years (*Psychoanalysis: Evolution and Development*, p. 122). The three joined forces when the first two reached the United States in the early 1930's (*ibid.*, p. 196). See also the Biographical Sketches, *infra*, pp. 233-37.

particular difficulties in this respect, for its misunderstanding at large has proceeded apace with its absorption into the intellectual heritage of our own time—which may be two ways of saying the same thing. Prolific writer that he was, Freud kept his leading concepts in a state of flux, as might be expected of a man whose chief motivation in life was to find out, to discover. As a result, his continued acquisition of fresh knowledge necessitated frequent and unabashed amendment of what at one time were plausible hypotheses. As one legend has it that Marx once denied being a Marxist, so another has it that Freud exclaimed on one occasion, "Moi je ne suis pas un freudiste."[1] Eric F. Goldman's canny observation is worth repeating: "Freud, like so many seminal thinkers, was less important for what he meant to say than for what he was said to mean."[2] After too long a period of sharing honors with his earliest collaborator, Josef Breuer, Freud stated in no uncertain terms, "Psychoanalysis is my creation."[3] It was created as an experimental improvement in the then current practices of neurology, in that it regarded "nervousness" not as the result of lesions in the nervous system but as disruption of mental processes. The new demonstration of causation, or etiology, was to be a psychic one, not a somatic one. Rounding this out into a body of medical knowledge would have occupied an ordinary man for a lifetime. Extraordinary man that he was, Freud exploited the findings of psychoanalysis enough to give it the attributes of a *Weltanschauung,* "an intellectual construction, which gives a unified solution of all the problems of our existence," covering all questions of human life and interest.[4]

For centuries it had been the practice of philosophy and its younger sister, psychology, to equate "mental processes" with "consciousness." The material with which these disciplines were accustomed to deal was what occupied sane, normal men in moments of ratiocinative reflection, as subject, of course, to the rules of logic. Freud dispensed with this naïve tradition at a blow. The first edition of his greatest work, *The Interpretation of*

1. Numbered notes (primarily source citations) will be found at the back of the book, pp. 239–66.

Dreams (1899), was not a best-seller by any standards,* but by the time Freud introduced psychoanalysis to the lay public at two series of lectures at the University of Vienna in 1915–17 he could boldly state that the essential feature of mental life was that it was unconscious, that consciousness consists only of isolated fragments of the total. He believed that this "decisive step towards a new orientation in the world and in science" was of a magnitude comparable to the revolutions of Copernicus and Darwin. It had in common with them the infliction of an outrage on human self-love. Copernicus had shown the earth to be a mere mite in the immeasurable vastness of creation; Darwin had shown man to be an animal and a descendant of animals; psychological research was showing man "that he is not even master in his own house," having to be content with only shreds of information about the unconscious aspect of his mental processes. This unwelcome disclosure, Freud felt, was the core of the revulsion that greeted the new science. Emotional reactions stood in the way of accepting the idea of an unconscious, for "no one is desirous of becoming acquainted with his unconscious, and it is most convenient to deny altogether its possibility."[5]

Freud valued his discovery of the unconscious so highly that he ruled the acceptance of unconscious mental processes—among other fundamentals—to be a *sine qua non* for analysts. Only the division of mental life into conscious and unconscious permitted understanding pathological mental functioning. Consciousness was but one property of mental life, and not a necessary property at that. When Adler stressed the strivings of the conscious ego at the expense of the unconscious, Freud considered him to have wandered from the proper subject matter of psychoanalysis; this difference was responsible for Adler's split from the psychoanalytic movement.[6]

Nor is "unconscious" only an adjective describing a style of

* Ernest Jones states that it took eight years to sell the six hundred copies (*The Life and Work of Sigmund Freud*, I, 360). I have accepted throughout Jones's masterful documentation of Freud's *vitae*, though when it came to evaluating his work I have been wary of his unstinted adulation of the master.

mental functioning; it is also a noun referring to a topographical location.* In *The Interpretation of Dreams* Freud used the figure of speech of a larger circle, the unconscious, enclosing a smaller one, the conscious, the latter being as reliable a source of knowledge of the former as our sensory organs are in communicating the outer world to us—that is to say, imperfect. This inner (and unconscious) psychic reality, furthermore, must not be confused with outer, material reality; to the individual, "the unconscious is the true psychic reality," a complete psychic process in itself.[7] That which the individual does not ordinarily know of himself runs *pari passu* with his conscious knowledge of himself, is ordinarily outside the jurisdiction of his cognitive powers, and is yet his real psychic self. Thus man could no longer be master in his own house, the house of his psyche.

The frank materialism that underlay Freudian psychology would itself have assured it an unfriendly reception. Its opponents were also horrified by the importance it placed on sexuality, and in particular on the sexual life of infants. Finally, no small part of the opposition was due to anti-Semitism. Five of the "Committee" of six that gathered around Freud, after the split with Jung, to propagate the new doctrine and preserve its purity, were Jewish.†

Exactly what this fresh formulation portended it would have been hard to say in 1899. To Freud it offered splendid possibilities for psychotherapy. It is beside our purpose to enter into the details of psychoanalysis as a therapeutic method, but its broad principles include the following. If it be true that the neuroses constitute "disorders of the ego," or what is commonly called the conscious mind, by the action of forces lurking in the unconscious, and if it be true that the psychic conflict cannot be resolved until the contestants meet on even ground, then it is the task of the

---

* The diagram on p. 111 of the *New Introductory Lectures* makes this clear.

† It has even been suggested that one of the reasons why Jung and some of his Zürich colleagues were accepted into the movement was to "form a protective coating" for its almost solidly Jewish Viennese membership. (Schoenwald, pp. 126, 134. See also Jones, II, 69–70.)

psychotherapist to aid the patient to substitute "something conscious for something unconscious." In reliving—abreacting—the repressing experiences as new editions of early conflicts, the patient transfers, as it were, the precipitating crises onto the analyst. The transference is the crucial part of the analysis, "the battlefield where all the contending forces must meet." In recognizing this conflict for what it is, in using the technique of free association to raise the repressed to the level of consciousness where the matter may be brought to a rational decision, the dead hand of the past is lifted and the individual may—in words strangely familiar to political scientists—"become his best self, what he would have been under the most favourable conditions."[8]

The "best self" theory is familiar from the writings of such disparate political philosophers as Harold J. Laski and T. H. Green.[9] The rationalistic bias of nineteenth-century European liberalism was congenial to what we shall see was the rational basis of Freud's own system. The modernized version of liberalism, the program of liberating the individual's energies so that he may live the good life on a higher plane, according to his rational best self, finds an echo in the psychoanalyst's aim of aiding the patient to resolve his psychic difficulties by the use of reason. A revised liberalism charges government with the responsibility of providing the conditions in which liberated energies can operate at their optimum. Freudian psychoanalysis, by analogy, accepts the task of helping to clear a free field for the activity of the rational faculty.

Part of the Freudian revolution was the eradication of the hitherto clear distinction between the healthy and the neurotic. Neuroses were now seen to be but variations of normal mental life; the demarcation was no longer discrete but continuous. As Harold D. Lasswell put it, the dividing line between normal and abnormal "is not a cliff but a slope, and case histories of the sick are not too different from those of the well." Hardly any normal condition does not show signs of neurotic traits. Moreover, as Ernest Jones afterward remarked, psychopathology opened a route to psychology in general, perhaps the most practicable route.[10]

To the charge that it was illegitimate to formulate a psychology of normality on the basis of pathological material, it was easy to reply that all types of mental life find their expression in the common experience of dreams. Other types of everyday behavior, such as slips of the tongue or absences of mind—parapraxes, in the technical term—and certain types of wit and humor, which all people share, told the same story.[11] The unpracticed layman passes these by without notice; the skilled analyst recognizes the most petty nuances of behavior, expression, and posture as clues to the workings of the unconscious. This "rubbish-heap, as it were, of our observations" could yield gems if one knew how to interpret what one observed.[12] But the surest path to the unconscious was the first-named: "The interpretation of dreams is the *via regia* to a knowledge of the unconscious element in our psychic life."[13] The analyst, in probing behind the manifest dream-content to the latent dream-content, unravels the dream-work by the technique of dream interpretation Freud devised, and finds the dream to be in all cases the symbolic fulfillment of a wish.[14] Conjecture over the nature of these wishes was to occupy Freud for years to come. It gave rise to his theory of instincts.

Although Freud called the unconscious "the Kingdom of the Illogical,"[15] his clinical practice required him to formulate some explanation of its workings. Before he was done, Freud was to devise two theories of instincts, with an intervening hypothesis that was too short-lived to be systematized. The resemblance of Neo-Freudian formulations to the first theory requires an exposition of it here. Freud's early psychoanalytic work led him to postulate the existence of two basic instincts, the ego and the sexual, with all others to be subsumed under them. Still hewing to the materialistic line, Freud considered an instinct to represent a constant inner somatic source of stimulation, to be set apart from external stimuli. The instincts are to be distinguished not only by the bodily region whence their respective excitations are derived, but also by their respective objects and aims. True, the aim was always the same, the satisfaction accompanying discharge, though it was capable of being changed from activity to passivity. More important, however, was variability in object. The readiness with which one object could be exchanged for another, or the possibility of exchanging oneself for an external object, gave rise to the various perversions and narcissism. To complicate matters still further, the instincts can remain pure or be intermixed with one another.[16]

The two inclusive instincts comprehended between them a good deal of human activity, as indeed they had to. There is also a poetic charm about the theory, for it is both simple and comprehensive. The ego-instinct aims at the preservation of the individual, the sex-instinct at the preservation of the species. Both of them are inherently pleasurable to the individual, for if the mental apparatus can be said to have any purpose, it is in obtaining pleasure and avoiding pain. The pleasure principle automatically regulates the entire activity of the psyche.[17] A biological view of hedonism reveals pleasure to be connected with lowering stimulation, with removing excitation. Energy demands release in a particular direction, and in so doing removes the displeasure that invariably accompanies tension.[18]

It seems that a strict materialism at last gives the long-sought psychological vindication of philosophical hedonism. Everything depends, of course, on the validity of the concept of instincts. It was an acceptable hypothesis in Freud's time, but, as we shall see, it did not satisfy the *Weltanschauung* of a succeeding generation of psychoanalysts. In effect, what Freud was doing was universalizing a phenomenon that was prevalent in the society he knew, the insistent, almost demoniacal, frustration of a basic human urge whose uninhibited indulgence could wreak great social dislocation. If the supreme pleasure of the sexual act were pressed into the service of propagation, which normally takes place with the onset of puberty, the sexual aim would be altruistic while still retaining the purpose of procuring pleasure, Freud maintained. But normality and the blessings of altruism were not to be had cheaply. Sexuality had to be put in harness; the development of erotic felicity could suffer morbid disturbances by the repression of the sexual instinct.[19]

In the meantime, Freud had to justify the equating of "pleasure" with "sexuality." A Benthamite Utilitarian could base an ethic on pleasure without doing violence to contemporary mores; Freud had to make out a convincing case. With the moral courage of his scientific convictions, Freud observed that sexual gratification releases the greatest amount of somatic tension, and hence was the pleasure most people sought most persistently. Society itself had acknowledged the potency of the sexual instinct, for its most rigorous repressions were directed against it. The proof of this relentless restraint lay in our dreams, which are generated above all by unfulfilled unconscious wishes so intense as to confirm that "no other instinct has had to undergo so much suppression, from the time of childhood onwards, as the sexual instinct in all its numerous components."[20] As a corollary, all methods employed by the organism during its development for securing pleasure are correctly regarded as phases in the maturation of sexuality. Thus there are good grounds for saying that the infant, too, has a sexual life, and it is erroneous to exaggerate the distinction between infantile and mature sex life. In fact, what we know in adult sexual life as perversions all occur in infancy, and hence "perverted sexuality is nothing else but infantile sexuality, magnified and separated into its component parts." The perversions are regressions to the stages of pregenital sexuality wherein, during sexual maturation, the erotogenic zones of the body successively come to the fore and meet with disciplines imposed from without. The oral phase is followed by the anal, the phallic, and, after a latency period, the culmination in genital sexuality.[21]

With this broader concept of sexuality Freud could conjecture that nothing of importance happens in the organism that does not assist in the excitement of the sexual instinct. The fact that during psychotherapy sexual overtones invariably entered into the transference, though they were neither sought nor induced by analyst or patient, was "unshakable proof" that neurosis origi-

nated in sexual life.[22] The equating of the sexual with the pleasurable left man a pleasure-seeking animal, as he has ever been
known to be, but in the eyes of his adversaries it also left Freud a
"pan-sexualist," as he has since been known. In psychotherapy,
"sexuality" had to be construed strictly, but for purposes of philosophical speculation it meant not merely genital gratification but
all that Plato had meant by love in the *Symposium*: love of self,
of family, friends, for humanity in general, for concrete objects,
and for abstract ideas, as Freud insisted more than once.[23]

For its part, the ego-instinct operated to modify the pleasure
principle by the supervention of the reality principle. Unmitigated hedonism cannot persist in a world of limited resources.
The grim force of economic need requires some renunciation of
pleasure-seeking activities in the interest of survival of the species
and the diversion, by sublimation, of sexual energies to goals of
social value. In the name of society, education takes up the task
of restraint by teaching avoidance of the pleasures attendant on
purely and persistently hedonic activity. Society depends on the
supremacy of the ego-instinct; the individual pays the price of
renunciation in terms of neurosis. The neurotic conflict is between ego-instincts and sex-instincts.[24]

The first theory of instincts had within it the seeds of a social
philosophy. With civilization founded on the renunciation of instinctual activity—more specifically, the cramping of the sexual
instinct—the resultant social pathology furnished ample grist for
the mill of any psychoanalytically oriented philosopher with liberal inclinations. In an early article on "civilized" sexual morality and modern nervousness, Freud himself was outspoken in his
criticism of the impaired marital relations and degeneration of
character that result from suppression of sexual instincts except
for legitimate procreation:

> On the whole I have not gained the impression that sexual
> abstinence helps to shape energetic, self-reliant men of action,
> nor original thinkers, bold pioneers and reformers; far more
> often it produces "good" weaklings who later become lost in

the crowd that tends to follow painfully the initiative of strong characters.*

Abram Kardiner avers that Freud had no intention of undermining European sexual mores and was far from advocating sexual profligacy as a preventive or curative measure for neurosis. Going further, Erich Fromm argues that if anything, Freud was too conservative, for he lamented sexual repression without a concomitant and equally forceful criticism of his society. In point of fact, when Freud lectured to a public audience his comments on the subject were a bit more moderate than the above quotation would lead one to anticipate. Then he confined psychoanalysis to critical observation of conventional sexual morality and found it could not support society's attitude toward sexual problems. With a trace of irony, he held society's moral code to require more sacrifices than it was worth and to be based on neither honesty nor wisdom.[25]

In the last decade of his life Freud retreated from the "unwarranted responsibility" of training psychoanalysts to be subverters of contemporary social institutions. The goal of therapy, normality, he held to be not emancipation from social standards, but the obtaining of the optimal psychological situation for ego functions, referring, however, to the intrapsychic situation, not to the social situation. "I should go so far as to say that revolutionary children are not desirable from any point of view."[26] The Neo-Freudians were to have different ideas about the social uses of psychoanalysis.

Considerations of social philosophy apart, the initial theory of instincts proved unequal to the demands of even clinical practice. During the First World War the dreams reported by patients were often not wish fulfillments of the sexual instinct at all, for many of them repeated traumatic experiences. Their concern with self-preservation subsumed both instincts under the rubric of narcissism, or self-love, and revealed the self-contradiction of the twofold

* "'Civilized' Sexual Morality and Modern Nervousness" (1908), p. 92. Thus the culmination of the repressive civilization of Orwell's *Nineteen Eighty-Four* is revealed in the pronunciamento, "We shall abolish the orgasm."

theory.[27] When Freud enunciated the first theory of the instincts in the *General Introduction,* it was already obsolete.

The persistence in Freud's thought of a dualistic approach was at the bottom of the new instinct theory elaborated in 1920 in *Beyond the Pleasure Principle.*[28] The opposition between Eros and the death-instinct is the basis of the philosophical speculations which, more than clinical practice, occupied Freud for the last twenty years of his life. It is hard to avoid the impression that intellectual manipulation came to mean more and more to Freud, and careful observation less and less. Meanwhile, the lure of a definitive *Weltanschauung* brought forth a theory that embraced the eternal themes of life and death, love and hate, and, with some imagination, "all the problems of our existence."

Eros, Freud theorized, is the basic instinct that has as its purpose the establishment of ever-greater unities, first individuals and then tribes, races, nations, and, ultimately, humanity. It enables the germ cell to survive its temporary shelter in the individual and reveals its conservative nature by preserving life from dissolution into the antecedent inorganic state. The death-instinct, on the other hand, is the basic instinct that has as its purpose the undoing of connections, destruction. As "the most powerful obstacle to culture," which presses Eros into its service, the death-instinct likewise proves its own conservative nature by providing the motive force for the inertia that is "inherent in organic life" and culminates in death.[29]

With respect to the individual organism, its development is accounted for by external forces. This is so because "the elementary living entity would from its very beginning have had no wish to change." As these stimuli are acquired over the generations they are "accepted by the conservative organic instincts and stored up for further repetition." Thus the progressive appearance of instincts is a deceptive one. The final goal of all organic endeavors is a previously existing state of affairs, ultimately the desire of the organism to perish after its own manner.[30] With instincts as essentially conservative, not to say reactionary, forces, it would be hard for Freud to avoid a conception of human nature as backward-looking, or regressive, insofar as instincts were the instigators of psychic activity. And the introduction of progressive trends into the personality would necessarily make for a perhaps ineradicable conflict as a permanent feature of human nature.

With respect to society, the proximity of organisms provides a temptation to gratify the destructive instinct, and it is the task of Eros so to mitigate the natural state of *homo homine lupus* as to furnish the conditions necessary for common effort to meet the demands of economic want; the common interest in work will not of its own suffice. In words heavy with the realization of a foreboding prophecy, Freud summarized the evolution of human life and works as follows:

> The natural instinct of aggressiveness in man, the hostility of each one against all and of all against each one, opposes this programme of civilization. This instinct of aggression is the derivative and main representative of the death instinct we have found alongside of Eros, sharing his rule over the earth. And now, it seems to me, the meaning of the evolution of culture is no longer a riddle to us. It must represent to us the struggle between Eros and Death, between the instincts of life and the instincts of destruction, as it works itself out in the human species. This struggle is what all life essentially consists of and so the evolution of civilization may be simply described as the struggle of the human species for existence.

The two instincts corresponded more or less to the polarities of attraction and repulsion that were the province of physics, and, as with them, questions of good and evil were beside the point, one instinct being as indispensable as the other. Eros and the death-instinct are "in opposition," yet at the same time they rarely operate in isolation but are always "alloyed" with and serve to modify each other.[31]

It is not clear how both types of relationship are to be carried on simultaneously. There is, in fact, a large dose of metaphysics in evidence throughout the theory of Eros and the death-instinct. Freud seemed more interested in rounding out a system of philosophy than in composing a new theory of neurosis by inductive observation. It is noteworthy that the sexual component of Eros is considerably reduced in emphasis, compared with its predecessor sexual-instinct. Eros is more of a universal force than a biological substrate, and the death-instinct seems to be more of a logical counterpart to it than something that could be perceived at work on the psychoanalytic couch.

More incisive criticism of the instinct theory will have to be left to the Neo-Freudians. We turn next to a vital element in the structure of Freud's thought: the libido theory. The essence of it can be quickly stated. Libido, "a quantitative magnitude, though not at present actually mensurable," is the energy that supplies Eros, the motive force of sexual life directed to an object. "There can be no question that the libido has somatic sources," i.e., that it is a material phenomenon. Stored up in the ego, it is mobile when "cathected," or discharged, toward objects, though it may also float freely during states of tension or be recouped into the ego narcissistically.[32] It is libido that activates the erotogenic zones successively during the sexual maturation of the individual. There is no term analogous to libido for describing the energy that supplies the death-instinct. Freud protested vociferously that broadening libido into a general psychic instinctive energy (thus equating it with Bergson's *élan vital* and robbing it of its exclusively sexual import) would lose all that psychoanalytic observation had gained. When Jung did so, it brought about his split with Freud.[33]

Questions of objective verification aside, the libido theory at least had the virtue of durability, persisting in Freud's thought through all his turnings in instinct theory and social philosophy, and reaffirming Freud's incorrigible materialism.[34] It also gave a solid grounding in human nature for the motive power for such constructive activities as men undertake, while similarly anchoring Freud's own humanistic views. Libido was the energy for Eros, and "love alone acts as the civilizing factor in the sense that it brings a change from egoism to altruism." That applies both to sexual love and to the desexualized, sublimated love of men for each other arising from common labor.[35]

Yet the theory's biological and material foundations were to have the defect of limiting the horizons of any world view. With a constant amount of libido available in the organisms to be cathected toward objects, the range of Eros is circumscribed *ab origo*. It is as though the wages-fund theory of economics had been transposed into a psychological context: an increment of libido to one party must necessarily mean a diminution in the amount available to other parties. The agents in any such relationship are competitors, and there is no possibility of augmenting the prize for which they vie. Thus religious ties, while creating a community of love among those libidinally bound together, result in cruelty and intolerance toward outsiders. Again, with the death-instinct ineradicable, a formula for ending war may have to be an indirect one, positing the promotion of bonds of nonsexual sentiment among men and the reinforcement of their identification with common purposes. Furthermore, to obtain cooperation in the work of maintaining civilization, their limited amount of libidinal energy compels men to divert some to each other, thereby reducing their sense of family responsibility and abetting the hostility of women toward culture. Finally, the divergent trends in the individual, one toward individual happiness and the other toward unity with all humanity, result not from the antagonism between Eros and the death-instinct (which, Freud notes, are probably irreconcilable anyway), but from "a dissension in the camp of the libido itself." Such a strain may be more than Eros can endure: "Who can predict his success and the final outcome?"[36]

Again metaphysical considerations seem to be uppermost in Freud's mind in his concept of libido. It is not easy to verify how this "quantitative magnitude" with "somatic sources" is to be "cathected," or discharged, toward objects, for the action is not observable as a stark material event. The indispensability of libido appears to lie rather in the philosophical completeness it gives to Freud's thought, and it may be to the point to interject Brill's rumination to the effect that he could not help comparing Spinoza's *substantia* with Freud's libido.[37] One may speculate whether the companion theories of the instincts and of libido were intended to have a poetic as well as a scientific quality. It is suggestive that just as the gods of Greek mythology reigned over the affairs of men but were believed to be ruled in their turn by inexorable fate, so the interaction of the instincts "gives rise to the whole variegation of the phenomena of life,"[38] and Eros, at least, is determined by fluctuations in libido. However, to find the direct route to Freud's larger meditations we must proceed with his theory of the structure of the mind.

The topographical metapsychology received its definitive treatment in *The Ego and the Id* (1923), though other writings, in a less technical vein, are more instructive. The oldest and most basic of the mental provinces is the id. It contains the organism's inheritance, especially the instincts, and thus represents the essence of individual organic life, the satisfaction of innate needs. This core of oneself, completely within the unconscious and in some place in direct contact with somatic processes, has no intercourse with the external world. As the locus of the instincts it is "a chaos, a cauldron of seething excitement." The quantitative factor of the pleasure principle alone having relevance to its operations, it is indifferent to good and evil alike. "Instinctual cathexes seeking discharge—that, in our view, is all that the id contains."[39]

The ego is that cortical layer of the id which is modified by contact with the external world. By channeling the influence of the latter onto the id, it counters the pleasure principle with the reality principle. It is indispensable in performing that service for the id, for the blind strivings for gratification of the id would doom it to annihilation. The function of preserving the organism thus belongs to the ego, and hence it alone is susceptible to anxiety. Its perceptive character is the counterpart of the id's instinctive character. It is the ego that we are certain of when self-conscious. "The ego represents what we call reason and sanity," said Freud, "in contrast to the id which contains the passions."[40]

Chronologically, the final part of the psyche is the superego. It is a portion of the external world that the ego has relinquished as an object and incorporated into itself. There it performs the functions formerly undertaken by the surrogates of the external world, the family (and notably the father) and their substitutes and successors—teachers, public figures of note, and ideals. Since parental influence represents, in addition, racial, national, and family traditions, the superego, as conscience, carries on vicariously the expectations of man's higher nature, the censorship of morals. With the function of a censor vis-à-vis the ego, it judges the latter and hence is the source of guilt; the anxious dread of criticism in the ego manifests itself as the need for punishment. The relations of the superego with the ego duplicate the cajolery and discipline of the parents over the child. "The superego is in fact the heir to the Oedipus complex and only arises after that complex has been disposed of." Freud specified, in addition, that, like the other elements of the psyche, the superego is a concrete entity, not merely the representation of such an abstract quality as conscience.[41]

Actually, the ego is the weakest party of the three. It is trapped within the triangle of the three forces of the external world, the superego, and the id. It is hard enough for anyone to serve two masters, but to reconcile the demands of three often divergent tyrants is sometimes beyond its capacity. This "poor creature" is especially at the mercy of the id. Freud described the ego as both an unwilling ally and a humble slave of the id, in that it strives to make the id acquiesce in the demands of the external world and resorts to a strategy of sycophancy to do so, "like a politician who sees the truth but wants to keep his place in popular favour." It is not to be wondered that the ego so easily gives way in its labors and suffers the disorganization that is neurosis.[42]

In a difficult paper Freud explored the subject of anxiety and found it to be a function of the ego (and not, as hitherto thought, of libidinal instinct repression). The three varieties of anxiety, objective, neurotic, and moral, relate respectively to the aforementioned three dependent orientations of the ego.[43] It is clear that Freud considered the ego a receptive agency, not an entity with an integrity and an initiative of its own. The dependent position of reason boded ill for any social philosophy, for this residuary legatee of biology and experience could hardly be relied upon as a buttress of individual or social stability. That Freud was a firm believer in the value of reason will be shown later, but he gave the impression of undermining his own position.

The Oedipus complex is the cornerstone of the Freudian system. It is at once the key to infantile sexuality, to repression, to the origin of neurosis, to the interpretation of dreams, to psychoanalytic therapy (and in particular the transference), and to acculturation and the maturation of the psyche. It is the connecting link between psychoanalysis and anthropology, and between ontogeny, the development of the individual, and phylogeny, the development of the species. It lays bare the rationale for the social order and is the point of departure for understanding mythology, religion, art, semantics, and group behavior. Freud raised it to the level of a shibboleth to separate those who followed psychoanalysis from those who opposed it.[44]

First adumbrated in *The Interpretation of Dreams*, Freud's observations of infantile behavior and the fruits of clinical experience—first and foremost his own self-analysis—led him to realize the fundamental truth in Sophocles' version of the Greek legend.[45] Oedipus' unhappy lot symbolizes the two desires of every man: to slay his father and to have sexual relations with his mother.[46] Love for one parent and hatred for the other are fostered in the infant's early family experience. The interpretation of dreams revealed this plainly enough: the wishes of which dreams are fulfillments are regressive to infancy and are erotic in content. Psychoneurotics manifest these feelings in exaggerated form, and so the Oedipus complex is at the nucleus of neuroses.[47]

But it is apparent that not only early conditioning is responsible for the urges to parricide and incest. The tragedy of Oedipus has universal appeal because "his fate . . . might have been our own, because the oracle laid upon us before our birth the very curse which rested upon him." Freud speaks of an Oedipus "whose *destiny* it was to slay his father and to wed his mother, who did all in his power to avoid the *fate* prophesied by the oracle. . . ."[48] There is thus more than just an interpersonal relationship at work here. It is nothing less than the biological inheritance of the organism itself. The two repressed wishes are not only infantile but archaic; that is, they relate not only to ontogeny but to phylogeny. Freud had observed that, rather than take the immediate, shortest route to its final form, the germ of every organism recapitulates— "even if only in a transient and abbreviated fashion"—its antecedent structures.[49] Could there not be an analogous psychic recapitulation of the species in the individual? Psychically speaking, if the individual's experience not only is a repetition of his own past but reduplicates—in transient and abbreviated fashion—the past of the species as well, then what experience does not supply, the archaic heritage does. To put the matter bluntly, "the archaic heritage of mankind includes not only dispositions, but also ideational contents, memory traces of the experiences of former generations." The archaic heritage does not have to be reacquired but only awakened.[50]

It is of course obvious that the hypothesis rests on the now discredited Lamarckian thesis of the hereditability of acquired characteristics. Freud sought to give a psychoanalytic underpinning to Lamarck, in that the creation and transformation of organs should be considered a somatic response to the psychic power of unconscious mental images, what Freud called "the omnipotence of thoughts." And by Ernest Jones's testimony, Freud was from beginning to end an obdurate adherent of Lamarckism.[51] On this assumption, if what the unconscious contains is "a general possession of mankind,"[52] that is, if the human race has an archaic heritage, psychically speaking, then there is a parallel development of individual and species, with correspondent experiences. And this time the recapitulation is psychic, not merely physical. Considering the crucial role of the Oedipus complex,

Jones has good reason to say that Freud had located a fundamental link between the data of psychoanalysis and of anthropology.[53] The hypothesis was daring, its implications breath-taking. The Oedipus complex is the nexus of Freud's *Weltanschauung*. Without it his thought is a collection of fragments; with it a system of cosmic proportions becomes possible.

Let us pause at this point to survey the central position of the Oedipus complex in the Freudian system, referring first to the elements already discussed. That the Oedipal desires reside within the individual's unconscious is proved by the latent dream-content: "It may be that we were all destined to direct our first sexual impulses toward our mothers, and our first impulses of hatred and violence toward our fathers; our dreams convince us that we were." That being so, what we know of neuroses invariably locates their core in the Oedipus complex. Indeed, "a more or less distinct phase of neurosis" lies along the path of every child's acculturation,[54] for repression of incestuous and parricidal impulses is the *sine qua non* of socialization. As Jones puts it, the child's recapitulation of anywhere between twenty and fifty thousand years of mental evolution leaves hardly any children unscathed; neurotic manifestations are the inevitable accompaniment.[55] In the transference, then, the analyst is a "reincarnation" of one of the patient's parents. Onto the analyst are transferred the emotional reactions that indubitably were directed toward his prototype of infantile days. Overcoming the resistance to such a suggestion and its implications is the essential work of the analysis, and the patient's ego is strengthened by this deepest of self-knowledge.[56]

It is hardly a coincidence that the two instincts, Eros and the death-instinct, correspond to the two halves of the Oedipus complex, incest and parricide. The severe restriction placed on the instincts by repression in the individual is accounted for by the terrible urges they seek to fulfill. Magnified onto a social scale, not only is there a universal prohibition upon incest, but Freud speaks of that sanction as "perhaps the most maiming wound ever inflicted throughout the ages on the erotic life of man."[57] The origin of the prohibition against parricide will be taken up presently. Again magnified onto a social scale, the destructive instincts must be opposed by whatever obstructions culture can summon. Taking the two sets of socially imposed inhibitions together, one could not dispute the contention that civil society rested upon an extraordinary degree of denial of instinctual satisfactions. Culturally fostered privation ramified into the entire area of human social relations.[58] In summary, the price of civilization is discontent.

The Oedipus complex is also consistent with the theory of the libido, by way of infantile sexuality as manifested in the libidinal phases of development. When the phallic phase is reached, that is, when the libido seeks genital cathexes, the quest for gratification via the parent of the opposite sex brings the Oedipal prohibitions into play. Incest is categorically forbidden, and repression of the instinct for it is accompanied by repression of the instinct to wreak vengeance on the menacing parent. Both renunciations are incorporated as the superego; the ensuing latency phase signifies the impossibility of fulfilling the Oedipal urges.[59]

The introjection of parental authority as the superego and the completion of the development of the topography of the psyche—that is, the resolution of the Oedipus complex—bring up the matter of the origin of the prohibition against parricide. In *Totem and Taboo* Freud utilized what he considered to be the best anthropological material then available to substantiate his challenging hypothesis. He undertook a historical reconstruction of primitive society on the theory that the ontogenetic vicissitudes of the Oedipus complex were a recapitulation of the phylogenetic experience of the species in its earliest times.

Primitive religion, totemism, began in the aboriginal form of group life, the primal horde. The incestuous desires of the young males for the mother, who was the exclusive possession of the elder male, precipitated their expulsion from the horde by the father. The exiles were soon to take vengeance, for they joined forces, slew the father, and consumed his remains. Cannibalizing

the victim was a natural act because the brothers desired to identify themselves with the envied yet dreaded father of the horde.
They took on his strength in performing this primitive ritual. Subsequent totem feasts commemorated the act, the act that marked
the commencement of civil society, morality, and religion. For
their sense of guilt impelled in the sons an eternal renunciation
of committing the crime, and moreover they renounced the retrieved women as well. Thus arose the two fundamental taboos
of totemism, corresponding exactly to the two repressed Oedipal
wishes.[60] The physical incorporation of the father and of the authority he represents corresponds of course to the figurative incorporation of parental authority in the individual's resolution of the
Oedipus complex.

Freud tried to guard against the imputation that his theory
would have founded civilization upon a crime by stating that, like
neurotics, primitive men overvalued psychic reality as against actual reality. Therefore the mere wish to kill and cannibalize the
father had sufficed to arouse the moral reaction that created totemism and taboo and with it civil society.[61] But it was of no avail
for his reputation or for the consistency of his anthropology. By
a literal interpretation of primitive events, the veneration of the
totem animal in primitive religious rites was an attempt at recon-
ciliation with the murdered father, a symbolic agreement, as it
were, by which his protection, care, and forbearance were secured
in return for a pledge never to repeat the homicide against his
symbol, the totem animal. It also served to allay the sense of guilt.
Renunciation of the women had an additional, utilitarian, purpose, since it precluded rivalry among the victors for the spoils
and thereby preserved the new social organization from destruction. A prohibition against fratricide joins those against parricide
and incest. With the exaltation of the slain father to a deity, a
more sophisticated form of religion emerges. The appearance of
godlike kings transfers the patriarchal system to society politically
organized.[62] The evolution of the social structure is now complete.
In all its essentials, so is the Freudian system.

2

THE
FREUDIAN SYSTEM:
IMPLICATIONS

IF THE DISCOVERY of the existence and influence of the unconscious had raised a storm of indignation, if the positing of the death-instinct proved unpalatable to many, if the contents of the Oedipus complex were too shocking to be true, the theory of the primal horde and the origin of civil society made Freud a more controversial figure than ever.[1] The critics relied chiefly on more extensive and authoritative research and the comparative study of cultures which were being developed in the late 1920's, and on the consequent repudiation of the universality of the Oedipus complex. In Jones's controversy with the most vociferous of Freud's faultfinders, Westermarck, he accused the latter of dealing always with conscious motivation, and thus ignoring the fundamentally unconscious nature of the phenomena in question.[2] From what can be learned from the literature cited, it appears that neither party fully understood the other's position. It was the old story of the polar bear and the whale, the antagonists being unable to find common ground on which to thrash out the matter. The Freudians were oblivious to the relevance of empirical anthropology; their opponents could not understand the ideas of unconscious motivation and symbolic fulfillment thereof. Harold D. Lasswell appears to take an unreasonable stand when he questions the competence of anthropologists, notably Malinowski, to challenge psychoanalytic hypotheses,[3] but these early critics could hardly reply that they had made the most of their opportunity. If the polemics ended in a victory for neither side, as appears at that stage of the contest, it was because the anthropologists failed to accept psychoanalysis as an investigatory technique, and so Lasswell was at least tentatively justified. It was not until later students, notably Abram Kardiner, combined the two disciplines that a constructive and meaningful criticism could be made.

To a present-day reader the polemics are pretty stale anyway. In point of style the palm would have to be awarded to Freud.* The anthropologists are not particularly enthralling; Freud's writing still charms, his daring still amazes, his agility at ordering apparently irrelevant or conflicting material into significant explanations still provokes admiration. It is not for want of imagination that his hypotheses have not entirely stood the tests of time and science. Much of what he said about the beginnings of civilization must necessarily be conjectural. We do not need a Burke to tell us that a veil must be drawn over the remote past; it is there anyway. Attempts to pierce it, contradictory to Burke's advice, will have to be speculative, but all the same they are not worthless. A political philosopher could easily raise a defense against the accusation that anthropological material does not provide historical confirmation for Freud's speculations. There was no ethnological foundation for the social contract theories of the Enlightenment either, yet it cannot be denied that they have a certain creative value for political philosophy. Franz Alexander suggests that the entire construction, as it culminates in the Oedipus complex, is a theoretical generalization of the universal necessity of the family as the nucleus of social organization.[4]

In any event, Freud extrapolated some fascinating ideas from the theory. The Oedipus complex, we recall, recaptured the essence of the Greek legend from which it takes its name. If psychoanalysis could delve into its hidden meaning by the interpretation

* Freud was awarded the Goethe prize for literature in 1930, though not for *Totem and Taboo* in particular.

of dreams, could it not turn the same trick in probing the meaning of other myths? They took were obscured by the passage of time; they too dealt with the forgotten history of peoples. Myths, legends, fairy tales, folklore, in all these areas we find the same symbolism. Their parallel to the symbols of dreams was convincing.[5] *Totem and Taboo* was, in the last years of Freud's life, succeeded by a yet more brilliant—or reckless—*tour de force* of this kind, *Moses and Monotheism.* Freud's wide-ranging imagination took up the hypotheses of Moses being an Egyptian and monotheism being a modification of the apostasy of Ikhnaton. Historical material combined with the psychoanalyst's careful attention to minute detail resulted in some startling disclosures. The particulars of his analysis do not concern us here, but Freud's delineation of the character of Moses pertains to topics of more immediate interest to political science, those of group behavior and political leadership.

To Freud, what holds groups together is a direction of libido onto the leader in his role as a substitute for the ego ideal, or superego, and a more general dispersion of libido among companions in the group. The leader is a deputy of the father of childhood.[6] It is not surprising, therefore, that group behavior is similar to that of an infant, or, to be more exact, to that of infants *en masse,* the primal horde. These are its characteristics:

> The dwindling of the conscious individual personality, the focussing of thoughts and feelings into a common direction, the predominance of the emotions and of the unconscious mental life, the tendency to the immediate carrying out of intentions as they emerge. . . .

The two compendious theses that explain group psychology are the intensification of emotions and the inhibition of intellectual functioning, in both of which the group members tend more and more to approximate each other. The group leader is again the dreaded father of the primal horde, and the group wishes to be dominated by authority and force.[7]

There is a strange admixture of feelings of the group for its leader. They exemplify "the coincidence of love and hate towards the same object" that Freud called "ambivalence." Although the origin of ambivalence was obscure, it was fundamental to our emotional life, he maintained. As may be expected, it can be illuminated by the Oedipus complex. In primitive society the totem animal is a symbol of the father; killing it is forbidden, but once it is ceremonially killed, a holiday follows during which the totem is mourned amidst the celebration. Hatred was expressed in the murder, love in the ensuing remorse. Parricide being forbidden in civil society, the prohibition, internalized as the superego, results in a sense of guilt which is reinforced by culture as a necessary concomitant of its growth. Ambivalence is another expression of the conflict between Eros and the death-instinct. Culture obeys Eros, knitting men into a mass; the death-instinct is repressed and society preserved, but at the price of psychic inquietude that may well reach unbearable proportions. As long as external objects remained toward which to direct aggressive inclinations, a group could be unified by Eros.[8] In a type of organization (if it can be called such) that represents regression to primitive mental activity, the direction of aggressive impulses outward would not be too difficult. Here the character of the leader entered.

Regardless of the need of members of the group to feel loved by the leader, he can dispense with a reciprocal relation and is not to be regarded as an equal.[9] In *Moses and Monotheism* Freud catalogued further qualities of the leader, or great man. His influence is due to the ideas for which he stands and to his personality. He is the father of our childhood days, displaying decisiveness of thought, strength of will, forcefulness of deeds, self-reliance, independence, the divine conviction of doing right, even ruthlessness. He is a figure to be admired, perhaps trusted, but above all to be feared.[10]

As applied to an understanding of political behavior, Freud clearly regarded group activity as basically irrational. One must be careful in using the word "group." The *Massen* of *Massenpsy-*

chologie und Ich-Analyse (the German title of *Group Psychology*) was rendered "group" in translation,[11] whereas it seems beyond question, from the material in the book and from its commencement with a discussion of Gustave LeBon's *The Crowd*, that the word should have been rendered "crowd," if not "mob." Perhaps it was well to avoid the pejorative flavor of the latter terms, for Freud, unlike LeBon, did not regard group behavior as necessarily destructive. If anything, Freud would be predisposed to regard groups with favor, for they manifest the libidinal ties which promote human solidarity.[12] Yet there are some disquieting aspects of the theory too. The three essays that comprise *Moses and Monotheism* were written immediately before, and published immediately after, the *Anschluss* of Germany and Austria in 1938.[13] Though ostensibly describing Moses, the resemblance of "the great man" to Hitler is inescapable. For that matter, any "great man" could fit the formula, and one is forced to the conclusion that it was intended to be that way. When Freud characterizes the mass of men as "lazy and unintelligent," it follows that the masses can be induced to labor and to renounce instinctual gratification only by exemplary individuals who are recognized by them as their leaders. And he believes the danger, if any, lies not in the harshness but in the flaccidity of leaders.[14] Freud's blind spot in political science was never so glaring. He seems to have been unaware of the illiberal implications of his theory of group psychology and leadership. Self-government for a community is out of the question from the beginning; rule by an elite is left as the only practicable type of government. Freud pays no attention to means of protecting the community from charlatans and strong-men, who can easily enough impersonate a man of authentic greatness. Rational conduct appears to be the attribute only of men acting individually; group behavior, being under the influence of libido, is *per se* irrational, a regression to the primal horde. Unwitting tendencies of this kind in Freud's work perhaps account for David Riesman's characterization of his influence as reactionary.[15] The employment of this theoretical outline to explain the actual practice of politics, however, was to await the pathfinding work of Harold D. Lasswell.

The analogue of group psychology in childhood behavior threw light on religion too. A proper view of religion in the evolution of man saw it less as a permanent feature than as "a parallel to the neurosis which the civilized individual must pass through on his way from childhood to maturity."[16] *The Future of an Illusion* took this point of departure for Freud's characteristically scientific view of another aspect of human life. It was easy to establish that the individual, faced with the inscrutable terrors of the natural environment, sought consolation, if not explanation, and that this, far from being a new situation, had had its infantile prototype in the helplessness of the child. "The derivation of a need for religion from the child's feeling of helplessness and the longing it evokes for a father seem to me incontrovertible."[17] The security that can be obtained by propitiating the gods is equivalent to the security the infant receives by honoring and obeying the father. The forces of nature are endowed with paternal characteristics and personified as gods. In the fashioning of deities, not only an infantile prototype but also a phylogenetic one is followed. Gods are only psychic products of man, "in every case modelled after the father" and dependent on our relation to him. Infantile impotence and the persistence of the wishes and needs of childhood into maturity, as an obsessional neurosis, explain the beginnings and content of religion.[18]

But "experience teaches us that the world is not a nursery." For the individual, those of his childhood neuroses that he does not outgrow can be cleared up by psychoanalytic therapy. But for humanity as a whole—recalling the phylogeny-ontogeny parallel—how was the obsessional neurosis of religious belief to be overcome? Freud balked at the idea of a neurotic civilization and sagely cautioned on the difficulties involved in overextending the analogy.[19] Religion was an illusion; there could be no doubt of that, because by definition wish-fulfillment was an inordinate factor in its motivation regardless of any relation to reality. Was not the answer to turn a deaf ear to the adjuration, *credo quia absurdum,* and fulfill the wishes in question by the application of the reason and the scientific method that marked maturity?[20] Freud's invincible confidence in the intellect now made its strongest manifestation, and with it a humanism all too often lacking in defenders of the faith.

A meek acquiescence in man's lowly part in the universe, said Freud, is itself irreligious, a view that no friend of humanity could take. Was it not advantageous to admit the hardships of civilization to be of human making and to strive to alleviate them, substituting the results of rational mental effort for the products of repression?[21] Ignorance remains ignorance, and gives no right to believe anything, even absurdities, but "there is no appeal beyond reason." Reason—the ego—alone can master the instincts—the id—whose excesses had brought about repressive social institutions. In league with science, the "education to reality" could proceed. "The voice of the intellect is a soft one, but it does not rest until it has gained a hearing"; nothing, in the long run, can resist reason and experience. On no account could religion illuminate the perils besetting the human species, much less stand as arbiter of science. Its preference for what is lofty to what is true is a repudiation of reality and of a rational probing of it, while science slowly but surely enlarges and perfects the realm of knowledge.[22]

Freud was a staunch champion of the intellect. To place him in the vanguard of the "cult of the irrational"[23] is to do him an injustice. Freud believed man's best hope for the future lay in the ultimate triumph of the intellect, which he equated with the scientific spirit.[24] In his exchange of letters with Albert Einstein on the possibility of abolishing war, Freud retreated somewhat in acknowledging as impossible the ideal solution of subordinating instinctive life to the dictates of reason, but looked forward to the strengthening of the intellect and a perhaps hazardous introversion of the aggressive impulse. The "psychical modifications that go along with the cultural process"—again the inheritance of acquired characteristics—had made some people not merely intellectual but constitutional pacifists; and while it might be long before such a disposition became part of the psychic heritage of mankind, it was certain that whatever made for culture worked against war.*

That the forces working for culture ultimately would triumph could be anticipated with some confidence. But the contest would be a hard one, and assuredly a protracted one too. Was it sheer accident that Freud had placed the ego in a weak position vis-à-vis the other components of the psyche? Aside from what psychoanalytic experience taught, the arrangement had a dramatic aspect too. Starting from a precarious position, one apparently destined for defeat, the protagonist, the ego, would sooner or later prove its mettle. Given a sufficiently formidable antagonist, the combat would be of epic proportions. The ego would triumph over seemingly impossible odds to turn certain doom into probable victory. Though it is hard to tell the artist from the scientist in the fashioning of this plot, it is no mere theatrical performance. The entire course of both phylogeny and ontogeny foretold the same result. As civilization had emerged from the primal horde, so a rational man would emerge from the domination of the emotional forces of his early life. If this was a philosophy of determinism, it was an optimistic determinism.

Freud's interpretation of the statue of Moses by Michelangelo, which stands in S. Pietro in Vincoli in Rome, also took an unexpectedly optimistic turn. Does it represent Moses about to smash the Tablets of the Law upon seeing the children of Israel worshiping the golden calf? With the meticulous attention of the analyst to the details of behavior—even sculptured behavior—that would reveal hidden motivations, Freud found enough clues to see a

* "Why War?" pp. 286, 287. Against this must be stood Freud's long-time interest in the occult. (See the surprising credence lent to it in *New Introductory Lectures*, pp. 47–81.) The apologia Jones offers for this unaccountable wavering (III, 375–407) seems to be unnecessarily elaborate. Aside from the influence on Freud of the occasionally erratic Committeeman Ferenczi, it can be just as easily explained as a not-too-happy ambition to utilize psychoanalysis in extending the frontiers of human knowledge.

more heartening significance in it. Moses had had the impulse to destroy the Tablets of the Law, but he checked his emotions. "He remembered his mission and renounced for its sake the indulgence of his feelings." It was in the posture of self-restraint that the artist had depicted the father of the Judaic tradition of Western civilization. The statue portrayed man's highest possible mental achievement, "that of struggling successfully against an inward passion for the sake of a cause to which he has devoted himself."[25] The mobilization of intellectual power could conquer the most intemperate of human emotions. Reason could control destruction if it could but find a higher cause around which to rally its energies. And what higher cause than the welfare of mankind could there be? The theme epitomizes Freud's own life and work. He allowed neither physical discomfort, academic ostracism, nor a certain disdain for the foibles of society to discourage him from his mission of adding to the knowledge that would make life more endurable. He saw, in Erich Fromm's words, "that only the understanding of man's passions can free his reason to function properly."[26]

One can be an optimist, philosophically if not temperamentally, if one does not expect too much out of life. No one acquainted with Freud's life history could accuse him of overvaluing the pleasures the human lot affords. Only to those who were careless or unscrupulous enough to misinterpret his writings was Freud an unmitigated hedonist who wanted to subvert moral standards to allow the shameless pursuit of sexual gratification. Erich Fromm contends that Freud's love life was "dry and sterile," and, for all the to-do he made of sexuality, he was a "typical puritan" himself.[27] There is nothing in this to surprise us when we recall that Freud considered sexual activity to be undertaken—one can almost say undergone—for the purpose of removing the tension aroused by the sexual instinct. Sexuality was not a good in itself. With pleasure equivalent to sexuality it was at bottom nothing more than the absence of pain. And so as a hedonist, Freud was both philosophically and temperamentally an Epicurean, with something of the Stoic intermixed, and not at all a Cyrenaic.

John Stuart Mill characterized his father as a blend of Stoic, Epicurean, and Cynic, and as to both personality and philosophy there is more than a passing similarity between James Mill and Freud. The gnarled, disenchanted Scotsman adhered to pleasure and pain as the standard of right and wrong but believed few pleasures to be worth the price they exacted. "He thought human life a poor thing at best after the freshness of youth and of unsatisfied curiosity had gone by." The joy of comradeship for its own sake is absent from James Mill's life; the individualistic pursuit of happiness, happiness as the absence of unhappiness, made his world go round. Hard-headed, tough-minded, scornful of opposition to the one true faith of Utilitarianism, he seems to have held civilized life to be exclusively intellectual life, and that to be attained at the sacrifice or suppression of emotional life. He turned a stern, almost ferocious, authoritarian demeanor to his son, applied discipline rigidly, kept maternal love at bay (the younger Mill makes not a single mention of his mother in the story of his life), made a superb reasoning machine of his son, and left him with one of the most atrocious Oedipal problems ever recorded.[28] There are numerous passages in the *Autobiography* of the scion of Utilitarianism where Freud's name could be substituted for the elder Mill's and the portrayal would be perfect, though Freud had greater success than Mill in rearing happy offspring.

Repression of emotions gave free rein to unsatisfied curiosity, for James Mill. Sublimation—that was Freud's word for it—was used by Mill and other of the Utilitarians to attack the then current social institutions with a searing broadside of logic that at the same time could find order in many of the complicated processes of society. Before they had finished, the Utilitarians had reconstructed—in some cases constructed outright—penology, legislation, jurisprudence, ethics, economics, logic, and virtually the British Constitution. It required but the acumen to see purpose masquerading as utility, and the intellectual (and political) agility to amend social institutions accordingly. Life and society could be arranged scientifically, for the universe too had a rationalist temper, correctly known as the principle of Utility.

So too Freud is the rationalist *par excellence,* perceiving order behind chaos. A system that is reputed to endorse the irrational forces of life has more of *telos* in it than first meets the eye. See how cleverly unconscious wishes disguise themselves in symbols to evade the censorship exercised in repression, how the apparently purposeless strivings of instincts in reality have as their aim the lowering of somatic tension, how the gratification of instincts subserves the well-being of the organism, how both Eros and the death-instinct conserve the organism, each in its own way, how neatly phylogeny and ontogeny parallel each other so that one can flit from the race to the individual and back again to illustrate the development of the one by the development of the other. Even the galaxy of dream symbols could be reduced to a few stand-ard ones with constant meanings,[29] not unlike the Forms Plato held to be the compendia of all human knowledge. It could be argued, and not whimsically, that both Plato and Freud attempted to build world systems on these not dissimilar bases. In sum, almost nothing is left to chance in a deterministic system, almost nothing is unpredictable in a materialistic conception of things. The solitary exception is the operation of reason, which alone can rise above normal limitations and open fresh horizons for the de-velopment of man and his society. If anything, Freud was too much the rationalist, striving to encompass all the works and thoughts of men in one titanic system.

Was Freud no more than a latter-day Utilitarian? Omitting from consideration any possible influence that might have come from translating some essays of John Stuart Mill in his youth, there is still much that Freud either drew from the British school or held in common with them. Bentham launched his philosophy from a study of the malfunctioning of English jurisprudence; Freud commenced from studies of pathology of a different sort. In addition, the strong rationalistic bias, the foundation in hedon-ism, the confidence, almost faith, in the possibility of improving the human condition by human means, the prevailing "liberal" tone—all these and more characterize both schemes of thought. But coincidence does not prove causality. Freud worked from an independent basis—psychoanalysis—that was not available to the Utilitarians. And his social philosophy traveled along highways and byways that the Utilitarians did not touch upon. Freud was by no means an adept of social science. Of the latter's three broad divisions, the political, the economic, and the social, Freud appears to have been notoriously weak in the first two, and more speculative than methodical in the last. We shall have to forsake the familiar Utilitarian moorings in trying to ascertain Freud's place in social theory.

A convenient point of departure is the question, What was Freud's ideal man like? As Plato's philosopher king was really Plato, as Machiavelli's prince was really Machiavelli—at least as each thought himself to be—so it may be that Freud's ideal man was really Freud, in whole or in part. In that case, the job of reconstruction is not too difficult. For one thing, the ideal Freudian man's sexual instinct receives regular, though not abundant, gratification. He exhibits genital, and not perverted, sexuality, propagating his kind while finding pleasure of his own—uniting, in Utilitarian fashion, universalistic with individualistic hedonism. Sexual repression is minimal; if repression is directed anywhere, it is toward the death-instinct, which is toned down to moderate self-assertion in relations with others. It is plain that Eros has triumphed in its combat with the death-instinct. Eros blesses the ideal man in his relations with his family and his friends, extending, even, to the benign feeling toward mankind that he has. Because his Oedipus complex has been resolved in infancy, the pressures of his superego are tolerable. He accepts law and moral standards, but they must not be thought to be above criticism. Insofar as they are beneficial, they have become constitutionally permanent with him, thus capping phylogenetic as well as ontogenetic development. Insofar as they are not, he has the wherewithal to protest or to rebel. For if there is any singular characteristic about Freud's ideal man, it is the supremacy of his ego. Having achieved the supervention of the reality principle over the pleasure principle, his ego is able to exert an easy mastery over his instincts as the result of natural growth and he is able to stand an independent, civilized man. Nonconformity does not mean psychosis for him and he is not beset by any neurotic disability now that his instincts have been tamed. Eschewing the meaner indulgences of his passions, he is able to sublimate his psychic energies in a lifetime of work directed to ameliorating the human lot.

Admittedly, much of the foregoing is inference, and anyone can beguile the time away with that sport. But it is not idle speculation, for assuredly Freud's ideal society would be subordinate to his ideal man rather than vice-versa. Freud's ideal society must next claim our attention, though as we shall see, even a reconstruction will be inadequate. The ideal society would provide the conditions for the flourishing of the ideal man. Therefore, one thing is certain: it will not have a strong resemblance to the Vienna Freud knew. As Plato loathed democratic Athens, as Machiavelli contemned strife-torn Italy, so Freud had less than friendly feelings toward bourgeois, neurosis-ridden Vienna. That means, above all, that the repression of sexuality exerted by society will be considerably lightened (though not completely removed) and directed instead toward the death-instinct, insofar as the two can be disentangled.

Beyond that, however, we are at a loss to proceed. Whereas the characteristics of the ideal man can be inferred with greater or lesser accuracy from Freud's *vitae,* coupled with the obverse of the pathological individuals he analyzed, the same cannot be done for his conception of the best society. The empirical data are missing in his writings, data which Freud had not bothered to collect. Since man, to him, was formed virtually independently of social influences, he apparently did not feel the necessity of studying social institutions. Hence, when the time now comes to consider any possible Freudian utopia, we find Freud not to have provided the materials needed to construct or repair the social institutions that would accommodate the ideal man. The most he could visualize was an admittedly utopian "community of men who had subordinated their instinctual life to the dictatorship of reason."[30]

In order to elaborate his thought on social matters we shall have to resort to the expedient of two extended comparisons, one with the social contract philosophers and one with Marx. With respect to both there are significant differences that disclose the Freudian system to be an important advance in the development of political and social thought.

The social contract philosophers, by whom are meant Hobbes, Locke, Spinoza, and Rousseau, took upon themselves the task of solving the problem of legitimating political authority and exploring the limits thereto. By opposing man to society, the problem was impossible of solution from the outset, as is now recognized. Yet the social contract writers fixed a framework for political inquiry that has lasted till our own day, and theirs is a fair standard of comparison by which to draw out the meaning of Freud's system. They began with a conception of a state of nature that was said to be antecedent to civil society. For Locke and Rousseau the state of nature was a not intolerable condition; for Hobbes and Spinoza it was a dismal state of affairs at best. For all of them except Locke, men were creatures of passion in it and became rational only in civil society. It need hardly be said that the state of nature was a convenient fiction. The social contract writers lacked a sense of history and mistook travelers' tales of exotic primitives for a science of anthropology when they bothered to consider the matter at all. Freud's position was somewhat stronger here. We can easily correlate the state of nature with the primal horde. Freud estimated it as neither good nor bad, for it preceded the morality that came only with civilization. He merely observed that the patriarch's instincts were freely gratified, a pleasure the other males had to forgo.[31] There or in civil society men were usually ruled by their instincts, though less so in civilization, where repression played so strong a role.[32] And to Freud the primal horde was a proved fact; what anthropology did not supply, the analogous developments of phylogeny and ontogeny did.

Thus for the social contract writers civil society was a conscious creation, the form of government was deliberately chosen, and for that matter government itself was at least in theory expendable. And whereas man-made law was absolute (here Locke would demur) and external to man, political obligation was optional. In the work in which Freud most closely approximated the exposition of a political philosophy, *Civilization and Its Discontents,* he described the institution of society almost in terms of a social contract. Communal life is possible, he said, only when several combine their strength against the strength of any single individual. It becomes the right which opposes the might of the would-be rebel. "This substitution of the power of a united number for the power of a single man is the decisive step towards civilization." Instinctual gratification was renounced for social stability.[33] The pleasure principle came to terms with the reality principle. But this is not the same thing as saying that civil society is a conscious creation. The inexorable necessities of phylogenetic development required the bringing of order out of chaos, just as the inevitability of ontogenetic development required the succession of infancy by maturity.[34] If civilization was less than perfect it was nevertheless inevitable, and in any case it was better than what had gone before.[35] With instinctual life the primary problem,[36] and not political authority, forms of government were a matter of indifference to Freud, though government and law were always necessary in society. Law was not quite so absolute as with the social contract theorists, for, as the cement of social cohesion, it was in large part supplemented by the recognition of a community of interest and the feelings of unity, even though it ultimately rested on violence.[37] But to Freud law was certainly not completely external to man, having in fact been incorporated in the superego as part of the process of character formation.[38] Hence political obligation was hardly optional; it existed in man before he was conscious of it.

With their psychology of consciousness (Spinoza being something of an exception) the social contract writers could be consistently rationalistic. They could ignore questions of character formation and the importance of sexuality therein (again Spinoza must be partly excepted). By contrast, a psychology of the unconscious and a realization of the importance of sexuality, in both of which Freud pioneered, enabled Freud to penetrate to the mainsprings of human nature with a telling truth that none of the social contract philosophers save Spinoza could begin to apprehend. As to the latter school, whether the supreme value was individual liberty (for Locke and Spinoza) or order (for Hobbes and Rousseau), whether they were materialists (Hobbes and Locke) or philosophical idealists (Spinoza and Rousseau), they could at all events be optimistic: the ways of power could be justified to man and the benefits of citizenship were seen to outweigh the advantages of such liberty as the state of nature afforded. Freud too, as we have seen, was supremely rationalistic, and because of that his highest value was the triumph of reason, whether it be achieved by liberty or by order. Freud's materialism has already been remarked on; his optimism was not so apparent.

Thus Freud ignored some of the conventional categories of political philosophy, for want of training and for want of interest, and did not undertake to solve traditional problems in a traditional manner. The social contract writers tried to reconcile man to civil society, and none of them could be said to have presented a consistent argument to support his conclusions even if one assents to the conclusions. Freud's excursions into social philosophy tried to reconcile men to culture, though he could not claim to have wholly succeeded either. While he, as they, pondered the relation of man to society, Freud was the more deeply troubled, and for deeper reasons. His attention to unconscious forces and to the intractability of instincts left him more realistic but somewhat less optimistic than the older school. In contrast to the comparatively staid musings of the social contract philosophers, Freud injected an element of drama into human affairs, a sense of destiny that eluded the most careful legal prescriptions. Not everything could be settled by a social contract, with or without a right of revolution held in reserve. Men were determined by forces that were but incompletely within their control. Because of that, his system is more akin to Marx's, and to that affinity we now turn.

A philosophy of determinism does not require a doctrine of materialism to rest upon, but it can be of help. Both Freud and Marx made the most of such a combination. For Marx the basis of society was to be found in the system of ownership and control of the means of production, distribution, and exchange; hence the *via regia* to the understanding of man and his works was an economic interpretation of the relations that depend on the forces of production and of the historical trends determining them. Freud's materialism was of a different sort. It lay in the somatic sources of the instincts and the ever-present libido. And whereas Marx visualized historical development in terms of struggle between two opposing classes—in our own day, between bourgeoisie and industrial proletariat—Freud could pass the observation, obvious enough to any who were willing to see, "that human beings consist of men and women and that this distinction is the most significant one that exists."[39] The one focused on capital and the cash nexus, the other on sexuality and the Oedipus complex. And hence the one explored the macrocosm and the evils of social institutions, while the other explored the microcosm and the pathos of individual psychic debility. Thus the two had less in common than first meets the eye, and most of that is superficial.

Both thinkers had a critical opinion of the warping effects of social institutions on men. But although they also shared a bilious view of religion, their systems led in opposite directions from this point onward. For the socialist revolutionary, social institutions were but a disguise for sheer exploitation of one class by another, and as such they were evil and unnecessary. The ultimate solution was communism: the abolition of private property and the exploitative social relations depending thereon. For the liberal psychoanalyst, civilization meant repression, and as such it was in our own time excessive but unhappily necessary.[40] There was no once-and-for-all solution but only a continual struggle in which one could look forward to the victory of science in assisting man to cope with an unfriendly natural and social environment.[41] As for the abolition of private property, Freud thought it was a nostrum that was pretty much beside the point. It would deprive men of an instrument of aggression but would not affect the differences in power and influence otherwise employed by the death-instinct; nor would it alter this instinct, which moreover had been regnant before private property appeared; nor would it affect rivalries springing from the sexual instinct.[42] Freud saw the real roots of social conflict to be buried in human nature, specifically in the insufficiency of libido and the irrepressibility of the death-instinct.[43] His was the view of the therapist concentrating on the individual, Marx's was that of the revolutionary and he concentrated on the ineluctable action of historical forces. And whereas Marx would remake people by remaking society, Freud appeared to think that society would take care of itself as people constitutionally inherited the improvements of phylogenetic development.[44]

Thus the two were at theoretical loggerheads on the matters of character formation and human nature. For Marx character was formed by the impact of economic institutions, though his writings are pitifully bereft of any explanation of exactly how that comes about. With that gap in his theory, he took people ready-made: men were consciously aware of their respective self-interests in the exchanges of the market place, economic units held together by the cash nexus of capitalist transactions. Freud, for his part, gave scant attention to the importance of social institutions in character formation, regarding the latter as a function of libido. Being more aware than anyone else of the potency of unconscious motivations, he scarcely ever considered men as adult, rational individuals capable of judging their interests properly; society was little more than an enlargement of the Oedipus complex.

Since the two had analyzed, each in his own way, the implacable forces that at present oppressed mankind and determined his development, and since each had built his respective analysis into a science, each could be optimistic, after a fashion, as these forces worked inevitably toward a desired goal. Marx, however, had the initial advantage. He hitched his wagon to what he believed to be necessary historical developments. His analysis pointed unfailingly to the proper course of action. As the industrial revolution swept all in its path and manifested itself in concrete political situations, its denouement could be directed and hastened by the vanguard of the working class, the communist party. The socialist revolution could be managed and not merely awaited. By comparison, the psychoanalytic movement was but a feeble implement to assist in realizing a more distant and only highly probable outcome. The glacial progress of phylogenetic development could hardly be a spur to those who craved immediate results and it did not permit more than the vaguest specification of the lineaments of the future ideal society. The reason is that the Freudian utopia is to be found in the sanctum of the psyche. More than Marx he saw that the axis of the universal swirl ultimately had to pass through individuals. For all the lurid passages in *Das Kapital* describing the condition of the working classes in England, it is plain that Marx regarded proletariat and bourgeoisie alike as but the instruments of economic development. His commiseration with the industrial proletariat is patently counterfeit. Admittedly it is difficult to feel compassion for a historical force; it cannot be said that Marx ever succeeded in evincing such feelings authentically. The fact that Freud penetrated to the living realities behind such forces and encompassed them within his system—made them the very center of his system—marks him the superior thinker on that score alone. The union in Freud's thought of the spirit of humanism with that of scientific inquiry makes it a distinct advance over that of Marx.

Utopia for utopia, the Freudian one would in the long run probably prove to be the more efficacious and enduring of the two, but it would be a very long run. Some unhappy premonitions may therefore be pardoned Freud. Nevertheless, his pessimism, his allegedly gloomy view of the future prospects of mankind, has been considerably exaggerated by many students of his thought. Assuredly no man who had undergone thirty-three operations for cancer of the jaw and had spent the last sixteen years of his life in unremitting pain without the indulgence of an anodyne could be called a defeatist (and, it will be remembered, these were the years when his most important writings on social philosophy appeared). Considering, on the one hand, his view of civilization as tantamount to forfeiture of individual happiness, and on the other hand the limitless vistas to human progress he saw opened by science, it might be fitting to call Freud a pessimist for tomorrow but an optimist for next week. The tragedy of Freud's system was that the premises of orthodox psychoanalysis did not permit the construction of a philosophy that would sufficiently take account of social institutions in realizing his humanistic aspirations. That deficiency the Neo-Freudians were in large part to remedy.

For those who like their political philosophy to have the sweep and grandeur of cosmic theory, a farewell to a Freudian approach will be painful. Cavil as the critic will, he has to grant Freud's titanic achievement of synthesizing so many fields of human knowledge into one comprehensive scheme. For all his clinical work, for all his practical application of psychoanalysis to therapy, Freud is nevertheless the latest of the great system-builders. His thought belongs more properly to philosophy than to medicine. A student of social thought must, from the very nature of his own discipline, admire the style of Freud's integration of knowledge into a connected body of ideas from which he proffers explanations of social as well as psychic phenomena. None of the Neo-Freudians, in this writer's estimation, has matched the scope of Freud's genius; perhaps one such mind in a century is all that can be asked for. Notwithstanding this disadvantage, a less impressive display of the imaginative faculty may yield less grandiose and at the same time more tenable conclusions. The logical place to begin is with Neo-Freudian revisions in the master's system.

3

THE BREAK
WITH FREUD

IT MUST BE an audacious critic indeed who would propose root-and-branch modifications of so majestic a system as Freud's, one that is architectonic in structure, comprehensive in scope, solidly grounded in clinical experience, and thoroughly integrated. The Neo-Freudians were not so rash as to reconstruct psychoanalysis *in toto*; in this respect they differed from Adler and Jung, whose respective emasculations of Freudian doctrine left the original discipline unrecognizable. Neither have they quibbled with minor particulars and offered a series of piecemeal qualifications that left their work within the bounds of orthodoxy. Taken in the large, the Neo-Freudians have attempted the delicate operation of so revising Freud's ideas as to separate the wheat from the chaff, retaining the essentials of Freud's principles while modernizing them to comport with developments in clinical practice and the conditions that confronted psychoanalysis in America.

What factor was most responsible for bringing about the Neo-Freudian movement—the disappointments in conventional methods of analytic therapy that began to appear with disturbing frequency by the 1920's, the characteristically American predilection for applying science to the solution of social problems, or the noticeable difference in pathological material in the New World—cannot be ascertained.[1] Doubtless each ingredient, and perhaps others, was of different weight with each analyst in inducing the

Neo-Freudians to query so formidable a structure as Freud's. Although each of the Neo-Freudians has had his own contribution to make in reshaping Freudian psychoanalysis, it is Karen Horney who has made the most systematic and thoroughgoing critique of orthodoxy, and much of this chapter will be devoted to her theoretical reformulations. Other figures, however, were not deficient on the topic that first engages our attention.

From the exposition of Chapter 1, it should be apparent that the focal point of any assault on the Freudian system would sooner or later have to be the Oedipus complex. This the Neo-Freudians undertook, not for the purpose of rejecting the concept outright but with the idea of desexualizing it, so to speak. Instead of visualizing the Oedipal situation as one revolving about the activity of the erotic and death instincts, the Neo-Freudians regard it as an interpersonal relation which may, on occasion, take on sexual connotations, but which is fundamentally a matter of authority and insubordination rooted in the family. In truth, Horney regards the Oedipus complex as an outcropping of more deep-seated difficulties in the Freudian system, specifically the instinct and libido theories.[2] Her remarks on the first subject, therefore, may be taken as the initial skirmish in a controversy that engaged her colleagues at somewhat greater length.

Horney doubts that the virulent jealousy reactions that are at the core of the Oedipus complex have the universality in our society—to say nothing of other societies—that Freud thought. The atmosphere in which the child grows up may be so emotionally unhealthy as to precipitate the fear and hostility whose repression culminates in the basic anxiety that provokes Oedipal behavior. That behavior is, typically, the clinging of the child to one parent for the sake of reassurance; in the large, it is a neurotic need for affection. These are not instinctive reactions; they result from the family atmosphere and are artificially generated: "The attachment to the parents is not a biologically given phenomenon but a response to provocations from the outside."[3] Hence the Oedipus complex is not a primary process itself, says Horney, but the outcome of other processes, in particular the cultural conditions that stir up rivalry, beyond the family as well as within it. "The competitive stimuli are active from the cradle to the grave."[4]

Moreover, the accumulation of infantile experiences builds a character structure from which adult difficulties may flow. Since the feelings or attitudes of the family relationship are, in reality, present in all human relationships, it is disturbances in these latter relationships, and not merely the isolated repetition of infantile experiences, that are important in generating neuroses. The totality of early experiences that molds character must be considered, and that means paying less attention to the constitutional inheritance and more to the cultural influences that shape the individual, notably the crucial experiences of childhood.[5] Last, neither is the sexual component of the Oedipal relationship all that it appears to be. What is fundamentally a dependent relationship in infancy may take on a sexual coloration, but sexuality usually accompanies an attempt to allay anxiety. It is in actuality a manifestation of the neurotic need for affection, and hence sexual difficulties, as they appear in dreams and fantasies, signify disturbances in interpersonal relations; they are the effect, rather than the cause, of a neurotic character structure.[6]

A not dissimilar line of thought is taken by Erich Fromm in his reformulation of the Oedipus complex. He too stresses its origin in interpersonal relations, to the consequent diminution of its sexual aspect. With somewhat more of a culture orientation than Horney, owing, no doubt, to his early training in sociology, Fromm buttresses his ideas with anthropology more than with clinical experience. To Fromm what is called the Oedipus complex results from the child's reaction to the parental authority that is exercised to form his character. In training the child to want to behave the way he has to behave in social living, that is, in the acculturation process that replaces outer force with inner compulsion, parents provoke an assertion against their own irrational authority, the authority that thwarts the child's independence and spontaneity. The child destined for neurosis, however, endeavors to remain attached to the protecting figure of the mother. The craving for maternal closeness is not essentially sexual but one of dependence.[7] Freud's stress on the sexual nature of the attachment—in which, incidentally, he ascribed adult rational sexuality to the infant— overlooked "the intensity of the irrational affective tie to the mother," the fear of leaving her completely as a mature individual. The appearance of sexuality indicates an abnormally strong at- tachment, not a sexual root. If anything, sexual desire is unsteady in its object and during adolescence helps liberate a child from the mother.[8]

Noticing that Freud's formulation of the Oedipus complex left the father in the elevated position of respect while degrading the mother to the object of incest, Fromm points to "the strictly patriarchal attitude" prevalent in Freud's time. It was not always so. Antedating contemporary patriarchal society, with its defer- ence to man-made law, the predominance of rational thought, and man's effort to change nature, was matriarchal society, where the ties of blood and soil reigned supreme and man was in har- mony with nature.[9] We may anticipate Fromm's major thesis by remarking his idea that, both as individual and as species, man's natural growth away from the primary ties that characterize in- fancy and matriarchy, respectively, presents him with the "am- biguous gift" of freedom, and with it the problem of once more relating himself meaningfully to nature and to man.[10] When Oedipus guessed the riddle of the sphinx he in reality solved the problem. Piercing the symbolic language in which the riddle was cast, he was able to save mankind (Thebes) by affirming that man himself is the answer to the most perplexing of the riddles he must face.[11]

Dealing with the Oedipus myth proper, Fromm interprets it as not being concerned with sexuality at all but with authority and the attitude toward it, one of the basic aspects of interpersonal relations. The incestuous relationship is a secondary element; the essence of the myth, he believes, is the rebellion of Oedipus against paternal authority, Oedipus' accession to his mother being but one of the symbols of the son's victory. Sophocles' recounting of the legend, after all, is a trilogy. The same theme of the tyrannical father-son relationship fills all three plays. If the plays symbolize anything, it is the age-old feud between patriarchy and matriarchy as systems of social organization.[12]

It is Abram Kardiner who offers the most far-reaching criticism of the limitations stemming from Freud's version of the Oedipus complex. He is at one with Horney and Fromm in regarding the Oedipus complex as the result of a family situation, one that is not necessarily sexually tinged. As part of the emotional inter-actions of parents and children, its contemporaneous restrictions on the child's sexual activities are secondary to the disciplines relating to security and support. In the almost symbiotic relation between mother and child, it is security and support that the child prizes most; left to fend for himself, his efforts would end in certain failure. If the total relationship of the child to his parents is considered, the restrictions they impose on him are accepted for the sake of the benefits they bring.[13] The sexual ingredient is but one ingredient—and not an essential one—in this relationship, for sexuality and love are not identical. The human capacity for love is vast because human dependency is relatively long-lived; and love develops about the nucleus of dependency. For that matter, intense love can exist without sexuality at all. In love, it is concern for the security and welfare of the loved one that is paramount. Therefore, "the complex is an end product, an effect, rather than a cause."[14]

Kardiner finds that the Freudian contention that Oedipal impulses are phylogenetic acquisitions has had deleterious effects on the value of anthropological research. The theory of a universal human nature and the evolution of a universal society, with anthropology confirming institutions (such as the Oedipus complex) as survivals of prehistoric times, may have suited nineteenth-century anthropological thought, but it does not do justice to the dynamic aspects of social institutions. These lose their significance when the Oedipus complex is treated as a phylogenetic survival instead of as the consequence of the institutions which in actuality first gave rise to it. The Oedipus complex is phylogenetic "only in the sense that man is helpless at birth and forms a marked attachment to the stronger figures about him."[15] In failing to distinguish the sociological from the biological components of the Oedipus complex, Freud overlooked the impact of social institutions, which vary from one society to another and leave their idiosyncratic stamps upon their respective members.[16]

Kardiner is protesting that a preoccupation with the historical aspects of culture ignored its dynamic effects and relegated anthropology to an ancillary status (which his own work has done much to rectify). With him, anthropology moves from a confirmatory to an investigatory discipline, as a full-fledged ally of psychoanalysis. Paired with the adaptation of psychoanalysis that he refined for just such work, psychodynamic biography, Kardiner's use of anthropology has revealed a basic personality peculiar to each society that is a function of that society's primary institutions. The basic personality necessarily varies from one society to another according to the methods of adaptation to the environment dictated by primary institutions. The Oedipus complex, in consequence, will have a different configuration in each society, depending on the prevailing social organization. In all cases, however, it is "a definite indication of retardation of development," a persistence of a dependent attitude. The persistence of a dependent attitude and the prominence of the Oedipus complex are in direct proportion to each other. In the process, "the individual seeks to make the object of dependency his sexual object as well." Prolonged dependency can be equated with a failure in ego development.[17]

Our discussion of the Oedipus complex may have given an intimation of the direction in which the Neo-Freudians are going. There is a decided movement away from the instinct and libido theories and an inclination to explain psychic phenomena with reference to interpersonal relations. The focus of interest has shifted from the microcosm, so to speak, to the macrocosm, and the generating forces of human behavior are seen to be due less to the inherited constitution of the organism than to the social conditions that confront him as a maturing individual. Their resultant stress on ego-psychology points to the environment as the more significant agent in precipitating individual and social pathology, and the opportunity for formulating a social philosophy is considerably broadened. Some attention to the Neo-Freudian rejection of the instinct and libido theories will prepare us for pursuing this line of thought.

The Neo-Freudian revolt against the orthodox theory of instincts centered upon the proposition of the death-instinct and the philosophy of human nature that underlay it. One Neo-Freudian, however, contested the very concept of "instinct" at the outset. Kardiner denied both the existence of and the possibility of securing clinical evidence for a death-instinct. Aware of the value for the social sciences of observable behavior, he cautions that instincts, precisely because they are assumptions, cannot be observed: make the assumption, and behavior is blamed on instincts. One can observe behavior, but one cannot observe instinct. "One can draw conclusions about behavior; about instinct one can only philosophize."[18] Likewise, Harry Stack Sullivan, for his part, dismisses the concept of instinct almost with contempt, seeing little space for instincts in "our incredibly culture-ridden life" unless the prefix "human" is added, leaving the term "so broadened in its meaning that there is no particular sense in using the term at all."[19]

But it was the philosophizing of the orthodox dispensation proceeding from an instinct-theory that especially galled the Neo-Freudians. Here it must be recalled that the net effect of Freud's final formulation of the instinct theory was to substitute a death-instinct for the ego-instinct. Thus, in so far as man expressed his individuality it was in a destructive manner, destructive by turns of social bonds or of himself. Karen Horney spoke for the newer *Weltanschauung* in eschewing the negative, deterministic implications of a death-instinct. Ascription of an instinctual character

to self-destructive drives left upon them "the stamp of finality."
Seen as such, they have no origin in specifiable, alterable psychic
conditions. They are postulated as a permanent part of human
nature, and man is left with the sorry alternatives of suffering
himself or turning the drives outward and making others suffer.[20]
In contradiction, Horney's experience as a psychoanalyst pointed
to the defensive nature of hostility and its direct proportion to
the degree the individual feels hurt and endangered. Hostility is
provoked; it may be an adequate reaction to a nettling situation.
The release, by analytic treatment, of the underlying anxiety, she
found, enables one to become more affectionate and tolerant
toward others. Such could not be the case if destruction were
instinctual.[21]

Turning to the more positive aspects of the question, Horney
asserts that, generally speaking, destruction is not undertaken for
its own sake but to defend what one conceives to be one's safety
or happiness. "It seems to me that any kind of self-assertion is the
expression of a positive, expansive, constructive attitude toward
life and toward the self."[22] Harry Stack Sullivan, drawing on his
clinical experience, later corroborated this opinion with the remark that "there is immanent in human personality a striving
towards a way of life that is not destructive to others." Man can,
after all, live in peace;[23] there is no inherited death-instinct to
present an insurmountable barrier to it. Pursuing this question
to the ultimate, Franz Alexander denies war to be an inevitable
result of a death-instinct. The potential of aggressive behavior
in men is provoked by frustrating circumstances. Diminish the
frustrations attendant on the individual's maturation from dependent infancy to independent maturity, and the repressed hostilities also diminish. Appreciation of external factors means "war
cannot be explained from human nature alone."[24]

Horney's ever-greater attention to the positive aspects of behavior, psychopathological and otherwise, signified what purists
would call a glaring Adlerian tendency in her approach that also
infected her colleagues. Many students have noted the similarity

of Horney's ideas to Adler's, all too often overlooking her advances beyond his initial revolt and thus neglecting much of her own original thought.[25] Her incipient apostasy did not result in her expulsion from the Freudian group until 1941, although the unfriendly review of *The Neurotic Personality of Our Time* by no less a personage than Ernest Jones, followed by a review of *New Ways in Psychoanalysis* of similar tenor by another Freudian,[26] indicated the handwriting on the wall. Midway in her career Horney had intimated the more affirmative view of human nature that was to mark her later work when she held that "man brings into the world a vital necessity to expand." In the drive to seize as much from the possibilities of life as one could, destruction was wrought on those who would be hindrances. "Not a will for destruction drives us, but the will for life itself it is that compels us to destruction."[27]

The year before her death she spelled out the differences that separated her group from the Freudians.

> Man for us was no longer an instinct-ridden creature, but a being capable of choice and responsibility. Hostility was no longer innate but reactive. Similarly, egocentric and anti-social cravings, like greed or the lust for power, were not inevitable phases of man's development, but an expression of a neurotic process. Growing up under favorable conditions, we believed, man would develop his inherent constructive forces, and like every other living organism, would want to realize his potentialities. Human nature was no longer unalterable but could change.[28]

The Freudian instinct theory, Horney claims, had shifted emphasis from the heuristic concept of conflict to the contentious concept of instinct. By reversing the emphasis, by removing the limitations of an instinctivistic and genetic psychology, the way is clear to seeking the genesis of neurotic conflicts in the life conditions that mold character—specifically, disturbances in human relationships. Unencumbered by a theory of instincts, an ego-psychology can be elaborated, and that ego will not be the "submissive slave" of the instincts and therefore almost inevitably a neurotic phenomenon. It will be a total personality structure whose conflicts are precipitated by imbroglios with the environment.[29] The formulation of a workable theory of character would, of course, require abandonment of the concept of libido, on which Freudian characterology depended by way of sexual development.

It cannot be said that the Neo-Freudians relinquished the concept of libido with any degree of reluctance. A comprehensive survey of human development would have to include more than sexual development, their declination ran. Even an enlarged meaning of "sexuality"—pleasure—achieved by interjection of the libido theory, whereby character is conceived as reaction-formations or sublimations resulting from early disciplining of the individual, could not take account of the relevant sociological data. The violence the libido theory did to cultural influences on personality was too much for the Neo-Freudians to stomach.[30]

In Freudian theory, the movement of libido to different pregenital pleasure zones of the body in childhood, and its cathexis or frustration, yielded traits that, taken together, manifested themselves in adult life as character. Tracing the regression of libido to its fixation at the relevant stage of infantile development revealed the source of the habits and attitudes of such character types as anal, oral, and phallic.[31] Horney, for one, questions whether trends toward affection (oral character) or power (anal character) are aim-inhibited libidinal drives, and she challenges the idea that neurosis is due mainly to regression to pregenital levels. The theory of the imaginary peregrinations of an alleged somatic ingredient, she believes, rests on indefensible analogies and generalizations and dubious data concerning the erotogenic zones.[32] Like all the Neo-Freudians she agrees that infancy is of pre-eminent importance in character formation, but not for the reasons Freud gave. Infantile experiences may be the breeding ground for the basic anxiety whose repercussions in adult life give rise to the neurotic behavior that corresponds to the Freudian character types. The "deep feeling of helplessness toward a world conceived as potentially hostile" saps the infant's confidence in his ability to obtain the satisfactions and safety every individual wants. By substituting emotional drives, or needs, as refined into a character structure by early experiences, we see the genesis of the defensive strategies adopted by the individual; their compulsive quality makes them neurotic trends.[33] Greed, power, possessiveness, are only means of reassurance against anxiety, an anxiety that is generated by disturbed interpersonal relations in which a child may grow up. Moreover, it will not do to ascribe all neurotic behavior to mere repetitions of the experiences of infancy, focusing on that period alone to the exclusion of later developments. It is lifelong cultural conditions that generate neuroses, and these cultural conditions are not just incidental but "in the last analysis determine their particular form."[34] In brief, character is not a pathological residue of aim-inhibited libido, but a potentially healthy entity that matures within an environment. "A prevailingly sociological orientation then takes the place of a prevailingly anatomical-physiological one."[35] And while Harry Stack Sullivan specifically stresses the significance of the oral, anal, and genital zones, he just as specifically ties them to interpersonal relations, calling them, in fact, "zones of interaction." Relating to the interpersonal environment with these successively prominent areas of the body can leave lasting effects on character development.[36] No further than this will Sullivan yield.

If we may take seriously the figure of speech proposed in the first chapter, wherein Freud was pictured as regarding the instincts to be the counterparts of the determining and yet determined gods of Greek mythology, the Neo-Freudians seem to have worked a noticeable change in the character of the *dramatis personae*. The protagonist, man, is a comparatively free and responsible agent, an ego with a personality in his own right, working out his destiny in cooperation or conflict with the forces that surround him. An unhappy denouement will be a personal tragedy, not the inevitable consummation of cosmic necessity. We have moved from Sophocles to Shakespeare, from Oedipus to Hamlet.

Disparaging the importance of repetition in explaining current behavior entails rejection of the phylogeny-ontogeny parallel that played so prominent a part in Freud's thought. Development of the individual, Kardiner finds, notably his conscious systems, is connected with basic institutions. The significance of these institutions is not superficial, as compared with the attention orthodox psychoanalysis gave to unconscious systems. Neglecting them, in fact, and assigning the preponderating influence to phylogenetic factors, prevented Freud from examining current social realities.[37] It was, indeed, Kardiner's interest in social organization as a determinant of the intrapsychic apparatus that launched him on his studies of ontogeny in primitive cultures.[38] The inheritance of acquired characteristics on which Freud's theory depends does not take account of the role of social institutions in transmitting the material elaborated by fantasies, dreams, recollections, and myths. These reflect the pressures of primary institutions, says Kardiner; and, veritably paraphrasing Freud, fantasies "do not need to be inherited. Each individual can create them afresh."[39] Folk tales and religion relate to social organization as it channels human relations in solving the problem of societal adaptation. For such a purpose, a predisposed phylogenetic heritage is superfluous.[40] The current working of basic institutions, not a putative recapitulation of archaic experience, must engage our attention.

Once the theory of instincts has been disposed of, the interaction of the id, the ego, and the superego is seen to be but a specious explanation of psychopathology. Horney contends that, reduced to its fundamentals, the Freudian concept of neurotic conflicts visualizes them to be an inevitable conflict of instincts with the outside world, later introjected into the individual as the tribulations of the ego. The Freudian apology for a dearth of knowledge about the ego is that the historical development of psychoanalysis first directed attention to the id. But the hope of the school for an eventually comparable knowledge of the ego, Horney points out, had to be a vain one. A grounding in instinct theory from the very nature of the case precluded study of the ego, for such an entity could have no integrity of its own. What passed for an ego with the Freudians was bound to be a neurotic phenomenon. Only the liberation of ego-psychology from instinct theory would create a viable subject for study. Thus, a collision with the outside world is not inevitable for man. "If there is such a collision it is not because of his instincts but because the environment inspires fears and hostilities." The resultant neurotic trends perpetuate the difficulties; conflicts with the environment remain a vital part of neuroses. As Abram Kardiner puts it, "Neurosis is a freak of development and not a freak of nature."[41]

Actually, the Neo-Freudians pay little attention to the three-fold division of the psyche outlined by Freud. (On the whole, Abram Kardiner must be excepted from this generalization.) Sullivan says, laconically, he did not find the conceptions of id, ego, and superego useful in formulating problems.[42] It is easy to understand why. Once the theory of instincts had been abandoned, the locus of the instincts, the id, was conceptually useless. The ego, which stands in opposition to it in the Freudian theory of neurosis, had therefore to be given up too. And a superego hanging by itself was a solecism. Without a theory of instincts the Freudian topographical metapsychology simply collapsed. In Neo-Freudian writings it is true we hear occasional references to "ego," but then usually to differentiate their type of psychology from the "instinct-" or "id-psychology" elaborated by their predecessors. With the younger generation of psychoanalysts there is a distinct shift away from preoccupation with the etiology of morbid psychic phenomena in favor of a study of man's encounter with the environment, particularly in interpersonal relations. Thus in Neo-Freudian hands the classic topographical metapsychology perished less from damage than from desuetude. It is comparable to the passage from use of the sixteenth-century maps of the New World. They had once served a more or less useful purpose, but when outdated by subsequent explorations and refinements in cartography they were politely discarded with a minimum of polemics over their verisimilitude. The New World of psychoanalysis saw some cartographic casualties too.

By now the reader is due a closer acquaintance with the oft-recurring term "interpersonal relations," together with its most ardent exponent, Harry Stack Sullivan. It may be an error to embark on a discussion of Sullivan's ideas by way of his theory of interpersonal relations, for three posthumous publications of his[43] make it clear that the concept of anxiety is central to his thought, and in the only book he published during his life he acknowledged an inadequate statement of the theory of anxiety therein.[44] Furthermore, if the Freudian vocabulary is strange enough to tradition-minded social scientists, Sullivan's is still more alien, for he alone among the Neo-Freudians had no direct contact with the European school of analysts. He began his work as a psychiatrist with a special interest in schizophrenia, and as he matured he formulated his own vocabulary, which, although in many cases expressing concepts similar or identical to those of psychoanalysis, left his writings with an idiosyncratic flavor that does nothing to enhance their intelligibility.[45] Some ascribe Sullivan's incorrigible penchant for neology to his absorption with clinical work and the business of getting on with therapy, theory to take second place thereto.[46] Such an attitude speaks well for the scientific basis of Neo-Freudian psychoanalysis (an attitude not fully adhered to by all its exponents, as we shall see), however unhappy a reader's lot may be.

Now, if psychiatry ordinarily deals with psychosis, a psychic disturbance which is, in Freudian terminology, "a conflict between the ego and the outer world,"[47] what is that outer world if not other people? According to Sullivan, "If the term, mental disorder, is to be meaningful, it must cover like a tent the whole field of inadequate or inappropriate performance in interpersonal relations."[48] Sullivan expanded psychiatry to perhaps unmanageable proportions when he included in it everything pertaining to man in his personal and social life, his artifacts and his culture.[49] In actual clinical work, of course, the area had to be considerably circumscribed, but the significance of such a vision for a Neo-Freudian approach to social science is apparent. As a science, in Sullivan's opinion, psychiatry has to restrict itself to observable phenomena, "processes that involve or go on between people." The "inviolably private" was beyond its ken: "It must be concerned only with the human living which is in, or can be converted into, the public mode."[50] It does not study the individual in mental distress; it studies "disordered interpersonal relations nucleating more or less clearly in a particular person." Psychoanalysis would therefore be but one of several therapeutic techniques, though a vital one.[51] In effect, Sullivan converted all psychopathological studies into psychiatry. The term "neurosis" is absent from his writings (herein he differs sharply from Horney), being covered by the all-inclusive terms "mental disorders" and "mental illness." The feat was part and parcel of his renunciation of the Freudian topographical metapsychology and bore encouraging results in making schizophrenia amenable to therapeutic measures that employed psychoanalysis. By Clara Thompson's testimony, Sullivan was in fact one of the first to apply modified psychoanalytic techniques to the treatment of psychosis.[52] Sullivan felt there was good reason for his view, for no individual can exist unto himself. Communality with others is as vital to him as oxygen and water, and only a rare person can do without relations with others for any length of time without serious personality impairment.[53] One commentator put it more positively when she observed that interpersonal relations are indispensable to the acculturation process and that both the maturing and the fulfillment of some biological potentials demand interpersonal *loci.*[54] Lest it be thought that concentration on observable behavior would yield a superficial study that ignores unconscious motivation, Sullivan is careful to define "person" as comprehending imaginary, or fantastic ("eidetic" is his word) people as well, the awareness of whom is temporarily "dissociated" (repressed).[55]

Sullivan's concept of interpersonal relations apparently was influenced by the field theory of the physicist P. W. Bridgman. Scientific psychiatry, seen as the study of interpersonal relations, Sullivan says, requires the conceptual framework provided by such a theory.[56] Applying the physicist's approach to the matter, the

individual is seen to be comparable to a unit of electrical energy
activated by one social influence or another (in the analogy of one
critic) with no means of functioning except in immediate contact
with others. Thought and feeling are induced by an interpersonal
environment; social behavior reflects one's chance external relations.[57] What happens then to individuals as self-directed entities?
In truth, an exclusive regard for the network of interpersonal relations could leave individuals as mere nodules where the strands
intersect, or, to change the figure of speech, as so many knots in
a tangle of string, fortuitous phenomena that vanish when their
field does. It could easily lead to substituting the action for the
agent. Moving on a step, can "society" really be reduced to a
matter of groups of two or three people, and of larger, though less
durable, collections of such groups? What would become of situations where purposive activity (other than relations with others)
characterized groups? How explain emotions that can grip such
groups in time of war, or racial tension, for example? Finally,
how can such a view take account of the past, of history, other
than as a mere aftermath devoid of current impulsion?[58]

These criticisms point to a serious limitation on Sullivan's
efforts to construct the social philosophy with which he increasingly became occupied as the years passed. A concept of interpersonal relations based on the field theory was adequate for clinical psychiatry, where individual mental illness could be successfully diagnosed and treated, but it left something to be desired
when diagnosing and prescribing for social ills. Sullivan's closest
approximation to a social philosophy, the essay entitled "Tensions
Interpersonal and International: A Psychiatrist's View," traces the
tensions that produce wars back to the anxiety that individuals
necessarily go through in building their self-systems.* But while
wars and other types of social malaise are surely interpersonal
relations (of a sort), they just as surely involve more than groups
of two or three people. There is a missing link here, a link that

---

* Anxiety and self-system will both be discussed in Chapter 5; see also
infra, pp. 60–61.

would be filled by social institutions, the more or less standardized patterns of behavior involving all or nearly all the members of a society. Thus Sullivan's diagnoses of the ills of our times are on an individualistic level, lacking the realism that could be imparted by a sense of social conflict. And thus many of his editorials in the journal he edited, *Psychiatry*, have a highly moralistic flavor that students of *Realpolitik* would scorn. In the end, all forms of social conflict can be boiled down to you versus me, but in the dynamics of the immediate situation a good deal more has to be taken into account. Sullivan might have bridged the gap in his theory had his death not been so premature. His extant writings, however, are incomplete at a vital juncture.

Perhaps this indictment is too stringent. What Sullivan was inveighing against was, in his choice phrase, the illusion of personal individuality, "the ubiquitous superstition of the unique individual completeness of human beings," which, as we have seen, had no basis in fact. That old fallacy had equated the individual with his biological inheritance, but the truth was that to isolate a personality from relations with others exterior to oneself was "preposterously beside the point. . . ."[59]

To extricate himself from impending difficulties, Sullivan is careful to note that there are two ways of regarding the matter. One is the psychiatrist's, who postulates a "self" hypothetically in order to explain the activities people carry on with others (real or fantastic). A personality is "the relatively enduring pattern of recurrent interpersonal situations which characterize a human life."[60] As such, personality is beyond scientific grasp; the psychiatrist can never really know all about it that there is to know. However, it did not deny the individual a personality, for from his viewpoint it was quite another affair. To the individual, the "self" is composed of what Sullivan calls "reflected appraisals." These appraisals result from the focusing of attention by the "self-dynamism," or "self-system" (roughly equivalent to consciousness), on performances with significant other people whose approval or disapproval counts. They count because their disapproval can result in anxiety.[61] As a lifelong course of events the self-system is an ordering of the educational process that is composed of experiences sought to obviate or reduce anxiety-fraught occasions. The self may thus be called "the custodian of awareness," instead of the more commonly accepted term "consciousness." And, as a close student of Sullivan's thought maintains, this formulation does not deprive the individual of his personal identity, for a particular configuration of interpersonal relations is unique to each person. It is methodological redefinition, separating out the private and unique as unverifiable by scientific investigation.[62]

Sullivan's concept of anxiety will receive greater attention in a later chapter. Here we may pause to note that although he traveled by exasperatingly devious routes, Sullivan ultimately reached a conclusion completely in harmony with the tenets of his colleagues. The individual personality, for Sullivan as for the others, is not a by-product of a predetermined constitutional inheritance, and hence is not foreordained in its development. It is a consequence of constitution plus its interplay with the environment, as that environment is borne in the persons of others. The worst charge it would be possible to level against Sullivan is his having overstated a fact that the Freudians had all but overlooked. Mental illness could no longer be conceived of as individual, but as part of "a career line of interactions between individuals. . . ."[63] More than that, since mental illness arises from difficulties in interpersonal relations, psychopathology is of necessity a social more than a medical or a biological science. Therapy, therefore, would have to have primary reference to the cultural milieu. Once get rid of the notion that mental disorders are acts of God, says Sullivan, and they become "largely preventable and somewhat remediable by control of psycho-sociological factors."[64] These factors are often attributes of the social order. The therapist, chiefly concerned with the useless squandering of human talent, can hardly keep from visualizing a form of social organization where such problems will have been removed. A science of mental illness thus becomes also a science of society.[65]

The significance of the new theory for psychoanalytic therapy cannot be overstated. It too becomes a type of interpersonal relation, and the analyst takes on the role of participant observer. That is to say, he no longer merely stands aloof from the process, awaiting the transference of an infantile Oedipal situation and then guiding its resolution from a completely detached position, but, in Sullivan's words, he becomes "personally implicated in the operation. His principal instrument of observation is his self—his personality, *him* as a person."[66] Horney also sees the analyst personally involved in the transference, and it is the analyst's duty to perceive whether his reactions are those the patient wants to evoke, thereby obtaining closer knowledge of what is going on in the treatment. After all, neuroses ultimately express disturbed human relationships. One special form of these relationships is the analytical situation; the disturbances will appear in the latter as in the former. This is so because any encounter where emotional relations are present qualifies as a transference situation: they all contain irrational, emotional reactions, whether of infatuation or hostility. "In short, one can say people feel and behave just as irrationally outside the analytical situation as inside."[67] The analyst's aid is comparable to a friend's help, showing "emotional support, encouragement, interest in his happiness."[68]

Erich Fromm too criticizes Freud's "neutral, distant attitude toward the patient." Emotional assistance and psychological understanding, he feels, require the analyst to "reach out" toward the patient.[69] The orthodox technique for encouraging free association, which brings about the transference, had become a sterile ritual that yielded "free talk," inane chatter and reiterations that wasted much time and still left analyst and patient in an authoritarian-subordinate relation, the relation of a "normal" person to an "irrational" one. The necessary spontaneity was missing, Fromm believed, and it could be restored if the analyst prompted free associations with direct questioning and himself engaged in free association, the better to understand, to be "in touch" with, the patient by direct communication. "To interpret means to react with one's own imagination and free associations to the patient's utterances."[70]

Fromm, indeed, is dissatisfied with the more restrained forms of participant observation. His apostasy from orthodoxy goes to a perhaps untenable extreme here. It is plain that for him the analytic situation as it culminates in the transference is more of an emotional than an intellectual one. It is not mere quibbling to ask whether induced associations are truly free associations. But of greater importance is the question whether the procedure serves to strengthen the patient's ego-structure, his conscious self, or instead allows an emotional catharsis that does little or nothing to permanently reconstruct a damaged personality. Is the aim to be psychic rehabilitation or an interpersonal union with the analyst? And does the latter achieve the former? Franz Alexander thinks it does not, but does quite the opposite: a prolongation of the transference prolongs the patient's dependent attitude in a semipermanent regressive situation. Alexander's proposed innovations in transference technique are thus at odds with Fromm's. He would reduce the frequency of contact between patient and analyst so as to discourage the former's dependency feelings in the transference, and would consciously employ the analyst's personality in securing an objective yet helpful understanding in what is essentially a new (and not repetitive) situation.[71]

However much one may commend the more democratic flavor, so to speak, that Fromm would have the transference take in lieu of the superior-inferior relationship of orthodox practice, it raises certain complications of a practical kind. It must be difficult for the analyst to relate with the patient "from core to core," becoming one with him while retaining his separateness and objectivity, as Fromm desires. And when he speaks of the final act of understanding as an "intuitive grasp," an almost mystical element enters that perhaps carries the matter too far.[72] Fromm's ideas on the subject evince conceptions of mental illness, and of human nature in general, that will have to be called into question later on. For the present we can note that his zeal for a new dispensation in the clinic portends a similar predilection in his social philosophy.

At any rate, the gist of Neo-Freudian clinical psychoanalysis is not to visualize the transference as merely the occasion for managing repressed infantile experiences, as with Freud, but as one for correcting what Sullivan calls "parataxic distortions," a term meant to denote any fantastic representations of real persons whose impact helped generate the neurosis, by reconstructing this repressive situation.[73] For the Neo-Freudians were to expand the concept beyond its use in the clinic to a more general description of pathological reactions. The concept of the universal transference, or parataxic distortion, summarizes the fundamental truth that people's reactions stem as readily from unconscious motives as from conscious motives when a provocative situation arises. The conscious, rational mind is always poised on the brink of retreat to unconscious images of the self and others which, when reactivated, bear little relation to the realities of the current situation. Threats to the individual's security, or self-esteem, induce a recourse to a collection of defense measures that preserve psychic equilibrium, for the time being, but postpone or avoid a definitive coming to terms with interpersonal difficulties. It is touch and go all the way; a morbid and anachronistic pleasure principle can displace the reality principle at any given moment, when the stresses of interpersonal tensions become too much for a fragile self-system to support.

One further virtue must be claimed for the theory of interpersonal relations, regarding it now as a viewpoint taken by the Neo-Freudians collectively. It permits an intelligent reappraisal of the age-old dispute over whether instincts or environment determines human nature. This ancient issue is left a glorified logomachy as a result. The Neo-Freudians, we saw, discarded the concept of instinct entirely. The next step would be to stop treating "environment" as an abstract generality that glibly hypostatizes all that is not contained in "individual" biologically con-

ceived. The theory of interpersonal relations does just that, specifying what the vague term "environment" comprises so as to remove it from the realm of philosophical abstraction and spell it
out in terms manageable by the social sciences. The reason is that
with the Neo-Freudians the environment takes the form of other
people—that is, it is a social environment—notably the family as
it comes into contact with the individual in his younger years.
As such it is a specifiable group of people who, as bearers of culture, shape the individual's inherited constitution from an amor-
phous mass of potentials into a socially functioning unit. Thus
to Sullivan the self can be described as being formed by "the re-
flections of our personality that we have encountered mirrored in
those with whom we deal." The mother, "and/or her equiva-
lents," contributes the earliest and most significant part, the father
being second only to her.[74] And Erich Fromm is fond of referring
to the family as "the psychological agent of society," in the sense
of the family passing on to the child the character that makes him
a socially efficient individual.[75] Both these concepts will be taken
up again in the next chapter.

Franz Alexander has been especially insistent on this point.
Few other thinkers have wrestled as conscientiously as he with the
problem of reconciling human biological development with impersonal cultural uniformities. Assured that psychoanalytic insight into human nature provides a vantage point that other approaches do not have, this Neo-Freudian never forgets either the
humanistic implications or the methodological limitations of what
clinical experience has taught him. Alexander is ever aware that
the dual role of the psychoanalyst, as psychotherapist and as social
philosopher, is not only doubly opportune but doubly dangerous
too, for one can easily veer from the Scylla of treating individual
psychopathy from the standpoint of the anthropologist to the
Charybdis of treating social pathology as a mere enlargement of
individual neurosis. With circumspection and steady attention
to his subject matter, Alexander finds the nexus of the matter in
the interpersonal relations of family experiences.

The psychoanalyst, says Alexander, unlike the anthropologist, cannot be content with referring to general and constant cultural influences when trying to understand the human material presented by particular instances of mental illness. He must search for specific etiological factors which have brought about the emotional problems that vest themselves in concrete individuals. And these factors relate to childhood experiences that differ from family to family and for different children within the same family. Psychoanalytic experience proves beyond doubt that the "decisive factor" in accounting for the entire growth and functioning of the adult is the psychological management of the family relationships of the child.[76] This is not to say that the structure of a culture does not affect personality. So complex and rapidly changing a culture as ours offers a variety of ways in which individuals can experience its impact. What goes into the formation of a child's personality will depend upon the emotional needs elicited by the personalities of the child's parents, for "the most important factors in personality formation are the early experiences of childhood."[77] But at all events the psychoanalyst is not to regard his patients as "the exponents of cultural configurations"; they are individual people with individual problems and individual case histories.[78] Believing Horney to have swung from Freud's error of biological determinism to the polar error of general cultural determinism, Alexander, in a lengthy criticism of *New Ways in Psychoanalysis,* stressed that the subject matter of psychoanalysis is not groups but persons. "It is interested in the specific and actual influences upon the growing individual rather than general cultural trends."[79] For this neither a wholly biological nor a wholly sociological principle will suffice, for both fail to give proper weight to the influence of the parents' personalities.[80]

As far as it went, this explanation was simple and satisfactory. But a comprehensive view of neurosis and character formation left Alexander with the question of multiple variables. There are in actuality two classes of factors involved besides emotional experiences in the family: heredity and general cultural influences.

Heredity predestines "the whole rhythm of the life-span" and necessitates the adjustment of the individual to a "phylogenetically predetermined sequence of changes in its biological status," ranging all the way from dentition to sexual maturation.[81] Methodologically, as well as factually, it would be best to accept the hereditary human constitution as a given datum. If psychoanalysis could not manipulate it, at least it was a supremely adequate technique for studying hereditary constitution as it met the third variable, general environmental influences, when they became specific environmental influences. It is in the critical phase of childhood that constitutional intractibilia meet the demands of culture, the period when biological dependency must give way to emotional maturity. Hence the family situation is the focal point of all determinants and it is this that psychoanalysis reconstructs during psychotherapy.[82]

With these precautions in mind, it is possible to investigate the general cultural patterns for purposes of social philosophy. In so doing, one must turn the microscope into a telescope, so to speak, and see what trends characteristic of a nation are molded through the medium of the family to determine these very family attitudes. This is apt to be a difficult matter. It is all too easy to speak of fascism, for example, as "the paranoia of a nation," or to accept the facile generalization of "competitive civilization" without searching for the reasons that cause a given psychological attitude to develop and gain social acceptance.[83] Rather than plunge into a crude mass psychoanalysis, the analysis of a society at large as though it were an individual (after the fashion of Plato regarding the *polis* as the individual writ large), Alexander prefers a more cautious approach, as he appeals to sociology for cooperative endeavors. With psychoanalysis supplying the knowledge of psychological mechanisms and emotional processes, sociology can supply the study of the social structure affecting the human psyche. In tracing the etiology of group phenomena, the group must be examined sociologically in its cultural, political, and economic history, "corresponding to the individual life-history in psychoanalysis." A theory of social causation, explaining "precisely which psychological mechanism and which emotional attitudes, of all possible ones, will develop at a certain historical moment in a certain group," requires examination of the common, and no longer the individual, features of the group's members, as they relate to an actual social situation.[84] That is, in so far as there are emotional reactions so common as to be of societal (or near-societal) magnitude, psychoanalytic knowledge of them can be placed in a political, economic, and cultural context furnished by a history-minded sociology. Psychoanalysis provides the bricks, sociology the mortar. At all times it is necessary to remember that "the emotional relationships between members of the family are incomparably stronger determinants of character-formation of the child than the position of the family in a certain social group." The influence of family relationships "is vastly greater" on development of the child's personality than the intellectual, economic, or national-origin status of the parents. As could be expected, however, Alexander denies that early experiences leave an indelible imprint: what else does psychotherapy do if not bring about personality changes comparatively late in life?[85]

This trend in Alexander's thought merges with more extensive Neo-Freudian theories of character formation in society and leaves him in greater concordance with them than he seems to realize. Before broaching these topics, however, we had better summarize the pith of the Neo-Freudian break with orthodox Freudian psychoanalytic principles. First, the Oedipus complex has been (as we put it) desexualized; it is conceived of as but one type of interpersonal relation and not tied exclusively to the sexual development of the child. Second, the Neo-Freudians reject the instinct theory, moving away from the Eros–death-instinct dualism toward a framework of adaptation to the environment. That entails abandonment of the libido theory and its biological determinism and strict materialism. Next, there is a renunciation of the parallel of phylogenetic and ontogenetic development and a relegation of it to the area of philosophic curios, unsubstantiated by anthropological evidence. (Erich Fromm must be excluded from this generalization.) Then, according the ego a status in its own right, there is a pronounced shift away from an exclusive concern with the intricacies of psychopathology and a redirection toward the study of the development of individuals as going psychic concerns: an id-psychology, now outgrown, is supplanted by an ego-psychology. Finally, the Neo-Freudians pay less attention to infantile experience and its recrudescence in adult behavior and more attention to the environment and its effects, specifically by way of interpersonal relations: "It is a question not of 'actual versus past,' but of developmental processes versus repetition."[86] The path has been cleared for a new and dynamic social philosophy.

4

THE MAKING OF MAN

IT MAY WELL BE ASKED whether the Neo-Freudian revisions in psychoanalysis have not been so comprehensive as to utterly subvert its Freudian foundations. To put it another way, is it still legitimate to aver that the materials to be drawn from the revised discipline are truly of psychoanalytic origin? While purists may look askance at the innovators' position, a positive reply would not be hard to defend. In addition to training in the traditional concepts of Freud (with Harry Stack Sullivan as something of an exception), the Neo-Freudians can say, with Karen Horney, that

> the recognition of unconscious forces, of dreams being meaningful, the belief in the importance for therapy of the patient-analyst relationship, of recognizing and dealing with the patient's defenses, and the value of "free associations" are all part of a common heritage which forms the groundwork of psychoanalytic theory and method.[1]

None of the Neo-Freudians would take serious issue with the foregoing. What they have done is to broaden the scope of the discipline, to fill it with content that an instinct and sexual orientation could not contain, and give it firmer direction as a science with social import. To conceive the subject matter of psychoanalysis as the total personality in its adaptive activities, as does Abram Kardiner,[2] is to be able to utilize it to discover how human nature is formed in society. In evolving a methodology for tracing the conscious and unconscious impact of social institutions on the molding of individuals, Kardiner holds a pre-eminent place among the Neo-Freudians.

Summarily speaking, Kardiner is interested in finding how a society secures adaptation to its environment by forming within its constituent members what he calls a "basic personality." The latter may be traced to the operation of the basic disciplines of "primary institutions"; they form constellations of unconscious motivations in the individual which in turn are projected in the form of "secondary institutions" (or "projective systems"). Having eschewed the idea of "human nature" per se, he requires a method of research that will ultimately enable him to study the basic personality produced by Western society. For this purpose he worked out the technique of psychodynamics, refined into psychodynamic biography, and used it in conjunction with studies in anthropology. Kardiner's work is an implicit and explicit rejection of the Freudian principle that there is a human nature common to all mankind which secures an adaptation that is universal in configuration. Just as a society has an adaptational cycle, so the individual has his adaptational cycle within it and subject to the conditions imposed by it. Thus a constant, uniform nature is an assumption that empirical research shows to be false. "We must be extremely careful what factors we attribute to 'human nature,' " he says, "because there is no such thing; we know only specific types of 'human nature' under specific environmental and social conditions." The infant is helpless in all societies, which is precisely what makes him susceptible to the influences, pedagogic and disciplinary, that culture imposes. It is not enough to study unconscious constellations in general. One must study the connection between unconscious constellations and culture, in that way locating the sources of pressure on personality in its struggle toward adaptation.[3] Kardiner's new vocabulary may gain easier acceptance if we note, parenthetically, that "constellation" is his equivalent of the Freudian "complex," and that "family constellation" corresponds to the orthodox "Oedipus complex."[4]

With Kardiner the emphasis is on an ego-psychology. The ego-structure, which is the more conventional term for basic personality, is the individual's adaptational faculty which contacts institutions directly, and it is the relation between the two on which Kardiner focuses. Unconscious constellations are to be used as evidence, not of phylogenetic continuity, but of the pressures created by institutions. The individual's anxieties and the defenses he mobilizes are the internal adjustments necessitated by external reality, elaborated psychically and manifested in fantasy life.[5]

The basic personality differs from a concept like "national character" in that psychodynamics is a technique of investigation that can establish a cause-and-effect relation between cultural influences and personality patterns, yielding not a collection of traits but a basic personality structure seen as "a direct function of the institutions by which it is moulded." A record of life experiences is indispensable as a guide to the shaping of personality by institutions but psychodynamic biography goes beyond that in accounting for basic personality. It does not employ only the conventional and naïve method of conscious self-portrayal, but, using techniques of clinical psychoanalysis, it also rests on experiences whose meaning the subject may not understand, including, notably, such unconscious experiences as are revealed in dreams and fantasies.[6]

What are these primary institutions? They are the practices and customs that bring the problem of adaptation to bear on the individual. They answer to the need to satisfy human biological wants and include family organization, the formation of social bonds, methods of caring for children, infantile disciplines, patterns of feeding, weaning, anal training, sexual prohibitions, and techniques of securing subsistence. It is no wonder that the solution of these crucial problems creates pressures on the personality and that psychodynamic biography is the method needed to find the beginnings of the attitudes of the person toward others and toward his own capabilities. In locating the primary institutions of a society these questions must be asked:

> What are the direct experiences of the child in regard to infantile care or neglect; who are the objects with whom care,

solicitude, or neglect is experienced; and what are the consequences? What disciplines are instituted with regard to food,
sphincter control, and sexual activity, and by whom? What are
the obligations and responsibilities of the child?[7]

Primary institutions are relatively old and stable among cultural
patterns, having persisted because found to be utilitarian in serving the purpose of adaptation in the progress of social evolution.
Men do what they have to do so as to survive in as pleasing a way
as they can. A natural selection, in fact, can be proved to work in
social evolution as well as in organic evolution. The societies that
survive are those which exhibit "effective patterns of adaptation,"
adaptation of constitution to environment. Social collapse need
not result from outside pressure but can come about from internal
failure of the collective adaptation of the constituents.[8] The role
of sexuality, be it noted, is not of supreme importance, but the
role of the family is not to be underrated. "The family is the
locus of personality formation, and hence the most reliable avenue
for the transmission of culture," Kardiner says. It is here that the
personality most appropriate to the society is molded, and one
must be aware of the fact that the development of the ego will be
more or less affected depending on how close to infancy the basic
institutions operate. Once the basic personality, and with it the
emotions needed for social cohesion, are formed in the family, external blandishments are superfluous for the creation of morality.
Morality is not preached but built in; exhortation may reinforce
morality but no more. "Morality is built by constant interaction
with parents in early life."[9] In classical Freudian terminology,
acceptance of moral standards by the young child represents incorporation of parental authority in the superego. In Kardiner's terminology, this resolution of the Oedipus complex represents shaping of the basic personality to accord with the requirements of
adaptation to social living, which includes benefits as well as restrictions.

The resultant basic personality comprises "the effective adaptive tools of the individual which are common to every individual in the society." It includes "the mental and emotional processes" consistently displayed by a society of people living with the same institutions and environment. It can be predicted when the cumulative influences of the primary institutions are known. The interlocking of primary institutions, basic personality, and secondary institutions is so intimate that Kardiner could claim to be able to account for similarity in the basic personality of a society's members as well as the society's particular needs once he could establish that similarity in secondary institutions was due to systems of personality integration based on society-wide contact with primary institutions.[10] In any case, basic personality is to be distinguished from character. The former is a general cultural residue, the latter a particular variation of it possessed by each individual. Because the individual does not accept the acculturation process passively and is able to strike a compromise between his own adaptive equipment and institutional forces, he has something of a "margin of autonomy" that gives him this individuality, a smaller circle of personal attributes within the larger circle of culturally created possibilities.[11] It cannot be emphasized too strongly that basic personality does not comprehend the totality of an individual's characteristics. All the members of a society are not identical in every respect. There is no such thing as a societal stereotype superseding the several members' individual characters, after the fashion of Rousseau's general will superseding the collectivity of individual wills. As Ralph Linton puts it, basic personality is a norm, a construct, taken from the range of individual differences, "a common denominator, a series of fundamental characteristics upon which other and more variable elements of personality are superimposed" by individuals and groups.[12]

By "discipline" Kardiner means "the restriction or direction of impulses or activities which exist in some rudimentary form from the moment of birth." The disciplines to which the individual is subjected in the formation of his basic personality relate above all to the somatically derived needs of hunger and sexuality; others, being less important, can be created or emphasized; not being stereotyped, they account for the diversity found in human societies. The disciplines are most potent when begun in childhood and are thus incorporated into the personality structure, making the individual an often unwitting accomplice in perpetuating adaptive patterns.[13]

The basic personality finds expression in secondary institutions, or projective or reality systems, in Kardiner's scheme of things. They are the unconscious deposits in the individual of primary institutions. Resulting as they do from the traumatic experiences of disciplining and the anxieties they create, the projective systems are irrational and vary with the quantity of anxiety in the individual's growth pattern. They too are adaptive, serving "to relieve the mutilating effect of painful tensions." They take the form of taboo systems, religion, and fantasies.[14] Though projective systems do not include consciously learned reality systems, they are treated by the individual as external realities. Their unraveling by psychodynamic biography provides indexes of where institutional pressures impinged on the individual, and the primary institutions of a culture can be deduced from the pattern of secondary institutions the individual bears in his unconscious and reveals when his psychodynamic biography is taken.[15] Kardiner's conception of secondary institutions, or reality systems, as being the expression of psychological needs is something of a vestige of Freud's theory of the omnipotence of thoughts, wherein reality is believed by some to be the fulfillment of wishes. In the Freudian system, however, the theory applied to neurotics and primitive people, and not to normal or modern ones.[16] Kardiner's conception of adaptation to the environment, linked with the twin investigative techniques of psychoanalysis and an anthropology stressing comparative studies, thus focuses on the dynamic role of institutions, with a number of results important for the social sciences. It turns the tables on Freudian psychoanalytic principles in demoting the unconscious from the status of the alpha and omega of all psychic motivations to that of psychic record and witness of the activities of the ego in guiding the human career. In retaining the idea of the prominence of infantile disciplines Kardiner accepts Freud's theory of the paramount influence of the erotogenic zones in molding personality, yet without resurrecting the libido theory. The reference is not to gratification or frustration of libidinal cathexes but rather to institutional pressures as they become interpersonal relations in family life to act upon these zones: the emphasis is on social institutions and not on sexuality.[17] As a result, different conditions, reflecting different problems of societal adaptation, can be expected to yield different basic personalities, as in actual fact they do. Basic personality will thus vary with time and place; a viable unit for empirical inquiry and social philosophy appears, for basic personality is concrete and specific enough to be verifiable by scientific methods and yet comprehensive and flexible enough to serve as a basis for meaningful generalizations. On these grounds, therefore, there can be no criterion for postulating a fixed, uniform human nature with a universal history of culturally imposed neurosis. The true criterion has to be one of greater or lesser effectiveness in securing adaptation. General laws of human development and the possibility of a cosmic social philosophy have to be regarded as mirages. In compensation, however, the whole process of personality formation, as it varies from society to society and at different epochs in the same society, is open to study by the social sciences utilizing empirical methods of investigation. And moreover, that process is susceptible to conscious change and deliberate reorganization in order to improve the efficacy of institutional arrangements in developing basic personality.

Kardiner credits Erich Fromm with being among the first to introduce the methods of investigation of the social sciences—specifically, historical materialism—into psychoanalytic sociology.[18] Fromm's earlier works on the subject, all published in German, are quite consistent with the cultural relativism of Kardiner's theory. But Fromm is known to his American audience almost entirely by his writings in English, beginning with his provocative book *Escape from Freedom* (1941). In this and subsequent works Fromm unequivocally repudiates the objectivity of Kardiner's approach and adheres to an ethical absolutism. That is to say, while acknowledging, even emphasizing, the importance of social institutions in the formation of character, Fromm interjects a normative viewpoint by insisting that a character structure can be thus formed that is at bottom detrimental to the individual.

> Though there is no fixed human nature, we cannot regard human nature as being infinitely malleable and able to adapt itself to any kind of conditions without developing a psychological dynamism of its own. Human nature, though being the product of historical evolution, has certain inherent mechanisms and laws, to discover which is the task of psychology.[19]

The clay of the individual is in the potter's hands of his society, Fromm is saying, but when damaged vessels are turned out in large numbers there is something wrong with the potter. One must expect that if social institutions persist in fashioning human beings without regard to the minimal requirements of human nature, the products will be faulty. It is the prevalence of abnormal people in our society—by this standard—that provokes Fromm to level an ethical accusation against its institutions.

Fromm's demurrer on the methodology of cultural relativism signifies something of a cleavage in the Neo-Freudian school, although in a later chapter we shall see that Kardiner himself is not devoid of moral judgments. Being more concerned with refining a methodology, however, Kardiner tended to avoid ethical considerations in his works, whereas Fromm had already worked out his methodology by the time he came to the United States in the early 1930's. With modifications in it, notably an abandonment of strict Freudian principles and less stress on economic determinism, Fromm was ready to launch into social criticism with his first book in English. Therefore, his earlier formulations are much to the point of a discussion of those of his writings that are better known to Americans, aside from their own inherent interest and the achievement they represent.

Fromm's university studies in sociology and his subsequent
training in psychoanalysis put him in a position, he felt, to combine these disciplines in a fruitful union of Marxian sociology and
Freudian psychology. Historical materialism as it then stood, he
thought, had an inaccurate, or at best incomplete, psychology. To
hold that economic interests operate as psychic motives does not
by itself vindicate Marx's claim that the political and intellectual
history of every epoch is determined by the current type of economic production and exchange and the social order necessarily
dependent on it. Fromm observed that it was necessary to demonstrate that economic conditions per se function in all human
activity, ideology included. This called for a correlation of individual psychic disposition with the stage of development of productive forces. After all, laws of society as such do not act; it is
men who act. Psychoanalysis could show how particular economic
conditions affected the human psychic apparatus to produce given
ideological results; that is, it could show in what way ideology depended on the causative economic realities.[20] Fromm utilized orthodox Freudian psychoanalysis, both as a therapeutic device and
as a source of social theory, in order to make the demonstration.
As such it was an instinct-psychology, with special reference to a
historical perspective. It visualized human careers to be governed
by instincts, with the development of instincts to be understood in
the context of those careers.[21] As applied to the analysis of social
phenomena, psychoanalysis merely applied the method it employed in analyzing the individual, "comprehension of his instinct-structure from the total life experience." In Fromm's mind,
this was only a legitimate extension of psychoanalytic technique,
for psychoanalysis, in studying individuals, started from the premise of "the active and passive adaptation of biological facts, namely
instincts, to social factors."[22]

The key phrase is "total life experience" (*Lebensschicksals*);
it enables psychoanalysis to proceed from studying individuals to
studying groups, classes, or even societies.

It is those circumstances or conditions of life which determine
the mode of living and the conditions of life of the members

of a societal stratum beyond the individual differences in the life of an individual. . . . Hence, they are primarily economic, social, and political conditions under which a group lives.[23]

While still attaching pre-eminent importance to early childhood experiences, such historical knowledge was on the one hand a necessary prerequisite to the understanding of individuals. On the other hand, with a similar historical method one could understand "the common psychic attitude" typical of a group's members, "the totality of characteristic attributes" of a class or a nation. For the individual, psychoanalysis seeks the correlation between a specific career and specific instinct development. For the group the equivalent instinct-structure is to be sought in its counterpart of the individual's total life experience, "the economic, social, and political situation of that group." Let Fromm summarize for himself:

> Psychoanalysis appears to have all the prerequisites which make its method also useful for sociopsychological investigations and eliminate all conflicts with sociology. It seeks those traits which are shared in common by the members of a group and attempts to explain these common psychic attitudes in terms of the common total life experiences. These total life experiences lie, however, not in the sphere of the fortuitous and the personal, but they are identical with the socioeconomic situation of precisely that group—the larger the group the lesser it applies. Analytical social psychology hence means: the attempt to understand the instinct-structure, namely the libidinal, the largely unconscious attitude of a group, in terms of its socioeconomic structure.[24]

Society, Fromm theorized, had a libidinal structure that held it together over and above such mechanical forces as the police, law, and military coercion, or the rational interests of men. As the consequence of the confrontation of instinctual inclinations by social-economic conditions, this libidinal structure in large part determines the formation of the emotional attitudes of the various social strata. Employing the familiar Freudian concept of libido development, Fromm held that the strengthening or sublimation of the child's pregenital libidinal drives sanctions, by a kind of "social premium," the formation of a social character that is deemed normal or healthy in the society concerned. As determined by the group's sexual morality, regression of libido will intensify the oral and anal character traits that in social life are the most advantageous to the individual's advancement.[25]

It was here that the family played its key role. As the "psychological agent of society," the family is the means by which the society or the class imprints its own structure on the child and thus on the adult also. The family itself being the product of a given social and, more particularly, class structure, it is the relationship of the child to the members of the family that fixes the development of his instincts. The family funnels the psychic attitudes and ideologies of economic conditions into libidinal drives. Fromm was wary, however, of a too-easy analogy between individual neurotic development and social dislocation.[26]

With this method Fromm forged the missing link between historical materialism and psychological motivation. Since ideological motives themselves are explicable as mere rationalizations of libidinal needs, the most grandiose intellectual operations are reducible to a "material libidinal nucleus"; the unique importance of economic needs that had been the *idée fixe* of historical materialism could be done away with or, to be more precise, given its proper psychosocial context.[27] Fromm's achievement in uniting historical materialism and a dynamic psychology with the buckle of psychoanalysis is not to be underrated. More distinguished minds than his had been unable to fill the gap between economic institutions and psychological motivation. The foremost Marxist analysis of the organization of social institutions in the capitalist phase of economic development is shockingly innocent of a psychology that corresponds to the prevalent institutions. By contrast, the classic study of the origins of the spirit that motivated the development of modern capitalism completely ignores the impact of economic institutions on the social character evolving *pari passu*.[28]

Taken in the gross, Fromm's theory of the formation of social character is almost identical with Kardiner's. For Kardiner's primary institutions there are Fromm's economic circumstances; for basic personality there is social character; for basic disciplines there is the direction of libido by the total life experience; for secondary institutions, or projective or reality systems, there is ideology; and in both systems of theory the family plays a vital part. If anything, when it comes to cultural relativism, Fromm out-Herods Herod. A closer look, however, discloses Fromm to diverge from Kardiner in his adherence to the libido and instinct theories, and not even a closer look is needed to reveal the passivity of the ego in the whole process. As we have seen, a system resting on such a foundation is open to serious criticism, and this may have been the reason for Fromm's *volte-face* in mid-career that saw him switch to ethical absolutism. The cause is not clear, but if it were to come to conjecture this writer would guess that a comparatively objective methodology left Fromm no ground on which to base an unfavorable judgment of the social character that proved so receptive to totalitarianism in Nazi Germany. There must have been something drastically wrong (so Fromm may have thought) with a society that cultivated what he was later to call the authoritarian character structure. Fromm was observing what was to him a warped society producing warped individuals, and he may have taken it upon himself to excogitate a modified system that would explain the aberrations of both. Be that as it may, the new theory Fromm began expounding after his removal to the United States suffuses what is retained of the old system with a heady moral flavor.

Consistent with his earlier theory, in *Escape from Freedom* Fromm observes that the need for societal self-preservation elevates economic institutions into the primary factor in the determination of an individual's character structure; physical want forces him to accept the conditions under which he must live. Not that society has an exclusively suppressive function: the process works to the mutual advantage of society and individual. Acting in accord with one's character traits answers economic need while it affords the psychological satisfactions demanded by one's char-

acter structure.[29] In the formation of social character the society
does not exert a mere influence on the individual. It molds his
whole personality. The latter is determined by the social structure to such an extent that it is possible to infer the entirety of
the social structure from the analysis of a particular individual
living under its sway. Or, working deductively, if one has as complete a knowledge of a nation's history as the psychiatrist has of
his patient's life history, achieved by social, economic, political,
and cultural studies, one can understand how such circumstances
shape the character structure of most of its members. People's
thoughts and feelings stem from their character, and that, in turn,
is determined by "the socio-economic and political structure of
their society." It need only be remembered, in addition, that the
process of character formation works on a level beneath the conscious cognition of individuals.[30]

The family, in Fromm's newer theory, is still the psychological
agent of society. Leaving aside minor idiosyncratic variations, the
family transmits not only the educational patterns of their society
but also the social character of the class or society represented in
their own personalities, for the parents and their pedagogical techniques are alike determined by the social structure. Their character structures contain their social and class ethos, which the child
meets from the beginning. Childhood training is "one of the key
mechanisms of transmission of social necessities into character
traits."[31] With somewhat less emphasis, the concept of total life
experience survives in the new formulation. Fromm seeks not
isolated and fortuitous individual conditions but "the total structure of basic life experiences as they are essentially conditioned by
the socio-economic situation of the particular group."[32]

For Fromm the social character prevalent in a given society is
not a statistical sum of the character traits found therein but pertains to the function it fills, that of shaping the energies of its
component members so as to remove questions of behavior from
the area of conscious decision. *"Outer force is to be replaced by
inner compulsion"*; random energy is replaced by determined char-

acter traits. The resultant social character "internalizes external necessities and thus harnesses human energy for the task of a given economic and social system."[33] Ideology has no autonomous influence. It too is bound up in the adaptation of the individual to his society, Fromm holds. Ideas are potent insofar as they respond to the human needs that are salient in a particular social character. Their influence is proportional to their appeal to the "psychic needs" of their audience. When absorbed into the social character they become a stabilizer thereof.[34]

It is at this point that Fromm breaks with the comparatively detached position of cultural relativism. Fromm notes with alarm that, held to the types of behavior his society sanctions, the human being apparently has a restricted range within which he can function *qua* human being. Since virtually any activity can be made pleasureful, what may have social utility can actually be harmful to man. While statistical measurement of the genuine happiness of people in our culture is not available, Fromm is skeptical as to whether our institutions are serving their purpose of providing—in the Benthamite formula—the greatest happiness of the greatest number.[35] Fromm's concern as to the seemingly limitless influence of culture in determining character structure impels him to demarcate a line beyond which society cannot legitimately mold its members. The interposition of a criterion of legitimacy in a very real sense constitutes a resurrection of the dichotomy between the individual and the state that has plagued political philosophy since (in modern times) the days of the social contract philosophers and with it the problem of political obligation. Does the individual have a moral obligation to obey political authority? If so, to what extent? If not, then how justify coercion by the powers that be? Kardiner's concept of basic personality, and Fromm's concept of social character up to this point, had pretty much dispensed with the issue by showing it to be in large part a spurious one. Questions of political obligation do not make a true issue because one's attitude toward authority is not ordinarily a matter of deliberate reflection but is disposed of beforehand, unconsciously. It is built into individuals by the disciplines that go to mold basic personality. When the configuration of the basic personality has taken shape, one automatically renders unto Caesar the things which are Caesar's. There is no need for "outer force"; it has been replaced by "inner compulsion." The Oedipus complex is resolved, and with it the problem of political obligation. As for those instances which are not ordinary, those situations in which the political system presents conditions inimical to the continued development of personality and its relatively unfettered expression, they are symptomatic of what Veblen delightfully called idiot institutions. The ways of society—in this case, political power—are not serving their ostensible purpose. They are not securing successful adaptation for individual people. In a word, institutions are inefficient; they have lost their utility. To the newer Fromm, such institutions are bad; they have lost their legitimacy. The distinction is a fine one, but it is all the difference between a theory of utility and a theory of natural rights. It is the channel that separates Bentham from Rousseau, Burke from Paine. A theory of utility permits systematic, premeditated reform within the existing system. A theory of natural rights champs at the bit of what it contemns as palliatives and is inclined to unlimited reform—revolution or utopia-building. Thus Kardiner's *Sex and Morality* would revise sex education to accord with the changed needs of our society; Fromm's *The Sane Society* would refashion our social order outright. Most of the Neo-Freudians would find themselves among the utilitarians. Fromm would find himself in the school of natural right.[36]

Fromm's psychoanalytic equivalent of the natural rights theory takes the form of what he calls "humanistic ethics." Claiming that "there are immutable laws inherent in human nature and human functioning which operate in any given culture" whose violation inflicts serious damage on the personality, he implies that psychoanalysis has found certain psychological minima that set a limit to the adaptation of the individual to cultural demands. Adaptation cannot go on indefinitely. Culture patterns contradictory to man's nature induce psychic stresses that compel him to change the patterns, for man cannot alter his nature.[37] Fromm believes human nature is universal because of "the essential features of bodily and mental equipment" that all men share. These features are expressed in the "symbolic language" of dreams, myths, and fairy tales. Though forgotten by modern man, symbolic language is "the one universal language the human race has ever developed, the same for all cultures and throughout history." The relation between the symbol and what is symbolized is therefore intrinsic.[38] Fromm feels Freud had erred in stipulating that dreams can only be unconscious expressions of impulses of which we are consciously ashamed. Since civilization is a repressive agent, our dreams may represent not only what is primitive or indecent but also what is more intelligent and wiser. "My assumption is that dreams can be the expression both of the lowest and most irrational *and* of the highest and most valuable functions of our minds." The art of dream interpretation has to understand whether a given dream conveys one's animal nature or one's better self.[39]

The theory is an effort to meet Freud on his own ground, to utilize the interpretation of dreams and analogous phenomena for proof of a human nature different from that which orthodox psychoanalysis perceived. Fromm would stand Freud on his head, so to speak, using an orthodox investigative technique to uncover contradictory material. But it must be noted that Fromm himself is in error in burdening Freud with an ethical valuation of instincts. As we have seen, Freud regarded them as neither good nor bad. And when Fromm elsewhere characterizes Freud's theory of the Oedipus complex, with its twin impulses of incest and parricide, as "the secularized version of the concept of 'original sin,' " ethics being to Freud a "reaction formation" against man's innate wickedness, he repeats the same invidious allegation.[40]

The question may be raised whether his position is as valid and consistent as Freud's. It would appear to be not. It might be supposed that the immutable laws he ascribes to human nature are those he has discovered from empirical investigation of people in various societies, employing, of course, psychoanalysis as his technique. But it is quite clear—to this writer, at any rate—that Fromm obtrudes his own philosophical preconceptions of human nature into an area that one would have thought should be reserved for a science uncommitted to speculative presuppositions.[41] One cannot help note the strange paucity of psychoanalytical case material Fromm cites in his works. The substitution of references to the view of human nature of such humanistic philosophers as Aristotle and Spinoza is a subtle shifting of ground which, while it may lend popular or emotional appeal to Fromm's message, conflicts with the comparatively dispassionate basis used by his colleagues for their social criticism.

Undeterred, Fromm has to dispose of the criterion of normality postulated by "sociological relativism." A standard of normality must have reference, he says, to the "universal criteria for mental health which are valid for the human race as such," and not to the question of "adjustment to the ways of life in his society." A well-adapted person often becomes such by sacrificing his real self to the *ignis fatuus* of being what he is expected to be. Fromm's universal criterion, "valid for all men," postulates that men attain mental health if maturation follows "the characteristics and laws of human nature," mental illness being a deficiency in this process. Psychotherapy directed to a norm of social adjustment only enables the patient to conform to prevalent culture patterns in yet another way: to sink (or rise) to the general level of suffering of his society.[42] Humanistic ethics, on the contrary, posits the well-being of man as the criterion for good and evil. By holding that "there is nothing higher and nothing more dignified than human existence," it is his society, not he, that is to be thrown into the balance, and the society may be found wanting when judged by an objective study of the needs of man.[43]

A purportedly objective study yields a copious array of characteristics that Fromm conceives to be at the core of human nature. It may be questioned whether it is an empirical use of psychoanalysis that has revealed them. Aside from comprising what

Fromm's humanistic ethics holds to be "good," they are reducible to the more manageable group of relatedness, productiveness, and growth.[44] They all pertain to the thesis that is central to Fromm's thought, namely, that both ontogenetically and phylogenetically, man has irreversibly severed the primary ties that bound him (in the first case) to the comfort and sustenance of the mother and (in the second case) to his unity with nature.

Ontogenetically, man has an inherent tendency to develop and grow and to express the potentialities of life in its manifold aspects. The need to do so comes from within and is not imparted by exterior powers. Failure to do so, from infancy onward, produces dysfunction, unhappiness, and neurosis. Even the child, fighting against irrational parental authority, struggles for the more positive freedom to realize himself as a human being in his own right; neurotic adults bear the wounds of defeat in this contest.[45] However dramatic the process of maturation may be, it is actually a reluctant journey. The security and sense of orientation, the rootedness, provided by the ties to the mother are irremediably forfeited in the process of man's individuation; he is left with the problem of "how to overcome separateness, how to achieve union, how to transcend one's own individual life and find at-onement." Only in relating himself to his fellows can man find happiness. Since isolation is so unbearable as to be incompatible with sanity, the principal problem of ethics is that of man's relatedness to others. Fromm announces his kinship with Sullivan in visualizing individual psychology as social psychology, or the psychology of interpersonal relations.[46]

Phylogenetically, the emergence from matriarchal society launches the human race on its own path of individuation. Evolution releases physiological and psychological potentialities in the human species with their own dynamisms which have a tendency to express themselves once they have made their appearance. A healthy form of orientation is one which answers to the relevant stage of human evolution; a regression therefrom to an artificial unity with nature is a sign of social pathology. The evo-

lution of human religious beliefs and social organization, away
from the primitive and toward the sophisticated, has witnessed
the supersession of matriarchy by patriarchy and of the humane
aspects of interpersonal association by an aimless, feckless freedom.
Both ontogenetically and phylogenetically man is faced with what
Fromm calls "the human situation," the equally painful alternatives between progression and retrogression.[47]

There is a remarkable similarity between Fromm and Freud
in their treatment of the themes of individual maturation, individual regression, social development, and social breakdown. As
may be expected, only the Oedipus complex can weave these
tangled strands into an intelligible warp and woof. In the Freudian system, we know, the resolution of the Oedipus complex in the
individual internalizes a moral prohibition as the most formidable
barrier against incest. Violation of the prohibition entails regression to perverse infantile sexuality. Likewise, higher social organization necessitates inhibitions against the family becoming absorbed with its own interests. Violation of the inhibition means
social breakdown and a return to the primal horde in the state
of nature. The tragic truth is that the disruption of the family is
the *sine qua non* of maturation, in the individual and in society.
"Society, therefore, uses all means to loosen those family ties in
every individual, especially in the boy, which are only important
in childhood."[48] In his own way, Fromm is largely in agreement.
As to the individual, the affective tie to the mother must be severed
if individuation is to be attained. Dependence on maternal protection inhibits growth and hence is a pathological phenomenon.
As to society, or rather as to mankind, it is no longer merely the
family and the clan that extend the ties of blood and soil, but state,
nation, church, race, class, and parties also are forms of incest.
But the taboo on incest is the *sine qua non* of human development
to freedom. Since a return to a pre-human harmony with nature
does not solve the problem of human existence, "only the complete
eradication of incestuous fixation will permit the realization of
the brotherhood of man."[49] Fromm's use of the word "incest" is

rather a loose one. It serves to remind us of the fundamental difference between him and Freud on the meaning of the Oedipus complex: dependence versus sexuality.

In positing a necessary course of development as he sees it, in injecting a particular kind of teleology into evolution, Fromm gains the advantage of a moral ground from which to pass judgment on any society that does not sanction such development in its members or does not itself comport with a foreordained growth. Fromm's writings treat much of the various types of aberrant individuals and the specific type of an insane capitalist society, both topics to be discussed later in this volume. At the same time, in relinquishing a position of objectivity he lays himself open to criticisms of the very standards he applies in his judgments. It is easy to take issue with the type of social organization Fromm proposes as an alternative to capitalism, as will be done in another chapter; and a view of human nature based on a theory of natural law, while attractive in many respects, in reality evades the necessity of adducing empirical proof for its categorical asseverations—as, indeed, it is designed to do. Yet there may be a hidden route by which scientific evidence can be brought to fortify part of Fromm's moral battlements. In mentioning the attributes imputed to be inherent in human nature, he more than once alludes to a "striving for mental health," an "impulse to achieve psychic health and happiness," without which therapeutic efforts would be in vain.[50] If the clinical experience of psychoanalysis can demonstrate empirically what Fromm postulates philosophically, then perhaps some part of his system can be retrieved for the objective verification of a universal human quality. Let us consult what the less ambitious of the Neo-Freudians have to say about the powers of growth, the drive to be oneself, inherent in human nature.

Karen Horney, for one, was decidedly of a less speculative bent. Clara Thompson describes her as being "much more concerned with therapy than with theory,"[51] which, while underestimating Horney's very considerable contributions to the latter, points to the derivation of her ideas from practice, rather than from rumination. She often cites her clinical experience as the impulse to modification of a previous formulation, and her own development over the years is, in a way, confirmation of her final conviction of the innate capacity of the individual to grow. Horney states that her belief in man's constructive possibilities is "not mere speculation" but is based on the evidence of observed childhood development, clinical experience, and the changes that take place in psychoanalytic therapy.[52] One need not seek far in her works for reports of case material. So thick are they with endless catalogs of the shades and varieties of neurotic manifestations—one critic describes *Neurosis and Human Growth* as "a veritable handbook of neurotic etiquette"[53]—that the reader with an eye for glimmerings of a social philosophy is often hard put to detect anything of the kind. Although she is more modest than Fromm, the import of her work is, in this writer's opinion, more substantial.

In Chapter 3 we met with Horney's insistence on a "will for life" which, rather than a death-instinct, may impel people to destruction. It too was confirmed in psychoanalytic experience when dealing with the environmentally fostered anxiety that began in infancy.[54] Two papers on feminine psychology during her Freudian period further displayed her restiveness under orthodox theories of personality. In one she criticized an outlook that attributed feminine psychology to genital differences from the male which, she believed, overlooked woman's role in reproduction as a source of psychological gratification. In a second she found cultural conditioning, not biological sexual differences, responsible for aberrant female behavior.[55] Both essays pointed to the role of culture in impelling the neurotic trends that the Freudians mistook for normal feminine behavior. We know now what these preliminary rumblings foretold: a shift from an id-psychology to an ego-psychology which visualized drives of the ego to be on an equal footing with those of the id.[56] When the theory of the triple division of the psyche is likewise jettisoned, it is the accentuated conflict of drives per se that is seen to yield neurosis.[57]

In her first book Horney explored the conflicts between "those two drives which factually play the greatest role in neuroses: the craving for affection and the craving for power and control."[58] It is true Horney refers to these needs indiscriminately as "drives," "instincts," "tendencies," and "strivings," and it is almost too obvious that the need for affection and the need for power correspond fairly closely to the sex- and ego-instincts of Freud's first formulation of an instinct theory, although she simultaneously depreciated the sexual quality of the need for affection.[59] While it was not for another two years that Horney explicitly repudiated instinct theory, she would not have accepted the aforementioned "needs" as fundamental requirements of a universal human nature whose denial necessarily resulted in neurosis. She had already expressed the view that it was when drives conflicted with each other in ways the individual could not resolve that neurosis was precipitated. The etiology of neuroses was to pertain to conflicts in culturally imposed demands, which would differ from society to society. Cultural circumstances condition in very high degree individual emotions and outlooks, and a measure of normality would therefore have to have reference to social standards of action and feeling—although the standards involve time, class, and sex too. In our culture, competition seems to be an eternal nexus of neurotic conflicts, the problem of dealing with which is normal for everyone but exaggerated for the neurotic.[60] *The Neurotic Personality of Our Time* focused on the roots in our culture of the conflict between competition and success (the need for power) and love and humility (the need for affection). Two irreconcilable values are inculcated into individuals in Western society, that of success, which requires aggressiveness and self-assertion, and that of humility and compliance in accordance with Christian precepts. Normally two solutions are possible: to accept one and reject the other, or to accept both with resultant impairment in performance of both. The neurotic person is one who is notoriously the victim of these culturally induced difficulties: "We might call him a stepchild of our culture." In all cases of neurosis the common element is anxiety and defenses constructed against it.[61]

In the course of the critical exposition of *New Ways in Psycho-analysis* Horney interpolated what must be regarded as a tentative formulation of the motive forces of individuals. She observed that "man is ruled not by the pleasure principle alone but by two guiding principles: safety and satisfaction." The provocation to anxiety, which is at the root of neurosis, is a menace to what individuals feel to pertain to "the essence or the core of the personality." What the menace is will vary from person to person, depending on the central value concerned and hence on one's conditions of life and personality formation. The study of neuroses prevalent in our culture reveals marked similarity in the underlying conflicts, such as that between limitless aspiration for success and an enforced desire for affection. These are intensifications of the contradictory tendencies fostered by the cultural milieu which the individual cannot reconcile. She was thus led to hint at the possibility of an insane society, for the high incidence of mental disease is an index of a grave fault in our ways of living. "It shows that the psychic difficulties engendered by the cultural conditions are greater than the average capacity of people to cope with them."[62]

In her next major work, *Our Inner Conflicts,* Horney again saw neuroses generated by the incompatibility of solutions adopted by the individual to the difficulties imposed by culture, specifically between the attitudes of "moving toward," "moving against," and "moving away from" people with whom interpersonal relations provoked disturbances. There is a practical need to repress these inner conflicts from awareness. We desire inner unity because of the everyday need to carry on life, which cannot be done when one is torn by opposing drives; inner tranquillity and freedom are impossible when irreconcilable values persist.[63] Psychoanalytic experience proved, moreover, that this same need for psychic peace and liberty not only aided the patient to surmount his resistances but constituted the dynamism indispensable to the analyst's work.[64]

Here was the clue to Horney's final formulation of the nature

of neurotic conflicts and her affirmation of constructive forces inherent in the individual. It was not enough to say that the drives
toward neurosis were compulsive or incompatible. An amended
definition of a neurotic conflict would add that it could also be
one between healthy drives and neurotic ones, between "constructive and destructive forces."[65] Two important considerations must
be kept in mind when referring to constructive, healthy forces.
For one thing, their existence does not assume that man is "good,"
for that predicates a knowledge of what is good or bad that Horney (unlike Fromm) does not profess. It merely means that "under favorable conditions man's energies are put into the realization
of his own potentialities," which will vary with the individual's
temperament, capacities, and conditions affecting all stages of
his life. It matters less which of his potentialities he expresses—
whether they lead to the active or to the contemplative life or to
varieties of either—than that he develop his own unique potentialities. The healthier he is, the more he develops his individual
capacities.[66] Second, the impulse toward self-realization has a fu-
turistic aspect. It is a goal to be reached, and not a foreordained
one, either. Thus maturity, for example, is not an inherent faculty
but a goal. Nor is it clearly prescribed. "It is a kind of receptacle
into which everybody puts his personal ideals." In the words of
one reviewer of her last book, "Self-realization is not a finalistic
concept, nor is its goal a static one. It is a dynamic process, an
unfolding, a moving and developing."[67] One is reminded of Aristotle's conception of human virtue, or excellence, as a lifelong
process of maturation and exercise of man's characteristic nature.

Is there no connection between self-realization and the environment? Cannot a culture be conducive to, say, the realization of a
self with destructive proclivities? In *Neurosis and Human Growth*
Horney is concerned with the development of neurosis from the
basic anxiety of "a profound insecurity and vague apprehensive-
ness" to the creation of an "idealized image," wherein the individual unconsciously imputes extraordinary, even superhuman,
qualities to himself. It is the vain endeavors to actualize the ideal-

ized image by the neurotic solutions of expansiveness, self-efface-
ment, and resignation (enlargements of the triple movements of
against, toward, and away from, of *Our Inner Conflicts*) that en-
croaches upon and displaces the energies that normally are directed
to accomplishing the potentialities of the real self. When the individual is not given a chance to develop his real self, "that central
inner force, common to all human beings and yet unique in each,"
aberrant development ensues.[68] The real self, which Horney likens
to the ego of Freudian psychology save for the dependent status
Freud accorded the latter, requires congenial circumstances for its
growth. The basic anxiety can be forestalled by an atmosphere
that is at once cordial and resistant so as to impart to the individual an inner self-confidence in dealing with others and enabling
him to nurture his own thoughts and feelings. While a favorable
environment cannot guarantee growth of the real self, and while
events in interpersonal relations must take second place to intrapsychic developments, Horney is sure a totalitarian regime can
effectively deter psychic growth and by definition must so intend.
A regime furnishing the maximum freedom for self-realization is
the one to be striven for.[69]

A momentary digression on the three types of neurotic solution
of *Neurosis and Human Growth* may yield a greater appreciation
of Horney's reconstruction of psychoanalytic theory. Though these
types might be compared with the standard Freudian character
types, they are basically different. The expansive solution super-
ficially resembles the Freudian anal-sadistic character, as the self-
effacing solution does the oral-receptive character and the solution
of resignation seems like the phallic character. The basic difference is that to Horney these are neurotic solutions, whereas to
Freud they are stock character structures. To the one they are
deviations from the normal development of the real self; to the
other they are specimens of normality itself. There is no Freudian
equivalent for Horney's concept of the real self. Orthodox characterology was unable to construct a model of normal personality
structure, owing to the limitations of the libido theory and the

inability to progress beyond an id-psychology. Horney also shows greater skill in depicting the neurotic solutions as they operate in daily behavior and inner feelings, not leaving them as inert collections of general traits of personality as the Freudians tended to. She is able to do so because she does not regard neuroses as fixed states of mind or static personality dispositions. To her, neuroses are processes, or trends, developing, intensifying, and burgeoning out into dynamic systems of living. Having commandeered the psychic energies that properly belong to the development of the real self, their momentum persists as enduring character structures. They may, of course, be intercepted by psychotherapeutic measures.

Horney's intellectual development took her along lines that steadily diverged from Erich Fromm's application of psychoanalysis to social philosophy. A résumé of the titles of her chief books reveals this gradual shift in her studies. At the beginning of her American career she could write about the Neurotic Personality of Our Time as though there were a typical form of neurosis that had reference primarily to the external environment. Then, after developing New Ways in Psychoanalysis, she could turn her attention to Our Inner Conflicts for an explanation of psychic disability. Sharpening her tools of psychoanalytic insight, in her last major volume she investigated the relation between Neurosis and Human Growth, concentrating—in the subtitle of the book—on "The Struggle Toward Self-Realization." Her final position is thus very much like Fromm's, but it has far different implications. Both agree that the individual has an inner capacity for growth, both agree that the environment plays a vital part in promoting or impeding that capacity. But whereas Fromm prescribes a precise end toward which growth *should* tend, in ethical terms, Horney suggests several different ends toward which growth *can* tend, in psychic terms. Mental health for Fromm means a reintegration of man with his fellows, wherein he once more finds relatedness and an orientation; mental health for Horney means the integration of the individual within himself in which satisfactory interpersonal relations are but an element, though a very important one. Since to Horney neurotic trends are independent, though vicious, courses of development, they do not require constant replenishment from an exterior fountain of interpersonal relations, whereas to Fromm the psychic stream can rise no higher than its interpersonal source. In other words, to Horney interpersonal difficulties are a necessary but not a sufficient condition of neurotic development; to Fromm that condition is both necessary and sufficient. Thus Fromm will require a massive reorganization of society in order to consummate the ideal he sets for man; Horney will require only a more congenial environment to solve the difficulties that are, in the last analysis, within the individual himself. And where Fromm draws support from humanistic ethics to buttress his allegation of an inherent spontaneity in man, Horney is content to rely on clinical evidence to substantiate a hypothesis of the constructive possibilities of man. The distinction between the two trends of thought is perhaps exaggerated by this presentation, yet in a way they echo the different approaches of Freud and Marx to a social philosophy, with Horney settling down to more of a Freudian position than she might care to admit and Fromm reflecting more of a Marxian viewpoint than he might be willing to acknowledge.

To further round out the Neo-Freudian position we shall have to consider the theories of Harry Stack Sullivan on the question of the innate human capacity to grow as it is conditioned by the environment. While neither Fromm nor Horney seeks a biological substrate for the need for growth, Sullivan does: i.e., whereas the first two pay little if any attention to genetic factors, Sullivan finds a somatic origin for growth but locates its conclusion in interpersonal relations. Sullivan agrees with the view that a person evolves on the basis of inborn potentialities that serially mature, with corresponding facilitations or impediments in the environment. Innate capacities, flexible in their expression as the result of experience, can become more or less stable in their configuration, but not so stable as to merit the term "instinct."[70] Just as

one tries to reform dietary deficiencies, so one pursues experiences
to amend inadequacies in the acculturation process.

> Acculturation is necessary for the human estate. Growth im-
> plies incorporation of chemical substances for the somatic or-
> ganization, and of cultural entities for the personality. Defi-
> ciencies in either field may be disastrous. Noxious entities may
> be incorporated from either field.

Elaborating, one commentator suggested that the development of
a human capacity also evolves the necessity of using it, capacity
and suitable experience going hand in hand.[71]

Sullivan says there is much information to validate the concept of psychic growth, i.e., that personality tends toward the state
of mental health that is characterized by interpersonal adjustive
success. "The basic direction of the organism is forward." Barring a succession of psychic disasters, every human being "comes
fairly readily to manifest processes which tend to improve his efficiency as a human being," which Sullivan calls "the drive toward
mental health." Sullivan learned by clinical experience as a psychiatrist that, however blindly, people strive after improved mental health. No other hypothesis could explain the observable improvement patients exhibit.[72]

In effect, what Sullivan does is to equate "life" with "growth."
When it concerns the biological aspect of life, the equation is fairly
obvious even to the layman. Sullivan's innovation consists in extending the idea to psychic life, supporting his theory with the
evidence obtained from the careful observation of human behavior
that was his hallmark as a psychiatrist. Having denied himself a
theory of instincts as the "evidence" to substantiate such a view,
Sullivan turned to observation of the end-states at which human
activity is directed; that is, the beginning was to be sought in biology but the outcome was to be sought in discernible, describable
interpersonal relations. What he observed were "integrating tendencies." A dynamic element of individuals is discharged or resolved in a situation that is integrated for that specific purpose.

The resultant change affords satisfaction in a manner significant chiefly to one of the zones by which the organism relates to the environment. "This is the general statement of all interpersonal situations."[73] The features of integrated situations vary with the organism's psychic (and not chronological) age. Sullivan distinguished six stages in the development of the individual prior to adulthood: infancy, childhood, the juvenile era, preadolescence, early adolescence, and late adolescence. Their details are not germane to this discussion, but common to all of them is the need for the appropriate type of integration in interpersonal relations, from the tenderness of infancy to the intimacy of late adolescence.[74] Considering the importance of interpersonal relations, the individual's mental health depends on bringing about proper integrational situations. They are the *loci* for the release of tensions, the scene of energy transformations, both in observable activities and in the less accessible activities of the mind.[75] The tensions released fall under two classes of activity, satisfactions and security.

Sullivan relates tensions and satisfactions as follows:

> Tensions can be regarded as needs for particular energy transformations which will dissipate the tension, often with an accompanying change of "mental state," a change of awareness, to which we can apply the general term, *satisfaction*.

As one of the "great motors of human behavior and thought," the pursuit of satisfactions is connected with such bodily needs as food, drink, sleep, and sexual activity. Ultimately the pursuit of satisfactions can be traced to the physiological need to lower a heightening in tone of the unstriped muscles.[76]

As a psychiatrist, however, Sullivan is more interested in the second activity, security. The tensions impelling the need for security do not have an origin in the physicochemical and biological processes of the organism, but in interpersonal relations. Insofar as the components of this category of tensions are felt, they include anxiety. Activities undertaken to avoid or diminish such tensions aim at continuing or augmenting self-respect or self-esteem; Sullivan calls them "security operations." As reactions to disturbances in the equilibrium of established patterns of dealing with others, they are directed toward maintenance of one's feeling of safety as reflected by the esteem accorded one by others. Security therefore pertains to culture. The feeling of ability or power that its possession brings can be traced to the helplessness of the infant and a subsequent learning of actions and thoughts relied upon to shield him from the experience of insecurity and helplessness he once knew. So vital is the feeling of security that ordinarily it overrides in importance the satisfaction of bodily needs. A successful career of security operations lays the foundation for respect of oneself and, on the basis of that, respect for others.[77] While always chary of sweeping statements, Sullivan conjectures that the uncertain protection to peace of mind gained by security operations may be the mental disorder *par excellence* of modern man. He notes too that expertise in conducting oneself with others is recognized in our society to be one of the most efficacious means to achieving success, and therefore whatever impedes the perfecting or display of this skill is apt to produce acute insecurity. Since the gravity of mental disorder is roughly proportional to insecurity in status, therapy requires removal to a society in which vertical mobility is impossible, namely, a custodial institution.[78] Regrettably, Sullivan does not pursue this line of thought further with a sociological study of an open-class society as a generator of mental illness.[79]

Not the least startling feature of Sullivan's system is the absence of any mention of infantile sexuality.[80] It will be recalled that Freud enlarged the theories of libido and the sexual instinct to trace a continuing sexual development of a person from early infancy to adult maturity, save for the interruption of the latency period. The theory was less revolutionary than it sounded, for sexuality was made the equivalent of pleasure, although it involved the persistence and complication of unconscious motivations that no simple pleasure-pain psychology could comprehend.

Sullivan sees sexuality making its appearance in human development in the early part of the adolescent stage, which would be
roughly contemporaneous with the onset of puberty that marks
the end of the latency period for Freud. The reason for the difference between the two theories is easy to understand when we consider that Sullivan did not follow Freud on the idea of sexuality
being equivalent to pleasure. Sullivan specifically affirms sexuality
to mean what it commonly means, genital activity.[81] Thus the
infant can have satisfactions asexually, by gratifying the needs of
the various zones of interaction, while postponing sexual activity
proper—which Sullivan denominates the "lust dynamism"—to adolescence. What was infantile sexuality to Freud are infantile satisfactions or securities to Sullivan. And with a system of serially
maturing dynamisms to mark the stages of development, Sullivan
can dispense with a libido theory and its sexual connotations and
still account for the "pleasure" sought by the growing organism.

Again, Sullivan will have nothing to do with an Oedipus complex as Freud used the term. Indeed, in his description of the six
developmental epochs there is virtually no mention of the father;
it is always the impersonal "mothering one," the one who attends
to the infant's needs. The sex of that person is immaterial. To be
sure, the mother, or some female, will be the respondent in the
integrational situation centering upon the oral zone of interaction,
but it is not the mother or other female as an object of sexual
desire. And the sex of the person who stirs or allays anxiety is
likewise irrelevant, for the individual can get the same quality of
reflected appraisals of himself from either.

Sullivan appears to be on rather weak ground here, for there
is evidence aplenty of infantile sexuality even when it is understood to mean genitality. Clinical experience in psychopathology,
to say nothing of everyday observation, confirms again and again
this momentous discovery of Freud's. Yet Sullivan had few peers
as a clinical observer and he is not alone among the Neo-Freudians
in denying the sexual component of infantile interpersonal relations. Far from denying what experience affirmed, Sullivan re-

stricted sexuality to genitality, left infantile satisfactions as infantile satisfactions, and perceived sexuality proper as a dynamism called into activity at the appropriate stage of growth, adolescence, when we look for a person to exhibit sexual patterns of behavior. The individual would have a favorable reflected appraisal of himself if he evinced the activity expected of him when it was expected, and not before. The individual matures as a series of potential dynamisms that depend not upon "instincts" but upon interpersonal relations. With a concept of interpersonal relations Sullivan was able to retain a consistent theory of personality development while yet escaping the snares of a libido theory. And by visualizing maturation to be keyed to the seriatim activation of potential dynamisms he relegated sexual gratification to a position auxiliary to that of the growth of the self.

In sum, Sullivan confirms both Horney's conviction of the individual's need for psychic integrity, the security that wards off anxiety, and Fromm's conviction of the vital importance of relating oneself to others. Sullivan in reality synthesizes these two and shows them to be inseparable from the process of the individual's development. In placing security at the center of his system, Sullivan scans ahead to its denouement in the individual's career in interpersonal relations; he has, so to speak, paid his respects to biology. Sullivan's theories point to the futility of only seeking a biological seat for any of the behavior patterns exhibited by a person. Once grant that the individual has a psychic as well as a somatic capacity to grow, then it is less important to locate the derivation of this capacity than to locate the possible sources of disruption of the psychic unity necessary to its fulfillment. In finding them in the impact of cultural expectations on the individual and their cultivation of an anxiety that subverts mental equilibrium, it is less important to reorganize society to enable the fulfillment of specific potentialities than to mitigate those of its effects that do not permit the fulfillment of any mental potentialities at all.

5

THE INDIVIDUAL IN
WESTERN SOCIETY

ERICH FROMM, then, represents one of the two main streams of Neo-Freudian social thought. To change the figure of speech, there are two sides to the Neo-Freudian coin. One faces outward, to the social order whose impact can make for psychic dysfunction. The other faces inward, to the characteristic nature of that dysfunction in Western society. The former utilizes psychoanalytic data as the basis for excursions into the realm of social philosophy. Its attraction for social scientists, however, should not blind us to the significance of the disclosures of clinical practice. Clinical psychotherapy points uniformly to the interruption of the smooth, assured mental functioning of people as the impediment to realization of human potentialities through harmonious growth. It manifests itself as anxiety, an ineffectual and therefore insecure adaptation to social institutions as they are brought to bear in interpersonal relations. This chapter will deal with Neo-Freudian views on the dynamics of insecurity in its current context and the source of it in the evolution of social institutions. The following chapter will discuss the consequences of disturbances of mental equilibrium in various manifestations of social pathology in Western society.

For the sake of continuity it will be well to resume with Harry Stack Sullivan. The term "anxiety" has broad meaning for Sullivan. As interference with one's self-esteem, it is the opposite of the steady functioning of the self-system. Anxiety is indicative of the jeopardizing of self-esteem, denoting the exposure to risk of one's stature in the eyes of others (real or imaginary). In Sullivan's phrasing, anxiety is frequently understandable as "anticipated unfavorable appraisal of one's current activity by someone whose opinion is significant."[1] If desired, anxiety could be related to the tensing and relaxing of various muscles, in contradistinction to the tensions connected with the physicochemical satisfaction of bodily needs,[2] but it is more profitable to relate anxiety to its current function in impelling the self-system in interpersonal relations. And impel it it does: "A person who suffers insecurity is driven by a whip—anxiety—that hurts more than any of the individual whips of the biological needs." Anxiety is a sharper goad than any other, when it comes to interpersonal relations. The tension it represents is the aforementioned need for security.[3]

Thus anxiety is inextricably connected with the self, or, to put first things first, the initial concern of the self is with anxiety, with ascertaining its imminence and refining methods of lowering its intensity and avoiding its reappearance. It is the result of the educative experience of life that begins in infancy. This universal capacity of being susceptible to the uncomfortable experience of anxiety is used in all societies for acculturating their inhabitants. It can truly be said that all education begins with anxiety. Considering the self-system as a dynamism, it is seen to be "an organization of educative experience called into being by the necessity to avoid or to minimize incidents of anxiety." The security operations of this dynamism are those concerned with the avoidance of anxiety in the effort to protect oneself in terms of self-esteem.[4] The conception of anxiety as an educative experience is, of course, reminiscent of Freud's idea of the reality principle supplanting the pleasure principle.

It may be remarked that the self-system, as Sullivan uses the term, is something of a negative quality. It is a residuum, that which occurs as the result of shunning anxiety. Since anxiety is generated in interpersonal relations, the self-system is a creature of reflected appraisals. Keeping in mind Sullivan's contempt for "the illusion of personal individuality," the self is not a self but a self-system, not an entity but a dynamism. Sullivan alludes to "the fundamental postulate that the ultimate reality in the universe is energy," of which material objects are manifestations and of which activity is the dynamic or kinetic aspect. The psychiatrist is interested in the dynamism whose "relatively enduring patterns of energy transformation," recurrent in interpersonal relations, make up the human organism.[5] Again the field theory underlying the concept of interpersonal relations appears, and with it all the aforementioned objections to Sullivan's formulation. Horney was able to circumvent these difficulties with the idea of a real self, a self of hidden but nonetheless real potentialities, growing— or not growing—within society.

The concern of the infant in avoiding "drops" in the sense of well-being ("euphoria") is the lesson taught by anxiety in the child's first interpersonal relation, with the mother. Actually it is immaterial whether anxiety is induced by the mother or the mother's helper, and hence Sullivan's callous term, "the mothering one." The child's personification of the Good Mother, connected with the lowering of tensions in the achievement of satisfactions, or of the Bad Mother, connected with the undergoing of anxiety, lasts throughout life. All anxiety-laden experience in later life can be charged to the unconscious reactivation of this earliest experience of anxiety and its associated personifications.[6] Thus the beginnings of anxiety and of functions that have meaning only when referred to the concept of anxiety can be found in the nature of the family where the individual underwent his initial experiences. Steering shy of the Oedipus complex and all that it entails, Sullivan stresses that it is

> this *interpersonal induction* of anxiety, and the exclusively interpersonal origin of every instance of its manifestations, [that] is the unique characteristic of anxiety and of the congeries of more complex tensions in later life to which it contributes.[7]

Considering the experiences of life as a field of interpersonal relations, anxiety is of paramount importance as a motivating factor. The heightening or lowering of anxiety is the predominant influence in determining the quality of these relations. Most of the unsatisfactory experiences encountered therein can be traced to anxiety, as can a large part of the material presented to the psychiatrist. While anxiety does not initiate interpersonal relations, to a greater or lesser extent it guides and governs their denouement. Anxiety is almost invariably a pronounced factor in destroying interpersonal situations which in other circumstances could serve for the satisfaction of needs. It inhibits one's awareness of the elements in a situation that pertain to its incidence and to the *adresse* necessary to its successful outcome.[8] In a word, anxiety, more than anything else, shatters interpersonal as well as intrapersonal harmony.

If it will be recalled that, by Sullivan's definition, psychiatry has to do with the full range of interpersonal relations, then the material presented to psychiatry by anxiety will be enormous indeed. Since the realization of a person's capacities for interpersonal relations is coextensive with the quality and chronology of previous anxiety-laden experiences, reference must be had to "the particular sorts of inadequate and inappropriate ways in which one lives," extending from the primary unit of the family to such secondary units as the community or the nation. The social order is the source of a person's problems, problems which may signify difficulties inhering in that order. Because clinical experience justifies the assumption of everyone having problems in living, Sullivan thinks that society itself makes it impossible for anyone to find and keep conditions of life allowing happiness and self-esteem.[9]

Coming to the social order in the United States, Sullivan points a finger at the most vicious side of American culture, "our singular dearth of good prescriptions for intimacy and accommodation to other people," which contrasts ironically with Americans' success in manipulating natural resources. There are good reasons for Sullivan's intimations of an insane society when he is able to trace the source of the self-system to a society with a basically irrational nature. A plethora of behavior patterns have to be followed, he maintains, in order to carry on pragmatic and passable interpersonal relations, and these patterns are not perfectly rational. Were this not the case, personality development would not yield the warped, strained self-systems so commonly found.[10] Things have become so bad that nothing less than a "drastic readjustment of human personality and conduct" may be required for human survival. Here the psychiatrist ought to take a hand, Sullivan feels, in locating the causes of fear, anxiety, and the like, and by working to extirpate them.[11] Yet there is another horn to the dilemma. Is there a prescription for a more rational social system? Can we bring about a culture whose interpersonal relations do not so accentuate insecurity? The *deus ex machina* is not likely to be political disputation, Sullivan believes, for dearly held beliefs and convictions have a definite utility in themselves forestalling anxiety. A surrender or an objective evaluation of them would diminish one's self-esteem. With particular reference to politics, Sullivan concludes that "Argumentation, if it is not of the mildest kind, includes so much that is parataxic that the psychiatrist expects nothing useful to come out of it."[12]

Are we caught in a vicious circle, then? If the typical American political tactic of crusading for reform to eradicate evil only succeeds in mobilizing anxieties without appreciably diminishing their sources, is politics as Americans know it a *cul de sac*? If the amelioration of institutional pressures on the individual requires the periodic emotional orgies that characterize American political campaigns, to say nothing of the tensions daily created in the legislative struggle, then political action is worse than useless. Sullivan has no direct comment on the matter, but we may infer a tendency in his thought that most other Neo-Freudians confirm. The value of legislation in reducing sources of anxiety is not nearly so great as the more ardent champions of the good life seem to think. The very effort to consciously alter social institutions entails more psychic damage than its imputed benefits compensate for. But this is only a preliminary statement; we have yet to examine other views of the school on the matter. Perhaps the more specific relation of anxiety to culture that Karen Horney makes will be more suggestive.

That Horney is one with Sullivan on the concept of anxiety—minus, of course, his unique mannerisms of expression—may be seen from the following quotation:

> A neurotic development in the individual arises ultimately from feelings of alienation, hostility, fear and diminished self-confidence. These attitudes do not themselves constitute a neurosis, but they are the soil out of which a neurosis may grow, since it is their combination which creates a basic feeling of helplessness toward a world conceived as potentially dangerous. It is basic anxiety or basic insecurity which necessitates the rigid pursuit of certain strivings for safety and satisfaction, the contradictory nature of which constitutes the core of neuroses.[13]

Thus for Horney anxiety is fundamentally an intrapsychic difficulty, and remedies for it are in the first instance to be found within the individual. The cultural circumstances contributing to mental disorder may remain the same; the neurosis, however, refers to a disorder of personality, and therapeutic aims must be defined in that context.[14] Horney's aforementioned reliance on the person's native recuperative forces—the spontaneous strivings of the real self—in a very real sense serves to deflect the buoyant optimism suffusing all her books from questions of social pathology to those of psychotherapy. For all her acumen in tracing the source of anxiety and insecurity to the conflicts engendered by cultural conditions, the stigma of "inspired reformist" that one critic fastened onto Erich Fromm[15] could not be attached to her. Her keys to the kingdom of the good life unlock the doors of the psyche; other hands will have to fashion keys to the material world.

Notwithstanding her preoccupation with clinical practice, Horney, having a more pronounced cultural orientation than

Sullivan, is quick to place her finger on the major factor in our culture responsible for anxiety: competition. The principle of individualistic competition, she finds, not only is the economic foundation of our society but pervades all human relationships in it, extending even to the family, where the child is "inoculated" with it at the start. Parents are unable to give children the necessary warmth and affection because of their own competitively bred neuroses. Individualistic competition envelops our society's entire gamut of interpersonal relations, sexual, familial, and social alike, spawning "destructive rivalry, disparagement, suspicion, begrudging envy into every human relationship."[16] The tensions of competition create insecurity primarily in the economic field but in all interpersonal relations as well. Should the individual succeed, he fears the envy of others; should he fail, he fears their contempt; in the very process of striving for success he fears the retaliation of others likewise motivated. Clearly an atmosphere of endemic fear is not conducive to the social solidarity or individual security of cordial interpersonal relations. As a result, the individual is driven into isolation. Rampant potential hostility diminishes the security obtainable from human relationships; emotional insulation easily ensues.[17]

Isolation from others would be difficult enough to endure, but isolation from oneself, what is technically known as "alienation," exacts a heavy toll on mental energies. It galvanizes an intrapsychic conflict that places the neurotic person at odds with himself. This moving away from oneself develops into a self-estrangement that is the central disturbance in neurosis. As the real self is progressively detached from the conscious self, emotional and intellectual faculties become more distant, the sense of self-direction recedes, the feeling of inner unity is lost. The residue is "a numbness to emotional experience, an uncertainty as to what one is, what one loves, hates, desires, hopes, fears, resents, believes."[18] In the need to manufacture artificial ways of dealing with others by a pattern of neurotic defenses, the individual must unconsciously put aside his own genuine feelings and thoughts. The defenses supersede the real self: he who was once the driver is now the driven. In the confusion of the psychic situation, the individual no longer knows his identity or his purpose. He is oblivious to his own reality.[19] Although Horney persistently uses the word "neurosis," taken in conjunction with the concept of alienation it appears to cover all types of mental disease; thus she converges with Sullivan in all but terminology.

When it comes to individual psychotherapy, the personality must be reconstructed so that the patient's center of values is restored to himself. Analysis does not aim at abolishing the hazards of life. The goal is to aid the individual in relocating himself by retrieving his spontaneity and self-direction. Again Horney stresses that disturbed interpersonal relations are a contributory factor, not the crucial one, in neurosis, here diverging somewhat from Sullivan. The difficulties are intrapsychic; once the individual receives aid to find himself he reacquires the opportunity to progress toward self-realization. Abilities in interpersonal relations are important, but self-realization embraces competence in creative work and in assuming self-responsibility as well. Under analysis, the patient discovers the obstructive character of his neurotic trends that cut him off from himself. The self-knowledge that comes with disillusionment about them permits the liberation of the constructive forces of the real self.[20]

But when it comes to the vast majority of those unable to thus resolve their inner conflicts and find their real selves, the isolated, alienated individual is hardly in a position to make the choices among conflicting values that a rapidly changing civilization forces on him. With confused emotions and standards, the individual lacks the inner security required to renounce one or another of the competing values with which he is confronted. The almost universal alienation in our complex social system results in a decline of human values themselves; the multiplicity of contradictions leaves "a general numbness of moral perception" in which few ethical values are taken seriously.[21] The larger circle of universal competition prevalent in our society, Horney seems to be saying, contains smaller circles of contradictory values. In *The Neurotic Personality of Our Time* Horney suggests what some of them are. One is that between success and love which was already remarked on in the preceding chapter. Another is that between arousal of wants and the frustrations met with in attempting to gratify them. Last, there is that between ostensible individual freedom and the limitations which in fact surround one. These are typical of the conditions of life that make for emotional insularity, tension, hostility, and the sense of impotence, in generating neuroses.[22]

Still, Horney's insights are but the beginning of a more searching inquiry. True enough, she has specified competition as the mainspring of the anxiety that is at the root of so much of the psychic malfunctioning in our society. She also holds to the view that this competitive atmosphere has become institutionalized and perpetuates incompatible values that stymie the isolated denizens caught in their complexity. Social scientists, however, need an approach that is at once more historical, in taking account of the evolution of social institutions, and more dynamic, in surveying their current discrepancies. Let us see what Franz Alexander's work has to offer in this regard.

Alexander's membership in the Neo-Freudian group is perhaps the least certain of all, to judge by his own attitude. He has sometimes exhibited a reluctance to be so classified and has more than once taken pains to dissociate himself from thinkers of this cast of mind.[23] Furthermore, there is a persistence in his writings of more than the average Neo-Freudian quota of certain Freudian or quasi-Freudian principles, notably, the traditional topographical metapsychology, equivocal views on the Oedipus complex, a strong biological orientation, and a simple view of neurosis as regression. Yet despite his asseverations, Alexander's attempted withdrawal from the Neo-Freudian school is not as convincing as he would have it be. He capitalizes on an ego-psychology that recognizes the plastic nature of personality in a social context. He stresses the individual's capacity for psychic growth and imports the concept of adaptation to the social environment to fortify this stronghold of the younger analysts. His pathfinding studies of psychoanalytic therapy advanced beyond the Freudian concentration on an id-psychology. And his awareness of cultural development—his sense of history—goes hand in hand with his exploration of present social problems. One gets the impression that in repeatedly denying Neo-Freudian affiliations he bails his boat with a sieve. In succeeding pages of this book Alexander's inquiries into widespread pathological phenomena will receive attention. A résumé of his general system is a necessary prelude to a treatment of the material in his writings that bear more directly on the subject matter of this chapter.

Central to Alexander's thought is a biological conception of growth in terms of adaptation to the environment. Even rational thinking is a product of this adjustment, and therefore psychology can be classified as a biological science.[24] The emotional *contretemps* undergone by the individual in the process of growth are then explained easily enough in terms of an ego-psychology. It is in explaining the vicissitudes of social adaptation that Alexander has novel ideas to offer. The biological conception, however, requires some elaboration. From that viewpoint the organism's governing principle can be seen to be that of stability. This tendency to "preserve those optimal internal conditions under which the process of life is possible" is, in Alexander's opinion, a more precise formulation of the instinct of self-preservation. The ego functions as the agent of the stability or, more technically, the homeostatic, principle.[25]

But an organism is not destined for the happy security of a permanent equilibrium, for it has "the biologically predetermined" principle of growth within it. The requisite energy comes from the surplus beyond that needed to reduce tensions and assure self-preservation. Alexander accounts for sexuality by considering infantile erotic activities to be the necessary discharges of surplus energy whose retention would disturb the organism's equilibrium as surely as a deficiency of it would. At first aimless, random expenditure, surplus energy is, in maturity, the source of procreativity. On the analogy of water overflowing a filled container, the mature organism cannot itself grow further but turns "the tendency toward personal growth" into reproduction. When to this is added the contention that psychological growth is manifested in successive attitudes comprising "a progressive trend," plus the assumption of a "spontaneous impulse to learn," it can be seen that, more than any of the Neo-Freudians, Alexander affirms the natural capacity of the individual to grow and adapt.[26]

Of greater importance to acculturation, perhaps, is the utilization of surplus energy for creativity. Free of the exigencies of adaptation, man's creative ability can alter the environment to oblige his wishes. "Instead of adjusting to reality, with these creative faculties man can adjust reality to himself," and therein lies what is perhaps the most singular achievement of man.[27]

Opposed to the principle of growth is that of inertia, the tendency to economize energy. It impels the repetition of behavior that once afforded satisfaction. The reason is that the organism unwillingly abandons automatic habits that conserve energy, doing so "only because forced by the hard necessities of life" to adapt to new behavior patterns; it is always ready to revert to past behavior should such an adjustment be difficult.[28] Alexander likens the inertia principle to the repetition compulsion of Freudian theory,[29] thereby giving it the cast of a pathological phenomenon. Although surplus energy may not be the exact equivalent of libido, the opposition between growth and the inertia principle is quite obviously analogous to the opposition between the instincts of life and death in Freud's system.[30] And in both systems the adjustive agent, the ego, is in a weak position.

In Alexander's mind, the opposition between stability and growth can be enlarged into two complementary trends that rule human behavior. One is that toward stability and security, "the striving to secure the basic necessities for survival." The other is "the expansive or progressive trend toward new ventures into the unknown," a trend toward adventure and creation. In modern times a preponderating trend toward security signifies the exhaustion of energy in adapting to rapidly changing social and technological conditions, with little surplus energy available for creativity.[31] Contemporary art, for example, reveals to him a chaotic effort to reconstruct a rejected world of reality by drawing on "the primitive disorganized impulses of the id," instead of relying on the reasoning ego, thereby breaking the trend of self-discovery and progress that has marked Western civilization since the Renaissance.[32] But that anticipates Alexander's larger speculations in social philosophy. Suffice it to say here that the parallel between organism and society that Alexander frequently employs is of great value when to it is added the concept of adaptation to the environment.

In Alexander's system the ego is given the task of implementing the stability principle by managing the adjustment of the organism to its environment. Like the ego that Freud depicted, it too must mediate between the internal desires of the organism and the demands imposed by the environment. With maturation, the organism's self-preservation depends on the skill with which the ego secures adaptation. As needs become conscious via the central nervous system, the ego is thrown on its mettle, devoting its energies to continually harmonizing the organism's discordant desires.[33]

The struggle between the individual and his environment is not as unequal as may first appear. Alexander reminds us that the organism too is a conditioning agent, with a phylogenetic history older than cultural evolution. Far from being an "infinitely pliable object," a *tabula rasa* ready to receive passively any cultural imprint, the organism—or, to be exact, groups of organisms—determines and creates cultural patterns so as to fulfill biological needs as the organism develops. The biological orientation of psychiatry, extending and refining psychosomatic principles, brings that discipline ever closer to its origin, medicine, and helps to illuminate that oldest of human problems, the relation of body to mind.[34]

Thus the biological grounding of his psychoanalytic principles enables Alexander to stand at the crossroads of two riddles, that of the individual and his environment and that of the mind and the body. Although the second of these is tangential to the main interest of this book, it is worth noting that the connecting link which the central nervous system provides between the autonomic (vegetative) processes and the psychological processes is the fundamental principle on which the science of psychosomatic medicine rests.[35] As one of the foremost exponents of this science in the United States, Alexander has said, "My main interest has been the study of the influence of emotional factors upon bodily disturbances,"[36] which is an indication of his general outlook on social theory. Earlier, with perhaps too heavy a dose of Freudian materialism, Alexander had proposed the idea of the conversion of psyche into body, the latter being "the fossilized descendant" of psychic achievements in adaptation.[37] This formulation was a combination of Freud's theory of the omnipotence of thoughts, which held that among primitives and neurotics there is an overvaluation of the power of wishes to affect reality, plus Alexander's own innovation of adaptation to the environment. While such a suggestion is probably untenable if taken literally, Alexander retained the larger idea that somatic disabilities can make manifest psychic malaise, for, unlike Freud, Alexander stresses adaptation to the environment through the elaboration of an ego-psychology. Consequently, in conceptualizing the causes of neurosis Alexander turns to the broad frame of reference of adaptation to the environment and phrases it in terms of psychoanalytic psychology. Intellectually speaking, Alexander is a descendant of Darwin, as it were, with Freud officiating as godfather. The inability of the ego to harmonize the organism's self-preservative impulses with an environment demanding new behavior patterns is construed as failure of adaptation whose psychic counterpart is regression.

> All morbid phenomena might be explained by the inertia of the ego, its unwillingness or inability to deal with actual difficulties and its readiness to regress to previously successful but outworn adjustments.[38]

Neurotic conflicts most commonly result from the desire to regress to anachronistic ways of dependency, rather than to welcome mature and responsible ways. The task of psychoanalytic therapy is to redress the balance in the personality, relying on the equally natural regenerative powers of the ego, the equally spontaneous tendency of the patient toward recovery, which analytic treatment only assists. Nature heals, not the analyst; without this assumption treatment would not be undertaken.[39]

We have here the elements of a social philosophy. A successful adaptation to the environment demonstrates fulfillment of the psychic growth inhering in all human organisms. A failure of adaptation, manifested by various types of psychopathy that can be summed up as regression, is to be accounted for by the debilitation of the adaptive agency, the ego. A study of the causes of failure will focus on the institutional arrangements that stymie the individual in his quest for the conditions conducive to psychic equilibrium. Alexander thus joins those Neo-Freudians who have capitalized on an ego-psychology as an instrument with which to conduct a searching scrutiny of social institutions. His examination of contemporary American democracy points to some sorry conclusions. After twenty years of psychoanalytic experience, half of them in the United States, Alexander could point to the almost invariable occurrence of one emotional factor in his patients that underlined misgivings about democracy: insecurity.[40] In the search for the cultural causes of insecurity, Alexander puts the sociological string into his bow, though one fears that in the process he violates his own caveat against viewing the society as the individual writ large, for social disorganization is to him akin to individual neurosis, both being the result of refusing to adapt to new conditions.[41] Actually, Alexander spends little time on the breakdown of societies as functioning units. He is more interested in breakdowns of the component members of a society and the causes in institutional patterns, the dynamics of widespread neurosis.

Alexander agrees with the sociologists who characterize our era as one conspicuously marked by rapid social change, one that therefore necessitates a personal capacity for rapid adjustment, the exercise of the conscious ego as the instrument of flexible adaptation. Frederick Jackson Turner's theory of the influence of the frontier on the formation of American character and ideology gave Alexander the clue to the institutional discrepancies that are the upshot of social flux in America. The ideology inculcated as psychic desires does not match the reality to which adjustments must be made. Most of our youth are brought up under the influence of the values of pioneer individualism, but the independence, initiative, and integrity thereby inculcated find scant opportunity for exercise in the modern world.[42] Frontier conditions no longer apply to a standardized industrial society; the drive for individual achievement seems bound to be thwarted; so long as success is considered in terms of personal distinction, maladaptation appears to be inevitable.

The serious disturbance in our contemporary social structure that is constituted by prolongation of the frontier psychology Alexander thinks can best be explained by the concept of "cultural lag" made famous by William F. Ogburn. Basically, cultural lag refers to attitudes engendered by social institutions at one stage of social evolution that persist despite subsequent changes in the social structure. Individuals are impregnated with values that are increasingly obsolescent as they are more and more remote from newer social organization. Psychologically it means that "change in emotional attitudes lags behind change in social structure." There is a noticeable differential between the social structure as it exists today and the psychological attitudes which linger from the social realities of a bygone era.[43]

Subjectively, the discrepancies between old institutions and new conditions appear as feelings of insecurity and discontent. Some of Alexander's most impressive work, as we shall see in the next chapter, deals with the antisocial behavior that is a manifestation of the incapacity to adapt. Alexander also mentions revolution and political reform as social reactions to discontent, and he is convinced that an increase in neurosis almost always accompanies rapid social change, to the extent of neurosis becoming the rule and normality the exception.[44] As an analyst, however, he is more in contact with the typical derangement of our times, neurosis, which is a sign of, not the cause of, a disorder in social evolution.[45]

The neurotic fantasy life of regressive individuals accompanies a withdrawal from action that proves useless. A pathetic picture of the devastating effects of cultural lag emerges in the consulting room. There, where rationalizations and defensive mechanisms are stripped off, patients epitomize our society's emotional structure in their unfulfilled desires and the accompanying anxieties. They are psychically split asunder between "the prestige attached to independent achievement" and "the longing for security, love, and belonging" to some other person or group.*[46] The competitiveness of American society finds its echo in the typical psychic conflict between the strenuous effort needed to continue in the race and the secret craving for rest and security. Repression of the latter attitude is the usual tactic. The competitive effort is resumed with redoubled vigor, no longer with the practical purpose of eliminating a competitor but to display one's superiority while counterbalancing the self-reproach of repressed insecurity. Sometimes a refusal to acknowledge a dependent attitude leads to hyperaggressiveness that may culminate in dictatorial proclivities. At any rate, the connection between insecurity and aggressiveness cannot be doubted.[47]

Alexander has less to say about anxiety, insofar as it can be separated from insecurity, though to the extent that he does broach the subject and explore its implications he is in accord with Karen Horney. Anxiety, he says, results from repression of the hostile impulses called forth by the necessity of exchanging one form of gratification for another as the organism matures. Repression of these impulses enters significantly into the acculturation of the individual and, with anxiety, is to be found at the center of every

---

* One is reminded of the conflict between success and affection to which Karen Horney gave such prominence, and of that between individuation and regressive relatedness which is pivotal to Erich Fromm's system.

neurosis. Neurosis, as we know, is in reality a failure of the acculturation, or adaptation, process. It is a rejection of maturity and its accompanying responsibilities, with a desire to regress to an anachronistic dependency status.[48] Hence the liaison of an ego-psychology with a concept of adaptation to the social environment visualizes neurosis as regression. While Horney's treatment of the topic of neurosis is more subtle and complicated, she is in substantial agreement with Alexander on its connection with the demands of culture. As does Alexander, she sees the conflict between the values advertised by society—the liberty to determine one's own future in a full field of free opportunity that rewards one's efficiency and energy—and the actual situation; most people have limited possibilities of realizing the values.[49] And again like Alexander, in describing the striving for power that marks individual success in our society she finds that it may take the form of domination, a desire to humiliate others, or a tendency to deprive others. The power and prestige conferred by possession of wealth take on an irrational coloration when they are a protection against helplessness, insignificance, or humiliation. The compulsive nature of such striving disappears with the abatement or eradication of the anxieties impelling it.[50]

Returning to Alexander's exposition, we have to inquire what competition and insecurity forebode for democracy. He finds them to hasten regression toward a dependent attitude that is not in keeping with the maturity and capacity for decision that the generalized political responsibility of a democratic system presupposes. Democracy is menaced primarily by two factors. Emotionally, there is the unconscious regressive trend toward dependence. And economically, there is an insecurity stemming from badly organized production and distribution that encourages the emotional menace in the direction of a need for governmental assistance. The voluntary renunciation or postponement of some desires that is characteristic of a mature ego is less and less possible, and a trend toward an authoritarian, paternalistic regime may be set in motion. The obverse of this unhealthy tendency is that of a healthy ego, which is comparable to a democracy that acknowledges the validity of all private needs and, after a hearing, mediates and compromises among opposing interests.[51]

In turning his attention to politics, Alexander's analysis places him in a position to polarize democratic and authoritarian regimes. His attack on the latter type of commonwealth (if such it can be called) employs a revival of Freud's theory of group psychology that, even without the underlying libido theory, comes to much the same conclusion. Briefly, the leader there is in the stead of the figures of parental authority whom the neurotic seeks in his regressive outlook. Group cohesion is imposed from above and the stability of the regime depends on finding minorities to serve as scapegoats on whom to vent hostility. The authoritarian figures on whom conscience is modeled foster a psychic product that is the opposite of the conscience patterned on the loving, trustworthy parents of a democracy.[52] Although Alexander can make a comparison between regressive neurotics and authoritarian regimes, his freedom from the confines of the libido theory permits him to draw another analogy, between mature individuals and democracy. But as his mature individual depends on an unsteady ego, so his democracy rests on shaky foundations. The question of how to strengthen democracy led to two sets of proposals that are at first sight contradictory.

At one time Alexander advocated means of providing at least minimum security for everyone, including the replacement of economic anarchy by "government regulation based on the free consent of all interested groups" and an enhancement of the value of leisure for the expression of surplus energy in creative enterprises.[53] One wonders how "free consent" is to be wrung from those for whom the gospel of frontier individualism sanctifies the successful "adaptation" they have personally achieved (with or without neurosis). And the expenditure of creative surplus energy in spectator sports and ceaseless vigil of television productions leaves one in doubt about the virtues of leisure. In the second edition of *Our Age of Unreason* Alexander himself was not quite so buoyant.

A rewriting of the passage just referred to deprecates the misuse of leisure in a society where production of goods is considered the only worthwhile activity. The "new frontiers" of which he speaks, however, are yet to be exploited.[54] Experience seems to have taught Alexander that governmental underwriting of individual security had dangers of its own. A planned economy could too easily turn into a planned society, and the post–World War II disillusionment with the Soviet experiment warned him and others of the risks of the centralization of governmental power.[55] The political extremes of either right or left were equally subversive of a free society that, in accordance with the liberal tradition, stressed individual accomplishment—"the full development of the ingenuity and enterprising spirit of the individual"—while government, as a mediator, maintained an open field for all in order to preserve opportunities for the individualism that made progress possible.[56]

The political theory expressed here may be old-fashioned—the Liberalism of the nineteenth century—but it is quite in keeping with Alexander's theory of individual psychotherapy, which, as we have seen, similarly tries to strengthen the individual's efforts at self-management. Yet even fortifying democracy may not be enough in the face of the pervasive disintegration of the self that threatens to undo all of modern Western civilization. Unlike the generation prior to Alexander's, present-day men and women lack "an internally consistent value system as a central organizing and governing principle within the personality" and the self-confident, humane, creative *adresse* to life it imparts, he feels. Social role is replacing ego identity; functioning within an organization and group identity are supplanting individualism and the personally unique; conformity is taking the place of idiosyncrasy. In short, Alexander now fears nothing less than the spread of a mass society that will permanently transform human nature.[57] These forebodings had been pronounced some years previously by Erich Fromm, but whereas Fromm could claim the philosophical fastness of a natural law theory of human nature and the willingness to proffer social innovations to suit, Alexander, with his distaste for large-scale social action, would not turn the biological basis of his ideas to similar advantage. And so *The Western Mind in Transition* has a pessimistic tone not to be found in any other major Neo-Freudian writing and its author has still to excogitate a means for protecting the exposed position of the individualism he cherishes.

Thus while at one time—the 1940's—Alexander's suggestions for reform were akin to those later to be enunciated by Fromm, he soon doubted the wisdom of a hasty and radical, though attractive, alteration of social institutions as the pillar of fire to lead our society out of the wilderness of pandemic neurosis. If reshaping institutions worked at cross-purposes with, or even jeopardized, the higher value of individual integrity, the psychoanalyst would have to forgo the role of would-be social engineer. Alexander's outlook is not without reason. The encrustations of our patterns of behavior did not arrive overnight; they will not be banished overnight either. Though Alexander did not work from exactly the same standpoint as Abram Kardiner, he had enough of a perspective to see that institutions had their historical antecedents in centuries of development. There is a certain purpose in social evolution. Institutions are expedient because, in Kardiner's words, they "serve some end of the community that will aid in the comfort of its constituents and their survival as a social unit." While it may go awry in some of its details, the mainstream of social evolution cannot be amiss.[58] A historical perspective of that development, as found in Kardiner's work in this area, may drive the point home.

In studying the formation and operation of the basic personality in our society, Kardiner cannot say with certainty whether changes in institutions precede changes in basic personality or vice versa. Although the evidence at hand points to the likelihood of the former, specific causal relationships cannot be established in what is actually a process of continuous mutual change. Some features of the basic personality of Western man, and with them, methods of social organization and cooperation, have remained constant over the past forty centuries, which indicates that the primary institution of "the patriarchally oriented monogamous family unit with good parental care" and specific disciplines directed toward the child has continued without significant alteration.[59] The application of basic disciplines to the infant is chiefly the function of the mother, for the organization of this type of family unit secures a division of labor that keeps mother and child close together. "The most decisive factor" in the shaping of personality is the generally high quality of maternal attention and affection, in which scrupulous solicitude for the infant's bodily needs prevents the amassing of tensions while facilitating curiosity about and investigation of the external world together with some degree of assurance in dealing with it. The infant's ego is well launched; simultaneously the foundation is laid for a strong super-ego, for the child comes to idealize the mother because of the positive emotional response she instigates and her position as a source of security and satisfaction.[60]

Kardiner thus far seems to be at variance with the rest of the Neo-Freudians in that his colleagues uniformly regard infancy as the fertile propagator of a precarious ego and hence of anxiety. However, as an Oedipal situation revolving about dependency rather than sexuality, the family, in Kardiner's opinion, provides the venue for incipient difficulties. The strong attachment to and idealization of the mother, which in our culture "sometimes becomes maudlin," portends ill for the future. A prolongation of maternal protectiveness can induce a dependent attitude that blocks activity necessary for subsequent adaptations in the educational experience of later years.[61] Kardiner specifies what some of these "blocked-action systems" are. Outstanding among them are profound sexual difficulties, both in emotion and in activity. They result from an idealization of the mother that simultaneously degrades the sexual impulse (which is inhibited) and its object (which is deemed unsuitable for sexual gratification). Again, aggressive behavior takes a variety of manifestations, diversified forms of self-assertion being resorted to in reaction to infantile disciplining. Finally, attitudes toward authority also vary greatly, from excessive submission at one extreme to premature independence at the other, due to the exaggeration of the imputed parental capacities to inflict good or harm.[62]

The pressures built up in the individual by the primary institutions of Western society are released in the regularized patterns of behavior of secondary institutions. While in our cultural history the primary institutions have persisted with few alterations, it is a change in secondary institutions—the methods of dealing with external reality and the techniques of thinking—that furnishes the matrix for the understanding of contemporary society in its healthy and pathological aspects. The opportunities for consummation of institutionally created tensions are furnished by external reality, which includes both the natural environment and the social organization that is of human creation.[63] Since, from a psychological standpoint, a stable society is one in which the learned, habitual patterns of response of the component individuals are congruent with their social roles, social stability is fostered by creation of personalities predisposed to cooperation and trust; a society hindering the development of such personality patterns is one bound to be unstable. What Kardiner calls the "social emotions" are of paramount importance in procuring social stability. They include "the ability to have affection, to cooperate, to identify with, to develop conscience." The cultivation or encouragement of the social emotions conduces to a pattern of stability wherein social cooperation and effective living with one's fellows takes place. The negative of this situation, the onset of social collapse, can be identified by the prevalence of anxiety.[64] The genesis of the instability of our own culture, Kardiner thinks, is to be found in a change in the manner in which secondary institutions afforded relief for the pressures built up by primary institutions.

Kardiner's complicated analysis of the evolution of secondary institutions in Western society is unique in construing it in its psychological aspects. Economic, political, and religious changes are to be considered as reactions to, and not causes of, the psychic tensions produced by the constant basic institution of upbringing just described. He makes it clear that the decisive factor in the development of Western society was not an economic one but the introduction of the scientific method of dealing with material phenomena. For two reasons this development is of significance. An empirically derived reality system has powerfully enhanced Western man's control over nature by the utilization of manufacture, science, and so on. In addition, a reality system based on projection—religious systems—has been undermined. Between them the two have been responsible for the pace and direction of social change for the past six centuries. New social goals, new types of interpersonal relations, and a redefinition in direction for human development have resulted from precipitately augmenting Western man's control of the environment and of influencing his needs.[65] The replacement of religion by science as the effective reality system, Kardiner says, meant the replacement of deferred gratification by mundane success. "The changes in social organization were secondary to these." The claims of the feudal landowners and clergy to social pre-eminence by virtue of their ability to allay anxiety with religion were invalidated. Into their place moved the bourgeoisie and the masters of science, who now held the means of assuaging anxiety, and with it a claim to social superiority. The obsolescence of deferred gratification as a relaxer of social tension, however, did not affect anxieties flowing from intrasocial sources which, in fact, were enhanced by striving for status as the new means of self-validation. To the contrary, anxiety now permeates the relations of the members of the family to one another and of the family to the society; and to jeopardize family patterns and their regularized care of infants is to jeopardize culture itself.[66]

The altered method of self-validation, Kardiner asserts, had profound psychological effects extending to our own day. The individual psychological burdens of tension and anxiety could no longer be relieved by anticipation of post-mortem rewards. Socially created tensions have to be relieved by mundane success, increasing the social struggle to achieve it. The desperate effort to maintain status in the fluid social system exalted by the bourgeoisie, which extends ideologically from economic to political freedom, furnishes the psychological context for studying Western man's prevalent motives and anxieties. As a spur to anxiety, postmortem perdition has its modern equivalent of failure. And when terrestrial suffering lost its honorific value, direct action came to be undertaken as a protest against it.[67]

The direct action takes the form of a ruthless pursuit of success, which is now the equivalent of self-preservation and self-esteem. The individual is pressed into manifesting his self-validation by acceding to positions of power and prestige; tangible possessions are esteemed as safeguards from anxiety. The modern fluid social structure and the newer methods of self-validation place a premium on the individual whose character structure makes for self-assertion and competitiveness. "As long as the individual can pretend to some goal of success or security, he can claim some self-esteem." Prestige and economic power are today the universal currency in Western society. The virtues we prize now are daring and ruthlessness, and economic power is erroneously associated with sexual potency, as though achieving the one assures the other. What is lost in the process is the value placed on the social emotions.[68]

It is not to be expected that dog-eat-dog competition for success makes for social stability. Kardiner chooses three crucial points where social cohesiveness should be in evidence: "the tie of children to parents, of the sexes to each other, and of the men in common enterprise." With regard to the first, the power of parents to frustrate the all-important need of sexual gratification forms an unconscious image of them that may partake of a disciplinarian character. Kardiner states unequivocally that "there is no substitute for sexual gratification," and the diversion into other domains of energies that ought to be expended here can heighten social tensions that have no direct bearing on sexuality.[69] It is time to reorder our patterns of sex education so that it is consistent

and serves useful purposes. Sex morality no longer serves the needs
of social survival. The anxieties associated with parental punishment for indulgence in prohibited sexual pleasures mingle with
attachment to the mother and aggravate psychic conflict. Unconscious sexual goals may be relinquished in an effort to settle the
conflict.[70]

With regard to the second, the tie of the sexes to each other,
the wish to win love is subsumed under the quest for prestige.
The utilization of the power that comes of being loved or esteemed
is used instead for purposes of exploiting others for fear of being
exploited oneself. The necessity to be successful includes sexual
as well as economic success, and concern with sexual potency is
now a sign of social anxiety in addition to being a fear of sexual
disability.[71] Thus sexual relations can be and frequently are exploitative as well as amatory. They can be and increasingly are
sources of pride as well as of love. Since in Western society the
motive of self-esteem outweighs that of love, failure in sexual relations can be a blow to pride, and the threat to self-esteem of a
failure in sexuality brings on an anxiety that can dissolve this link
in social cohesiveness. Self-preservation—now referring not to bare
survival but to preservation of freedom from anxiety in the ceaseless quest for status and happiness—supersedes cooperative emotions; the egocentricity of the mates is breaking the bond of marriage.[72]

With regard to the third, the rugged individualism that de-
prives men of the fellowship of others in working toward goals in
whose benefits all participate taxes the individual's security by
necessitating the maintenance of defensive hostilities both within
and without the family. Even mitigation of anxieties connected
with sexuality is not likely to have much effect on the anxieties
stemming from the daily combat for status. On the assumption
that opportunities for individual self-validation are unlimited,
aspirations for success are unlimited too. But the opportunities
began diminishing in the twentieth century—here Kardiner strikes
a chord in which all the Neo-Freudians join—and the individual

began to show the strain of the competition. The emotional ties that man needs make him feel his isolation poignantly. In our own times members of the middle class are particularly susceptible to anxiety, largely because, with unlimited aspirations, their egos are driven to appalling efforts to maintain self-esteem.[73]

Kardiner's analysis of man in Western society is the broadest and in some ways the deepest of the Neo-Freudian school; it is also the longest by several centuries. His recasting into psychoanalytic terms of the historical evolution of Western social institutions furnishes the necessary perspective for understanding the generation and persistence of psychic dysfunctioning in contemporary American society. Looking backward, in one sense he gives historical reasons for the unsatisfactory resolution of a desexualized Oedipus complex in Western society, qualifying with definite institutional causes the universality of Freud's conception. Looking forward, in another sense he gives reasons for the incompatibility of what is loosely called the Protestant ethic, and its associated institutions, with a social stability that is ultimately to be measured by mental health.

Our résumé of Kardiner's theories rounds out the Neo-Freudian essay in social philosophy. When prestige attaches to success as measured by tangible manifestations of pecuniary assets, and when success so defined can be acquired only by individualistic competition, both social cohesion and psychic stability are menaced. Nor is this the result of a fortuitous circumstance: it has been the almost inevitable, if unforeseen, consequence of a revised value-system that has marked the development of Western society since the Renaissance. It is almost as though the development of Western society has reflected, in magnified form, the all but typical maturation of the individuals who now populate it—to reverse the familiar formula of ontogeny recapitulating phylogeny. That is, the growth of Western society under the guidance of the value of individualism has become an irreversible journey toward social instability. The counterpart in individual psychopathy is all too much with us. Let us recapitulate what the order of presentation of this chapter has disclosed. Neurosis, or, to speak more broadly, mental illness, was shown to be the upshot of insecurity and anxiety (Sullivan); insecurity and anxiety were shown to be generated most frequently—almost infallibly—by competition (Horney); competition was shown to be the necessary consequence of the quest for individual self-validation in an egalitarian society of conflicting values (Alexander); and our egalitarian, competitive society was shown to be the product of a long-term evolution of social institutions (Kardiner). Neo-Freudian social philosophy therefore seems to point to the melancholy conclusion that an extensive incidence of mental illness is inherent in modern Western society, to say nothing of an unavoidable trend toward social breakdown.

There is little satisfaction in nominating one's fellow citizens to candidacy for a psychopathic ward. Neither is much pleasure to be had from foretelling the impending doom of one's social order. The Neo-Freudians, on the whole, are averse to enjoying the cruel delight of playing Cassandra. The safest generalization that can reasonably be drawn from this chapter, and from the work of the Neo-Freudians as a school of social critics, is that the conditions of life in American society are notoriously conducive to the contraction of mental illness. The susceptibility of any given individual will of course depend on a variety of circumstances, most of them, probably, as they impinge on his early childhood experiences in the family. How many Americans currently suffer mental illness? How many are to be condemned to this plight under our present institutional system? It is impossible to say. Unreliable and incomplete statistical data, resting on conceptual differences as to what is to be reported in the first place, make estimation a futile exercise in morbid prophecy. Nevertheless, some studies in psychopathology have been made by the Neo-Freudians that may be useful in the evaluation of American social institutions. We may as well become better acquainted now with some of the denizens of our society who have not had the resilience to withstand the pressures of their cultural environment.

6

PSYCHOPATHY AS
A WAY OF LIFE

IT SHOULD be plain by now that instances of neurotic behavior are not isolated occurrences within the life history of a given individual. They are part and parcel of his total personality, fragments of a dynamic, if inefficient, going concern. The question of symptoms could easily becloud the matter. Whereas for Freud symptoms were sexual gratifications substitutive for those not obtainable in real life, achieved by regression of libido, Karen Horney was in a position to disparage the significance of symptoms once she had dispensed with the libido theory. Instead she has stressed that "every neurosis, no matter what the symptomatic picture, is a character neurosis." Beginning in infancy, life experiences combine to form a character structure from which later difficulties emanate. In the study and treatment of neurosis, Horney regards the neurotic character structure to be of central importance, symptoms not being the essential constituents but only the manifestations of mental dysfunctioning. Symptoms are a by-product and need not be present at all in what is fundamentally a disorder of character.[1]

In the light of this revised conception of neurosis there is more than an intimation of truth in the title of one of Franz Alexander's early articles: "Neurosis and the Whole Personality." The implication is that deviant behavior is not an ephemeral event of only passing interest; neither can its cause be eradicated merely by bringing repressed material to the conscious level, as Freud had hopefully believed in the early days of psychoanalysis. Alexander was one of the first to shift the emphasis of psychoanalytic studies from the repressed to the repressing agent. In so doing, he came to regard therapy as personality reorganization and not only (as hitherto) the making conscious of repressed material.[2] In the absence of therapy, neurotic behavior is the necessary though unsatisfactory adjustment to a society whose demands, when they become too heavy for a neurotic character structure, precipitate overt antisocial activity or press to the breaking point what is already a fragile instrument. This, in general, is the psychoanalytic explanation of various indexes of social distintegration, the overt signs of an overstrained character structure, and of the chronically impoverished mental life that may lurk beneath the most serene exteriors.

In exploring new pathways that were soon to carry him beyond orthodox Freudian limitations, Franz Alexander early sought an understanding of neurosis in the context of this total personality. Not content with adding to the already extensive knowledge of psychic morbidity—not content with forever discussing the repressed aspect of personality—he examined the repressing agent, the unconscious parts of the ego and superego, in *The Psychoanalysis of the Total Personality,* at this time retaining nearly all the orthodox conceptual paraphernalia. Within the book, however, are the seeds of innovations that bore fruit in his later writings. A preliminary summary of the relevant material is in order here.

In Alexander's elaboration of the Freudian theory of repression he found the superego to perceive instinctual strivings in the id that would violate moral laws if permitted to become conscious. Thereupon it signals the ego to repress, which it does automatically. In this way the ego adapts to conscience much as conscience adapts to social reality, though at the price of converting conflict with external reality into an internal conflict. Hence repression of the id by the ego becomes the means of avoiding conflict with conscience. Should the id obtain instinctual gratification the ego must needs be punished by the superego. That much is conventional metapsychology. By Alexander's new proposal, in the neurotic individual the interplay of the three elements of the psyche in repression of instincts leaves a residue of an unconscious sense of guilt and need for punishment, for the ego may anticipate the action of the superego by inflicting punishment on itself in advance, thereby justifying instinctual gratification.[3] By virtue of this conspiracy, as it were, between id and superego, the id expiates guilt and warrants its indulgence by seeking punishment of the ego. Although the individual is neurotic, each element of his total personality is satisfied: the id is indulged, the superego punishes, and the ego is relieved of conflict. But the victory is a Pyrrhic one, for it leaves the ego as the impoverished member of this malignant team. Hence therapy aims at strengthening the ego so as to properly reintegrate the whole personality. The corrupt superego is thereby to have its control of instinctual life wrested from it and returned to the ego; the id is to be confronted with a reinforced ego that is now in direct relation with it. "We must raise the level of the entire personality in the direction of the conscious ego."[4]

If the foregoing is complicated in spite of, or because of, its ingenuity, it serves all the better to illustrate how complex a heavy dose of Freudian metapsychology can be. Alexander admits to the deliberate personifications of id, ego, and superego,[5] which result in some nearly ludicrous passages. (In a later work he thought it wiser "to distinguish different functions of the mind" than to compartmentalize it in conventional fashion.[6]) Moreover, in his almost slavish effort to preserve his consonance with Freud he hides his light under a bushel, for there are a few noteworthy advances in the volume. The emphasis is on the study of the ego, as noted before. The idea of adaptation to the environment makes its appearance, if modestly. Alexander also employs Freud's theory of the recapitulation of phylogeny in ontogeny to make some remarks more germane to the discussion of this chapter. The relationships among the parts of the personality, he says, reflect human social relationships, in that neurotic instinct-regulating mechanisms correspond to the code of justice obtaining in primitive society. (Here we note an echo of Freud's equation of the neurotic with the primitive.) Neurosis bespeaks an archaic structure of personality based on punishment, and we recognize in it the primitive organization of society similarly based. "Social laws originated as projections of internal psychic relationships which then were reëstablished in the psyche by means of a reintrojection, albeit in a modified form." By analogy, therefore, in organized society a stern code of justice drives the would-be criminal from society and, when the law is broken, exacts retribution. In other words, just as an overactive superego must combat reactions against it, so severe justice breeds criminals against whom it must take retaliatory measures.[7] In both, the unconscious sense of guilt and need for punishment are instrumental. With these formulations Alexander was prepared to expand the psychoanalysis of the total morbid personality into an investigation of some social problems of our society; we must not be surprised if the last-named appears as implicitly morbid too.

Ernest Jones credits Freud's insight with inspiring a revised understanding of social pathology, which of course cannot be denied, and Freud himself looked forward to the day when research would be ventured into the pathology of civilized communities.[8] But it was the Neo-Freudians, more than Freud himself, who systematically developed those insights and fulfilled his hopes. The more spectacular evidences of a neurotic character structure, crime and juvenile delinquency, were what first attracted Alexander's attention to social pathology. His ideas on the topics, while setting precedents in the field, were still made largely within the confines of orthodox Freudian psychology. The study of criminality which he undertook in collaboration with the criminal lawyer Hugo Staub retains many concepts of the older school that are incompatible with strictly Neo-Freudian views. Such are the pleasure versus the reality principles, the division of the psyche into id, ego, and superego, a sexualized Oedipus complex, the libido and instinct theories (oddly omitting the death-instinct), the crucial role of sexuality, the libidinal phases of development, and civilization seen as repression. Alexander was to outgrow some of these concepts in later writings, but at the time they served him well in contributing a fresh approach to an old problem. Taken in the large, perhaps the most important message of *The Criminal, the Judge, and the Public* is one that is implicit in all psychoanalytic considerations of antisocial behavior, namely, that crime is not a form of moral perversity but a form of mental illness, that the proper attitude toward it is not one of condemnation but one of understanding, and that the proper remedy is not retribution but therapy.

In accordance with Freudian instinct-theory, Alexander finds that all human beings have a store of antisocial and hence criminal drives, with the tendency to carry them out when the ego liberates itself from the superego and does the bidding of the id. Under the pressure of social life, the reality principle supersedes the pleasure principle; renunciation of some instinctual life is grudgingly made but only in anticipation of compensatory gratification. "It is a sort of contract between the powers which restrict our instinctual expression and the instinctual demands of the individual." The social order is thus an equilibrium between present renunciation and expected gratification. But the right of revolution, as it were, is never abjured. When the emotional regulator of this precarious equilibrium, the "sense of justice," is disturbed, when the social contract is broken through exorbitant nonfulfillment of instinctual demands, the ego loses its confidence in the representative of the outer world, the superego, and with it its power over the id. In the rebellion the hitherto repressed instinctual drives are lived out completely and with no restraint.[9] This Freudian *Weltanschauung* underlies *The Criminal,* which generalizes from five analytic studies of instances in which the ego proved itself incapable of restraining instinctual tendencies in conformity with social requirements.

Omitting from consideration persons whose criminality is of an irremediable organic determination, Alexander classifies criminals into two broad categories. There is the neurotic criminal, "whose hostile activity against society is the result of an intrapsychic conflict between the social and anti-social components of his personality," and there is the normal criminal, "whose psychic organization is similar to that of the normal individual, except that he identified himself with criminal prototypes," that is, his superego is cast in the mold of a criminal.[10] It is significant that the book is devoted almost exclusively to neurotic criminals. Alexander specifies a "psychological etiology" for the neurotic criminal and a "sociological etiology" for the normal criminal. As Alexander soon realized, a study of the second kind, which is perhaps the more interesting if not the more momentous, would necessitate a Neo-Freudian approach that leaned on culture rather than on instincts as causal factors. He pressed the psychological etiology as far as it could go, however, making the most of conceptual limitations he was shortly to surmount.

Alexander feels justified in calling one type of criminal the "neurotic criminal" for a very important reason, which is that his is but a variation of the neurotic character structure. In the neurotic character there is a futile struggle to check antisocial tendencies. His life is a miniature dramatization of the conflict between individual and society, with the latter predestined to win. The neurotic character resorts to symptoms to gratify repressed instincts. The neurotic criminal finds his gratification in a real act aimed at the world, through overt antisocial behavior. Basically there is no difference between the two; the difference is outward, in that the acting-out of instincts is socially more deleterious. As opposed to the view of the criminologist, to the psychoanalyst "the neurotic criminal belongs to the group of sick people."[11]

Perhaps the most startling feature of the neurotic criminal character is his unconscious need for punishment. An imperfect incorporation of the superego (i.e., an unresolved Oedipus complex) left it "as a sort of foreign body" within the personality, resulting in a continuous tension between it and an ego striving to fulfill the demands of the id. Gratification of a forbidden wish arouses anxiety, a dread of the superego by the ego. Elaborating the concept in a later work, Alexander states that the need for punishment is the means for reducing the anxiety caused by refractory behavior. By virtue of this "sense of guilt," relief from anxiety demands punishment, from others or from oneself. The punishment once inflicted, the individual feels relieved "and the neurotic offender is emotionally ready for recidivism." To put the matter into a nutshell, "The core of the whole psychology of the neurosis is contained in the sentence that guilt is redeemed through punishment, through suffering."[12] Thus a criminal code based on the principle that punishment atones for crime is quite in keeping with the character of the neurotic criminal. He simply carries its logic one step further by considering punishment as his ethical warrant for fresh gratifications of censured impulses. This is obviously criminal justice defeating its own end, encouraging what it sets out to deter. The absurdity of penal law is illustrated by the finding that punishment cannot intimidate the neurotic criminal because of his unconscious need for punishment. He welcomes severe legal sanctions; "quite often he even actively seeks punishment"; in fact, anticipated punishment can be the chief motivation for lawbreaking. The persistently high rate of recidivism further substantiates this contention.[13]

If anything, Alexander holds, punishment answers to a public demand as a "defense reaction" of the ego against one's own instinctual drives. It protects the average citizen's psychic equilibrium from the anxiety lest his own superego be subverted and his own instinctual forces be given free rein to reactivate further psychic conflicts: "I am convinced that our failure in controlling crime is primarily due to our inability to study it in a calm intellectual way because it necessarily arouses in everyone horror, condemnation and the wish to retaliate."[14]

The implications of Alexander's analysis for conventional approaches to the administration of justice are apparent. Alexander insists that the neurotic character structure as a whole enters into the evidence of a case. The establishment of the fact that a crime has been committed is merely the location of an isolated event in a complex process: "One cannot abstract a deed from the doer." Without psychology the administration of justice in any real sense of the term is impossible; once apply this scientific attitude to criminal jurisprudence and a realistic attack on crime is in the offing.[15] It should be plain, Alexander thinks, that a proper understanding of personality—criminal and otherwise—must take account of the degree to which motivations are unconscious. Thus unconscious motivations may determine criminal acts even when the offender meets the time-honored standard of having conscious knowledge of the difference between right and wrong (the so-called M'Naghten rule). This is so because during trial only conscious motives ordinarily are exposed. The neurotic offender does lie, as accused, being driven to it by the necessity to invent plausible motivations because of the inaccessibility of true, unconscious ones. The possibility of a coherent, to say nothing of a true, explanation of his acts is accordingly almost nil. The individual will accept punishment rather than recognize the power of unconscious motives. "Man is never willing to admit that he may act at times without conscious intentions." In a word, the M'Naghten rule is obsolete.[16]

Then what becomes of individual moral responsibility for a criminal act? The right-or-wrong rule at least furnished some criterion, however erroneous, for fixing the onus. Does a psychoanalytic view of criminal jurisprudence dispense with this concept altogether? Alexander suggests a new standard. Everyone has but limited responsibility for his own acts, and since no act is performed completely under the control of the conscious ego every given act must be evaluated according to the comparative quantities of conscious and unconscious motivations entering into it. If considerations of responsibility are to be retained at all in a field where those of pathology should reign, a scientific concept, measuring "the degree and mode of participation of the Ego in a given act" is what is called for. In dealing with a criminal, the crucial factor should be definite knowledge of the extent of ego participation in the commission of an act.[17] What Alexander does is to throw the burden where it belongs, on society, and remove it from the offender. To carry the matter to its logical extreme, responsibility cannot be imposed until society first gives the lawbreaker the opportunity of taking on practical responsibility for his acts. That means preventive psychoanalytic treatment of offenders who are more under the influence of unconscious motivations than the normal individual. It is a parallel to the individual acquiring responsibility for his dreams after psychoanalysis. Only at that point may the neurotic criminal be held legally responsible for his acts.[18]

Technical questions of guilt aside, the neurotic criminal still constitutes a menace to society. Alexander's distinctly humanistic outlook is reflected in his prescriptions for penology. It would be daring enough to propose that the punishment should fit the criminal, not the crime. Going even further, he holds that punishment which purports to be a therapeutic measure only treats the symptoms, and not the disease. For the neurotic criminal Alexander recommends the abolition of all forms of punishment per se and remission to an agency for psychoanalytic treatment. As with any neurotic character, the neurotic criminal is psychically ill. He is therefore curable; "medico-psychological treatment" is of the greatest importance for him.[19] Mere incarceration rids society of the criminal temporarily or permanently, but is in itself a confession of the inability to cope with criminality. Incarceration that is used not for revenge, intimidation, or the temporary segregation of dangerous individuals, but for rehabilitation, represents the only constructive aspect of a penal system, although to be sure prisons of today are far from meeting that desideratum. At bottom, however, it is a question of crime prevention. Reform of the deviant attacks the problem too late. "As in the field of medicine, prevention is the ultimate goal, and not therapy."[20] If it would be charged that psychoanalytic preventive therapy is decidedly impractical, because too costly, Alexander could reply (in a later work) that it is actually the more economical alternative to conventional methods of penology. One must not overlook the economic burden imposed on society by untreated offenders, an expense far heavier than providing proper treatment would be.[21]

The problem of prevention would of necessity loom larger when criminality was examined in its social context. When in a second work on the subject Alexander accorded a greater role to the cultural environment in the incitement to crime, the groundwork was laid for a social philosophy that comprehended institutional influences on behavior, which we have already examined. In *Roots of Crime* Alexander takes up the sociological etiology he had put aside in *The Criminal*. It is combined with a psychological etiology that results from seven psychoanalytic case histories of young offenders conducted in cooperation with the psychoanalyst William Healy. The concepts of the neurotic criminal and the normal criminal are virtually forgotten, although the continuity in personality development that makes for a neurotic character structure is profusely illustrated with dream material covering each subject's entire life history. Nevertheless, one feels that in *Roots of Crime* Alexander had to sacrifice a systematic conceptualization completely within the confines of Freudian methodology for a more comprehensive understanding that requires consideration of cultural factors. Indeed, while *Roots of Crime* was in preparation he acknowledged that neither a psychological nor a sociological etiology alone would explain crime. Since *The Criminal* he had learned to attach greater importance to social factors.[22]

In the later study Alexander retains the similarity between neurotic and criminal behavior, the one seeking symbolic gratification for repressed urges, the other overt transgressions. Also kept is the theory of the psychic social contract, i.e., the renunciation of some instinctual gratifications for the sake of the compensatory fulfillment of others. But this is merely a psychological priming for a charge that is ignited by sociological events. In the psychological *quid pro quo* it is harder to abjure freedom for no return than for requital of instinctual satisfaction. Therefore instinctual urges are more likely to subvert social restraints in "the discontented strata of the population."[23] The pleasure principle, in other words, revolts against an inadequately absorbed reality principle.

A social situation conducive to discontent encourages the expression in antisocial conduct of emotional conflicts that arose from the early family situation. In criminal activity "the rational conscious motives run parallel with the repressed motives," the current social situation only providing rationalizations for the reactivation of infantile difficulties. Adult delinquency, he found, typically continued childhood delinquency, and hence if there were such a thing as a criminal personality its development took place in childhood, "when all the important character trends are formed."[24] With a broader sociological etiology superimposed on an orthodox psychological etiology, the impact of contemporary social conditions can receive its due emphasis as a causative agent of crime and delinquency. What Alexander calls "an unfavorable social situation" facilitates the displacement of family-created emotional conflicts as reactions against society, thereby relieving a variety of accumulated frustrations in antisocial behavior.[25]

The shift from a psychological to a sociological etiology had important results for Alexander's thought. Criminal behavior, he now says, is not the spontaneous eruption of instincts in reaction to a mere material deprivation imposed by culture, for people living in conditions below even the lowest American standards do not always reveal high crime rates. For that matter, discontent may be expressed in other societies in organized revolution rather than in individual revolt as crime. Ideological trends too are of account, notably those involving attitudes toward social living, authority, and law. For example, a society, such as the American, that elevates material success as its supreme value encourages its members to sacrifice a value such as law-abiding behavior, should a choice be necessary.[26] There could be no question that a socio-logical etiology would lead away from theories of instinct and libido and toward a social philosophy, however loath Alexander himself has been to break so sharply with Freudian principles.

The unfavorable social situation in question impressed itself on Alexander upon his removal to the United States. His dis-covery of the quasi-heroic stature of the criminal in America, the adulation accorded him by the public "with a sort of adolescent hero-worship," pointed unerringly to criminality as a method of recovering a prestige that had been all but obliterated by a lev-eling machine civilization. "It is a pathological attempt to re-gain a lost freedom." An unconscious motive of prestige persists in criminal careers in America because of the conflict between "the traditional individualistic philosophy of success" and actual contemporary possibilities.[27] The individualistic ideology of the American ethos, elevating the ideal of the self-made man, says Alexander, is now in contradiction with the actualities of an in-dustrial society. (It will be seen that *Roots of Crime* adumbrated the social philosophy of *Our Age of Unreason*.) In a society where the elements of success are beyond the control of the individual and where success and independence are valued even above respect for law, crime is a pathological form of individualism. The sen-sationalism attached to criminal cases is due not alone to disappro-bation but to "a profound unconscious admiration of achievement and courage," regardless of their outcome.[28] The enduring nature of institutional realities seems to assure a plentiful supply of juve-nile delinquents for the future unless, as Alexander suggests, our traditional ideals are modified to comport with current conditions so as to help youth accommodate themselves to our existing so-ciety.[29] Some further words may be ventured on his correlation of juvenile delinquency with "an unfavorable social situation."

That situation should not be construed to refer solely to one of economic deprivation. Not only are crime and delinquency prevalent during prosperous as well as depressed periods but de-viants come from well-to-do families as well as from impecunious ones. The easy generalization that criminally inclined individuals typically come from economically impoverished families characterized by slum residence, broken homes, alcoholism, and financial insecurity, Alexander maintains, forgets that although these may be statistically recurrent factors, they are factors that are operative "only in a special setting and in combination with the reactive tendencies of certain personalities."[30] Alexander's insistence on examining psychopathy case by case, as a necessary complement to sociological (if not philosophical) dicta, means more hard work in the clinic and less facile juggling of statistics. He makes it plain that crimes are not committed for economic gain alone. Their roots are to be sought not merely among the economically underprivileged groups of the population; they are to be sought among the emotionally underprivileged groups, among those who receive insufficient emotional gratification from the operation of social institutions. Alexander works on the imbalance between the gratifications and restrictions allowed by social living, that is, the disequilibrium between the pleasure and reality principles.[31] In casting aside a pure theory of instincts, the source of difficulty could be traced instead to the inculcation of values and their increasing inaccessibility in the face of social realities. This change Alexander made in *Our Age of Unreason*.

Viewed in such manner, juvenile delinquency, like crime, becomes a manageable social problem. We are not at the mercy of remorseless instincts that are a permanent part of a fixed human nature. The republic need not collapse in the throes of pandemic psychic debilitation as successive generations of neurotic personalities proliferate like cancers on the body politic. By the same token, we need not await the coming of a utopia before taking action. Ideally, there would be no specious values with which to impregnate the young and thus generate deviant behavior. Although we are not permitted the realization of many ideals in this world, a conscious, deliberate reconsideration of our institutional arrangements may do much to avert later, more drastic, recuperative measures. If the question is one of where we are to apply our efforts, Neo-Freudian psychoanalysis points, as may be expected, to preventive rather than to remedial action.[32] To be sure, a society which, like American society, dignifies the values of pecuniary success and individual achievement, will pay much attention to economic policy. The amelioration of material deprivation, it is said, can go a long way toward lessening illicit or undesirable behavior. No doubt a uniformly higher standard of living can make life outwardly more pleasant for many people. But the question remains, what will it do to make life inwardly less turbulent? For when all is said and done, the problem is one of an inner, psychic conflict. In such terms, a stouter ego structure will do more than a fatter bank account. Economic security means nothing if it is not accompanied by psychic security. No Act of Congress can outlaw anxiety. Yet a sober reassessment of values, a critical re-examination of the American ethos, can assist us in determining whether the game is worth the candle, and, if not, how the rules of the game are to be changed. It is not too much to claim that a good deal of the progress made toward understanding and dealing with crime and juvenile delinquency has been due to studies of the type Alexander made. It may be that similar progress will be made on the basis of a Neo-Freudian study of another type of aberrant character structure, to which we now turn.

In *The Mark of Oppression* Abram Kardiner applied the technique of psychodynamic biography he had been refining over the years to an investigation of the basic personality of the American Negro. We recollect that by Kardiner's formulation, the basic personality is one which a society has perfected among its members as best suited to meet the problems presented by the necessity to adapt to its environment. In Kardiner's words, "It is a consistent feature of human personality that it tends to become organized about the main problems of adaptation," the adaptive patterns of the personality being necessary to permit functioning in the social environment. Putting aside the archaic idea that group characteristics are inborn, and operating from the premise that they are adaptive within the possibilities determined by culture,

Kardiner addresses himself to the question whether there is indeed a basic personality for the American Negro and, if so, what the causes are of its peculiar configuration.[33] *The Psychological Frontiers of Society* had charted the configuration of the American white man's basic personality; the later volume did the same for the American Negro. The employment of psychoanalytic techniques was to add a new dimension to the understanding of this most investigated group in American society.

It seems perplexing, he says, for the Negro to have a basic personality different from that of his fellow American. After all, does he not live in an American culture, are his patterns of adaptation not determined by social conditions common to all, does he not share the predominant American values of success (especially financial success), social mobility, liberty, and fair play? To be sure he does, but the impact of social conditions is different for the Negro for reasons that can one and all be traced to social discrimination. "The adaptation of the Negro is qualified primarily by the color of his skin—an arbitrary but effective line of demarcation." His depreciated self-esteem comes from membership in an outcast group, a group which moreover is denied the chance of self-validation in ways presently acceptable.[34] Forced to develop his personality within the ambit of the white man's culture —for the Negro is unable to improvise unaccustomed personal objectives in the midst of American society—there is not a single personality trait of his that cannot be followed back to the exceptionally difficult conditions of life that are his mark of oppression, says Kardiner. A total exclusion of the Negro from sharing in social, political, and intellectual opportunities, a systematic discrimination against him that touches virtually every phase of his existence, is at the bottom of the Negro protest. His plight is that of being in, but not of, the community. The inaccessibility to the Negro of the goals of a culture that he must accept leaves him with a distinctive personality that is a distortion of his white counterpart's.[35]

In a society that places a premium on individual accomplish-

ment, whose values of success, power, and security are all ego-
centric, a heavy load is placed on personal adaptation, Kardiner
reasons. Anxiety, which can attach to jeopardized self-esteem as
well as to uncertain subsistence, is acutely the Negro's lot. Receiving as he does what Sullivan would call unfavorable reflected
appraisals of himself from others, this incessant chafing pervades
his entire personality, compelling continuous unconscious resort
to compensatory stratagems that barely preserve an exterior veneer
for adaptive social relations of limited effectiveness.[36] Since self-
approval in anyone amounts to consistency between idealized and
actual images of the self, even in the absence of protest from his
conscience and in the presence of good performance on his part,
self-esteem is impossible for the Negro when he is invariably faced
with the poor reflection of himself shown in the behavior of whites.
"The final result is a wretched internal life."[37]

We are thus confronted with the ugly fact of a form of aberrant
personality structure that is seemingly institutionalized in American society. The characteristics of Negro behavior that deviate
from the white norm have been documented by sociological studies
that are, as Kardiner says, as extensive as any in the world. What
makes *The Mark of Oppression* unique is its employment of a
method of investigation that studies directly and intimately the
effect of particular social pressures on the personalities of the subjects. Statistical recording of raw sociological data do not demonstrate how the tabulated facts become part of the character structures of the subjects. "We cannot tell how the social institutions
are integrated into the life of the individual until we study the
personalities individually." Kardiner stresses the qualitative rather
than the quantitative nature of the investigations. So considered,
twenty-five psychodynamic biographies are more than enough to
establish the pattern and activities of the Negro's basic personality.
If the volume is to be attacked on any ground it can be done on
the adequacy of the sample. The authors are well aware of it and
plead in extenuation the time needed to prepare a more comprehensive sample (five years having been required for the twenty-

five).[38] One hundred cases, they say, would have been preferable, but that is not much of an improvement from the statistician's standpoint. Notwithstanding doubts that will have to be returned to in our final chapter, Kardiner's claim that psychoanalysis furnishes a technique to obtain direct insight into the operations of social institutions on the human psyche is worthy of our attention when it is turned to an analysis of a vexing social problem.

Kardiner advises us to pay special attention to such things as emotional attachment to the parents and the capacity to idealize them, social cohesion, male-female relations, and, above all, self-esteem systems.[39] Culminating in the impossibility of the Negro's achieving a satisfactory level of self-esteem, his basic personality reflects economic insecurity, harsh family discipline, fragmented and disorganized home and emotional life, and the inability to relate affectively to others.

We are familiar enough with Kardiner's approach to know where to commence a search for the source of the basic personality: the operation of the primary institutions imposed in early family experience. Limitations of space preclude a detailed presentation of the sociological and psychological components of the Negro's basic personality formation, and in any case the vivid, intensely moving narration of the book cannot be improved upon by this reporter. A summary account of the main features will have to do.

Kardiner finds that the intermittent employment of the Negro father undermines his position as the child's source of authority. It is impossible to idealize one who fails in his expected function of providing subsistence the inadequacies of which expose his dependents to the anxieties associated with survival. Paternal authority disappears when the father loses his status as the chief source of the means of support during his child's years of dependency, in our patriarchally oriented society. The responsibility is thus thrust upon the mother, whose employment opportunities are superior to and more regular than her spouse's. But a working mother absent from home is a fatigued and irritable parent who confronts her children with harsh discipline, a demand for un-questioning obedience, and only intermittent affection. As an ob-ject simultaneously to be feared and relied upon, her idealized figure is one of ambivalence. The emotional attachment of the child to the parents is already weakened when he has no one to idealize positively. Because the idealization of others has its origin in the idealization of the parent, the absence of social cohesion that is so conspicuous in Negro life also finds its beginnings here.[40] Speaking with particular reference to the lower class, Kardiner ascribes the lack of social cohesion to

> the lower affectivity potential that results from the broken home, the absence of dependable parental figures, the vanish-ing father, the working mother who has no time to care for her children, the loveless discipline to which the children are ex-posed, the inability to idealize parental figures who frustrate more than they satisfy dependency cravings, the distorted re-lations between the sexes, the female-dominance in a male-oriented society, the disparagement of the male ideal, the universal mistrust and essential isolation of the lower-class Negro—all this in spite of the fact that the Negro is an inter-minable joiner.[41]

Unsatisfactory male-female relationships are concomitant fea-tures of the Negro's basic personality. The female lowers her esteem of a male who often cannot fulfill his economic responsi-bility. Psychologically as well as economically the female acquires the dominant role in the Negro family. Currently, the partial conversion of roles between the spouses arouses mistrust and con-tempt in the female and fear and hatred in the male, yielding an inability by both parties to relate to each other durably. Retro-spectively, the female remembers her own father as an unidealized figure who leaves with her a fear and distrust of men; the male re-members his own mother in terms of dependence and hostility, while his paternal prototype was disparaged and contemned. Both parties thus approach sexuality with impaired emotional predis-positions; "The Negro is hardly the abandoned sexual hedonist he is supposed to be."[42]

With a more resistant environment to adjust to than the white man has, the Negro is less happy, he suffers more, his spontaniety and ease are destroyed. In an unending vicious circle, the inaccessibility of white ideals leads to aggression, anxiety, depreciation of self-esteem, self-hatred, and increased aggression. In view of the Negro's lot of laborious emotional circumstances, his faulty adaptation has no hereditary racial origin but is indeed "the mark of oppression." Kardiner closes the book with an admonition that the only way to end the consequences of oppression is to stop the oppression. He rules out education of the Negro as a method; reintegration is what he needs. "It is the white man who requires the education."[43]

One may question the value of education in ameliorating a tension-fraught situation that is, moreover, so enduring and accepted as to be almost a permanent feature of American life. We are forced to ponder the effect education will have on hostile attitudes that ultimately derive from the white man's own unconscious anxieties. For does not the white man have a vested interest in the status quo in order to maintain his own prestige? Will he not resist efforts to undermine a source—real or imagined—of what is a precarious enough self-esteem? We recall Sullivan's distrust of all but the mildest kind of argumentation for the reason that it kindled the very emotional reaction it was trying to extinguish, anxiety. Admittedly education need not be argumentation, and there can be little doubt which variety Kardiner has in mind. Kardiner's whole social philosophy is predicated on the utility of human efforts to solve the problems of human adaptation; it rests on a psychoanalytic psychology that demonstrates the integrity of conscious motives in securing psychic and material satisfactions. On the one hand, this attitude escapes the determinism of a closed system and sanctions the value of purposive research in the social sciences. And as far as it goes, Neo-Freudian psychoanalysis and, more particularly, Kardiner's use of psychodynamic biography make substantial and important additions to our knowledge of social affairs. On the other hand, however, a purposive social science, no matter how firmly based on reliable evidence, imposes certain obligations on its proponent, for it is incumbent on him to suggest concrete means of implementing the goal he perceives as possible. In this respect Kardiner's inquiries into individual and social pathology leave a good deal to be desired; Franz Alexander too, we saw, boggled at this awesome prospect. The same could be said for other Neo-Freudian studies of a kindred spirit, excepting (as we shall see presently) the rather different tack taken by Erich Fromm.

No doubt it will be retorted that the disclosure of facts is itself a sufficient contribution to knowledge to justify a scientific study, and that this is the case *a fortiori* when many of the facts lie buried in the hitherto inscrutable recesses of the human psyche. Implementation, it will be said, lies with those who make policy, public or private: the scientist, having discovered, is quits with his social conscience. That may be so. Yet it can leave some friends of humanity with an uneasy feeling, and one is tempted to censure the Neo-Freudians—Alexander and Kardiner in particular—for their "singular dearth of good prescriptions" (in Sullivan's phrase) for bringing about what is so eminently desirable. The truth by itself does not always make us free, let alone happy; the Neo-Freudians' confidence in men's ability to direct their own lives under the guidance of conscious motivations may be overrated. On their behalf it can be said that at the very least they are acutely aware of the institutional impediments to living the good life, however unsophisticated they may be in elaborating techniques whereby that life can be realized. All the same, doubts as to the value of their work persist and will have to be taken up again in the last chapter.

Thus far we have taken two cross-sections, as it were, of contemporary society to disclose two classes of victims of its malfunctioning. Limited in scope and incisive in analysis, they reflect institutional discrepancies and point to precise areas where remedial measures are called for, although they may be difficult to apply. Alexander and Kardiner considered definable groups of people with personality disorders susceptible of clinical diagnosis; their treatment can be pictured within the current institutional structure of our culture. The same cannot be said of Erich Fromm's views of social pathology. His panorama of psychic disorder in Western society, notably in the United States, does not easily admit of collection into the consistent manifestations of a neurotic character structure. Such a statement may seem at odds with Fromm's undoubted accomplishments in relating social structure to character structure, which we examined in Chapter 4. And it is also true that Fromm holds the aberrant character structure, or orientation, that is prevalent today to be "a dominant one only in the modern era," one that is "definitely a modern product."[44] The historical antecedents of this present-day phenomenon were presented in *Escape from Freedom*, where the Protestant revolution, and especially its Calvinistic aspect, were seen to have inaugurated the features we are about to look into. That is to say, although the new orientation is conspicuous only now, it is no accident but has roots extending back several centuries.[45]

In Fromm's view, twentieth-century capitalism needs a personality type whose traits include the ability to cooperate in large, impersonal groups, and the desire for unlimited consumption according to standardized, manageable tastes,[46] which seems to clinch the argument that there is a neurotic character structure of the type he describes. Still, one cannot escape the feeling that his analysis is at bottom a compassionate satire, as it were, of behavior that deviates from his preconceived norm for the good life. His inspired tone of moral conviction can stir any audience of humanitarian inclinations, but those who manage to preserve some detachment may reflect that at times he resorts more to exhortation than to documentation. A Neo-Freudian who has moved from the microcosm to the macrocosm with a vengeance diagnoses not neurotic individuals but an insane society.

But to appreciate Fromm we must at least tentatively grant that the character traits to be described are what he calls a syndrome, resulting from an organization, or orientation, of character. An investigation into the durable features of character structure permits the analyst to interpret thought systems "in terms of the unconscious forces which can be inferred from minute details of manifest behavior."[47] By removing the analyst's attention to seemingly inconsequential nuances of behavior from the consulting room to the street, so to speak, observation of parapraxes can be transmuted into observation of social pathology. And when the diagnostician of individual mental disease readjusts his perspective, he exchanges the role of psychotherapist for that of social philosopher. The tactic entails a task of considerable proportions, for it requires not so much perceptive analysis as the ability to synthesize material that cannot be quantified and measured statistically. A catalog of the features of the orientation he perceives to be regnant today is not without interest, and the perspicacity of his many telling, if miscellaneous, observations on contemporary conduct cannot be gainsaid. Actually, Fromm gave three renditions of today's typical character structure. In *Escape from Freedom* the syndrome was that of automaton conformity; in *Man for Himself* it was the marketing orientation; in *The Sane Society* it was explicated from the leading concept of alienation.[48] Furthermore, Fromm states that a person's character is usually a mixture of some or all of the orientations he perceived. "We always deal with blends," and characterization as a rule must make reference to a person's dominant orientation.[49] For convenience we may refer to the leading syndrome of modern society's typical citizen as the capitalist character structure. At any rate, as a Neo-Freudian Fromm is sure to note that he replaces Freud's concept of libido development by one of relatedness to the social environment as the basis for his theory of character development and activity.[50]

What are the features of the capitalist character structure? So variegated are they that some arbitrary classification must be resorted to. In the first place, the person with this character structure is a conformist. Having lost his individuality in escaping from the unwanted freedom thrust upon him by the conditions of modern society, he accepts the personality offered by the current social patterns and becomes as others are and expect him to be also. He no longer experiences aloneness and anxiety, for he locates his identity in the approbation and recognition of others; as such, he is "essentially a reflex of other people's expectation of him," playing a role received from others. He retains the illusion of free will, thinking that as long as outer coercion is absent he makes his own decisions. But forceful constraint has only been replaced by the more subtle "anonymous authority of common sense and public opinion," the authority of nameless, unidentifiable, but all-pervasive conformity.[51] He feels and acts as he is expected to, without spontaneity; his frame of reference is outside himself. Equality, rather than furnishing the opportunity for cultivation of the idiosyncratic, has the leveling effect of eradicating individuality: the resultant society of automatons bereft of their several identities parodies the principle of equality seen as equal potentialities and rights.[52] Ethical standards too are taken from others. Virtue is equated with adjustment to the patterns of behavior of others and vice is to be different, for to be acceptable one must not be different. Hence the goal of education is to learn how to get along with others, variously known as "citizenship," "outgoingness," and "togetherness." In return for security the individual pays the high price that comes of surrender of individuality and spontaneity. Life, biologically speaking, proves to be a poor exchange for death, or automaton conformity, psychologically speaking. Uniformity and mental health are as incompatible as uniformity and freedom, for the obstructing of one's powers necessarily impairs mental health despite the disguise of complete adjustment.[53]

In the second place, the experience of oneself as a commodity permeates the capitalist character structure. In a capitalist society, where exchange has become an end in itself, person-to-person relationships between individuals yield to "a spirit of manipulation and instrumentality." The laws of the market rule social and personal relations as they do affairs of exchange. Employer-employee dealings have an air of indifference that is echoed in the treatment of customers as objects of manipulation rather than as persons with wants to be satisfied, and in the attitude of the manufacturer who produces for profit without any great interest in what he produces. "Man does not only sell commodities, he sells himself and feels himself to be a commodity." Personal characteristics are transient, easily put on and slipped off, so as not to conflict with the demands of the market in personal qualities that places a premium on acceptability. Roles are readily changed in the absence of a stability and enduring integrity in the commodity of the self.[54] When material success depends on personal acceptability, the influence of the market infects the formation of the social character of the urban middle class and, through it, the population in general. The motto of modern man is, in the playwright Pirandello's excellent phrase, "I am as you desire me."[55] Others too are experienced as commodities, from whom a friendly detachment is maintained, while knowledge becomes instrumental in achieving success in practical ways instead of being pursued for its own sake. Relations of love fall under the same rubric of exchange of commodities. Love is "a marginal phenomenon" in a system where the capacity for love is rare.[56] Last, politics is also a marketing process. Like large commercial undertakings, political parties and their politicians vend their wares to the populace. People without will or conviction are manipulated in the masquerade that is universal suffrage. The rule of the majority that is always necessarily right is after the nature of a plebiscite, wherein the voter does little more than record his concurrence with one or another of the "powerful political machines" which captures his political independence.[57]

In the third place, or rather, seen under its third and most comprehensive aspect, the capitalist character structure is an alienated one. Abram Kardiner fears our society may become one "in which we live alone together, among but not with one another,"⁵⁸ but Fromm carries the matter further. He believes alienation in present-day society to be so nearly total that it must be the point of departure for an analysis of contemporary social character.

> Man does not experience himself as the active bearer of his own powers and richness, but as an impoverished "thing," dependent on powers outside of himself, unto whom he has projected his living substance.⁵⁹

As divorced from himself as he is from others, isolation, or merely being "different," is an experience of emptiness; the solution of conformity, of regaining the security and identity furnished by primary ties, is sought at any price by promiscuous and purposeless membership in groups of all kinds.⁶⁰ In modern society it is the alternative to insanity, which is alienation unlimited. Any orientation, no matter how irrational, is tolerable provided a number of people share it; mass madness is not unknown, and an entire society can mistake material, intellectual, and political progress for security and happiness.⁶¹ Indeed, modern society discourages spontaneous emotions and thinking, substituting the cheap sentimentality of popular entertainment and prefabricated thoughts.⁶² As a consumer, modern man is ignorant of the processes of production, as he is of all social forces determining social life, and consumes compulsively, without pleasure and without knowledge. Whereas in the nineteenth century the principle of saving was regnant in the middle class, in the twentieth the craving for immediate satisfactions by ever-increasing consumption is their attitude. No distinction is made among needs, and so sexual and material wants are both gratified with minimal delay.⁶³

Some of this unhappy story may be disputed in one particular or another. The sum total, however, we know all too well from our own experience. The personality warps, the arresting mannerisms, the annoying traits, are everywhere about us. We find them in friends and strangers alike. Oddly enough, we do not find them in ourselves. Palpable as they are to the observer of his fellows, these characteristics do not discomfort the observer himself. Unlike a reading of Horney's works, where even more elaborate descriptions of poor psychic performance strike an immediate response and make us shift uneasily, a reading of Fromm's catalogs of disorientation prompts us to glance sharply at others instead. The charge might be made that Horney's delineations are too vague, her generalizations too loosely constructed, her web of neurosis so intricate and far-flung that all are bound to be caught in one place or another. The obvious retort, and probably the true one, is that she is correct, because neurosis is more prevalent in our society than we suspect. Horney is only holding the mirror up to nature, and if our nature sees its own distorted image are we to blame the mirror? Fromm's mirror, on the contrary, is held up to society; it points outward, capturing the aspect of others and not of ourselves. The reason, as has been remarked before, is that Horney is more concerned with inner conflicts, Fromm more with interpersonal relations. While the one restricts therapy to the consulting room, the other depicts character disorientation as a prelude to proposals for social reorganization.

Obviously a society in which the capitalist character structure is prevalent is in a sad state of affairs, and no mere palliatives can be expected to be of any appreciable remedial value. When a culture in all its works is diagnosed as insane, only a wholesale revamping of institutions will do. Fromm's critique therefore points inevitably to political means to bring about desired ends. Yet he never gives serious consideration to the dynamics of the political process. Granted, with a maneuver of this kind he can steer shy of the problems bound to beset more moderate proposals for change; questions of how are often harder to answer than questions of what. But if the axiom of he who wills the end must also will the means has any truth in it, then Fromm has not rendered a full accounting on his philosophical debts. A strategy must be implemented by a scheme of tactics if it is not to be a mere fantasy, and that means, in this case, an examination of political techniques and of those in a position to exercise them. Perhaps Fromm knows what he is about in evading this area of study. For what are we to say if politics is portrayed as a field for neurotic activity par excellence? What if the road to salvation only terminates at the arena of the irrational? For that we must turn to the ideas of Harold D. Lasswell.

POLITICAL SCIENCE
AS PSYCHOPATHOLOGY:
HAROLD D. LASSWELL

ANY BOOK that treats of the application of psychoanalysis to social theory must take cognizance of the work of Harold D. Lasswell. No other political scientist has so doggedly striven to illuminate his own discipline with the realities of behavior disclosed by this cognate science. In so doing, his revelation of politics to be something other than the rational means to achieve rational ends has earned him a reputation for misanthropy that recalls the obloquy heaped on another realist, Machiavelli, four centuries ago.[1] With a style that is now terse, clipped, blunt, now recondite in the convolutions of an unfamiliar jargon, Lasswell was determined to propose to political science hypotheses that it was ill prepared to assimilate. Adopting the tactics of an *enfant terrible,* he has shocked a complacent fraternity with truths that have remained comfortably hidden for too long. He was perhaps the first to systematically explore the foundation of political behavior in emotional instability. In linking professed values to their unconscious formation, he pioneered in explaining the techniques of political action by their appeal to unconscious motives. He moved character typology from the clinic to the political stage and made provocative suggestions as to the dynamics of group psychology. Ever peering behind overt political activity to its emotional determinants, Lasswell has incessantly pointed to new frontiers that begged for further research. And after nearly three decades of work he is by his own account virtually in a class by himself in applying psychoanalytic psychology to political studies.[2]

Why, then, has an exposition of Lasswell's political ideas been postponed so long in this volume? Why has he been segregated from the Neo-Freudians proper? One cannot lay down hard and fast lines of distinction when considering so restless and experimental an intellect as his, but it may become clear in the following pages that to a very large extent insofar as he applies psychoanalysis to politics Lasswell draws his inspiration directly from Freud. The consideration he gives to the revisions in psychoanalytic theory made by the Neo-Freudians occurs relatively late in his thought. The orthodox elements in his formulations predominate, as we shall see in passing. Within these limitations, the writings of Lasswell's earliest period, encompassing the 1930's, explored to the fullest the implications of psychoanalysis for political science. When these limitations proved unequal to the search for the values underlying a democratic system and the ways of safeguarding it, Lasswell abandoned a psychoanalytic approach almost *in toto,* and spent nearly a decade on the politics of democracy. A final shift, to the politics of power, saw the emergence of other themes, some old, some new, in an ever venturesome academic career that may at last have found a scheme of things that can withstand a skeptical spirit and an animated imagination. In all justice to his inquiring mind, these latter turnings will receive some attention in this book. Aside from the interest they have in their own right, they are more consistent with his initial aims than may at first appear and bring him to an unexpected consonance with Neo-Freudian principles. For the most part, though, we shall be concerned with his earlier studies.[3]

At the outset Lasswell warns of the irrational component of mental activity. Reality testing utilizes free fantasy as well as reason, and exclusive reliance on logic does more to incapacitate than to prepare the mind as an instrument of reality adjustment. Drawing what is perhaps too sharp a distinction between the two techniques, Lasswell says we have misplaced our faith in logic. For purposes of reality testing, free fantasy is a necessary complementary blade to logic. For purposes of political analysis, it behooves the investigator to search for clues to unconscious motives by intensive analysis.[4]

Thus Lasswell could legitimately criticize the conventional biographies of noteworthy political figures for revealing nothing about their traits and offering no information about the kinds of experiences that made for variety in the political portrait gallery. If life history be conceived as a natural history, it will ferret out facts that are developmentally significant. With an obvious allusion to the libidinal phases of maturation, Lasswell demands that political biography select the principal epochs of development and recognize the patterns typical of each. "We want to discover what developmental experiences are significant for the political traits and interests of the mature." Developmental experiences are important because an adult is the consequence of an evolution that is yet an incomplete evolution, in that many of his infantile motivations abide, unmodified, in the face of events of the post-infantile world. These impulses persist in what Lasswell calls "primitive psychological structures" which continue to control his psychic and overt behavior "in more or less disguised form."[5] In Freudian terminology, adults fail to supplant the pleasure principle with the reality principle, and untamed instincts continue their sway in the unconscious. If Wordsworth could say the child comes from God trailing clouds of glory, Lasswell could say the child emerges as an adult containing "primitive attitudes [which] are often called into play as the unobserved partners of rational reactions."[6] In *Psychopathology and Politics* Lasswell reviewed the analytic case records of a score of political figures to drive home his point. All revealed instances of infantile or adolescent sexual aberrations, all revealed political careers to be compensatory gratifications for frustrated libidinal strivings. While not saying it in so many words, behind representative political careers Lasswell found the ineluctable workings of the Oedipus complex.

It was possible, then, to generalize clinical evidence into a political formula that is especially applicable to the political personality. Its three terms capitalized on the discovery of the persistence in mental life of chronologically obsolete but nevertheless psychologically vigorous impulses. Initially, there are the private motives of the individual as organized in infancy. Their nongratification during that period impels, second, their displacement from family to public objects. "The repressed father-hatred may be turned against kings or capitalists, which are social objects playing a rôle before and within the community." Finally, the displacement is rationalized in terms of public interests. The political personality, *homo politicus,* shares the the first term, private motives, with everyone, and the second term, displacement, with some. He is unique in his ability to rationalize the displacement in terms of public interests. When impulses are not gratified in the intimate environment of childhood, they are externalized subsequently. "A fully developed political personality combines certain motives with certain skills, fusing an emotional capacity to externalize impulses with enough skill to secure success." The private motives can recede from conscious awareness and leave the political man with the impression that his rationalizations are objectively true.[7]

It is possible, says Lasswell, that a repressed hatred of authority is the outstanding private motive, due to the child's exaggeration of the wisdom and might of the paternal figure. If that be so, then the state, as the symbolic successor to the father, is "the legatee" of attitudes toward him, which accounts for the prevalence of hatred in politics. At any rate, "the common trait of the political personality type is emphatic demand for deference," a displacement onto the secondary environment of frustration or overindulgence in the primary environment of the family.[8]

By utilizing the Freudian tenets of the Oedipus complex, the libidinal phases of development, and the unconscious as the locus of antisocial instincts, Lasswell was able to excogitate a character typology of *homo politicus.* Distinguishing the species of the genus by the functions they perform, there are political agitators, administrators, and theorists. Each political type has a different developmental history. The differences would pertain to the imposition of the three infantile disciplines of weaning, control of elimination, and prohibition of genital manipulation.[9] The biographical details Lasswell gleaned from studying psychoanalytic case histories of typical political personalities revealed the importance of the gratification or frustration of the individual's infantile sexual needs. Thus the agitator's libidinal strivings, having been rebuffed, took a narcissistic turn whose homosexual component is later displaced as a demand for response from more generalized objects, the agitator being exceptionally alert to the emotional disposition of other people. "High value is placed on arousing emotional responses from the community at large." An enormous urge for expression, as an indirect way of fulfilling unconscious impulses, suits agitators well to the fluid situations presented by war and revolution.[10] Administrators, on the other hand, "are distinguished by the value which they place upon the co-ordination of effort in continuing activity," displacing their affects onto more tangible objects. Performing their functions within the formal framework of an established hierarchy, they retreat, behind the barrier of red tape, from the assertion of authority that responsibility entails. Their unconscious inclinations are hostile to authority, often undermining their nominal devotion to the conscientious administration of public affairs.[11] Theorists, as the third group, "are usually recruited from inhibited types." An undependable early environment, with frequent alternations between indulgence and deprivation, makes them unusually sensitive to fluctuations in human attitudes; their inner crises are unresolved.[12]

It should be fairly plain that Lasswell adapts Freud's theory of aim-inhibited libido as the key to character development. His political formula stands for the sublimation of aim-inhibited libido in the form of socially acceptable activities. The attitude toward the father as a symbol of authority and the displacement of that attitude onto public objects represents an unsatisfactory resolution of the Oedipus complex. The agitator, with his propensity for verbal and written expression, corresponds pretty closely to the oral character of Freudian typology. The administrator, with his impersonal penchant for order, corresponds to the anal character. The theorist, marked by inhibition, corresponds to the phallic character type.

Lasswell held the three types to be typical, not exhaustive.[13] He never explored any others, however, and the reason is not far to seek. There are simply no others to be explored so long as the Freudian typology is adhered to. Within the confines of an id-psychology, it is impossible to account adequately for the behavior of the mature, or genital, character, who has successfully resolved the Oedipus complex and finds sexual gratification in socially acceptable ways. When political thinkers resort to philosophy as a compensation for a severely inhibited emotional life,[14] what is socially acceptable may be individually pathological. In these terms, political biographies are studies in neurosis and political science is a description of a more or less sophisticated primal horde. At any rate, Lasswell's training in the social sciences enabled him to do things with clinical material that Freud could not. These personality types were no longer to be considered in the context of psychoanalytic investigation with an eye toward therapy. In Lasswell's hands they become subjects for political analysis, with an eye toward a science of politics. Lasswell made a substantial advance in Freudian characterology by infusing these inert, clinical paradigms with a vitality that made them the active propellants of political movements. The universal, almost abstract, constructions that Freud made were now placed in a cultural matrix that provided a field for their dynamic functioning.

It is in his treatment of the activities of *homo politicus* that Lasswell's writings seemingly take on their most cynical tone. A volume that equates Politics with the study of Who Gets What, When, How, is bound to excite revulsion among those who take a more philanthropic view of the matter. But a sphere of conflict that extracts "all the vanity and venom, the narcissism and aggression, of the contending parties" would have to bring to the fore "those who get the most of what there is to get." If the proposition that those who get the most are to be labeled "elite" and the rest "mass" disturbs egalitarian value preferences, then Lasswell could retort that "the science of politics states conditions; the philosophy of politics justifies preferences." Restricting himself to political analysis, Lasswell examined "influence and the influential."[15] It did little good to insert the proviso that stressing the influential did not leave the mass altogether out of account, or that the mass could benefit from some political changes while the elite enjoyed maximum aggrandizement.[16] The basic proposition remains that political science concentrates on the careers of the elite as perceived through the analysis of personality. As he himself was later to realize, little else could be expected of a psychology that predicated an intense craving for deference as the mainspring of activity and that viewed political careers as compensations for low estimates of the self. When an unconscious drive for deference makes the political world go round, "a diagram of the pattern of distribution of any value resembles a pyramid."[17] A democratic society is *ex hypothesi* out of the question. What may begin, psychologically, in equality of condition is sure to end, politically, in inequality of distribution, especially when the values are those which can be secured only at the expense of other people.

We already know that for the political personality the supreme value is deference. For reasons that are not clear, Lasswell adds safety and income. However, these are to be construed as representative, and not exclusive, values; different groups of values would yield different elites, and in any event "values change more by the unconscious redefinition of meaning than by rational analysis."[18] The elite maximizes its accrual of values by manipulating the environment—the mass—by the use of violence, goods, symbols, and practices. Politics studies the changes in the pyramidal value hierarchy.[19] Should the elite be successful in foisting a myth upon the emotionally receptive mass, it can easily enough secure deference and income from it. Should it not, then there eventuates a revolution, in which ways of recruiting the elite are changed and the prevailing myth is altered. Myths, or symbols, are prime weapons in the arsenal of the governing few (the ideology of defenders of the status quo) or of those who seek to replace them (the utopia of would-be revolutionaries).[20]

Taken in connection with the concept of displacement, that of symbols provides a theory of group psychology that is in keeping with Freud's. Aim-inhibited libido secures identification with an object with whom emotional bonds cannot be established as an object choice for sexual acts. With the necessary requisite of aim-inhibited impulses whose libidinal component is diverted onto symbols that substitute for immediate gratification, the qualities of the object are introjected to establish the emotional ties whose growth is the surest cement of the social consensus.[21] The remoteness of political symbols from the common experience of most people ensures their easy utilization as receptacles for private affects waiting to be displaced. The universality and constant reiteration of a symbol leaves it "nothing but a focus for the cumulation of irrelevancies." The more generalized the symbol, the greater its popular appeal. "Symbols must be sufficiently vague," Lasswell specifies, "to enable the individual to transfer his private loves and hates and hopes and fears to the slogans and catchwords of the movement."[22] Emotional bonds provide the charge for a political movement that is ignited when symbolic definition of the group in relation to demands on the world is achieved. If symbols are not impostures, and if political movements are not mass delusions, Lasswell can at any rate speak of "remarkable monuments to human vanity" when referring to the collective symbols of nations, classes, tribes, and churches in whose name people indulge primal urges for power, omniscience, amorality, and security.[23] Could Lasswell be blamed for suggesting that the impulse, rather than the citizen, might be "the unit of political action"? If so, then the critic would have to take account of the effects of symbols on the personality, which run from slight alterations in the manner of verbal expression to the total change of a career as people offer their talents to a common cause.[24]

It is the function of propaganda to diffuse and manage symbols, to precipitate mass displacement of private affects upon these public objects with a rationalization in terms of the public interest. Its task is facilitated by the amazing ability people exhibit in vindicating private goals in terms of political symbols; it makes little practical difference whether it be done unconsciously, as rationalization, or consciously, as justification. Propaganda used to maneuver a symbol is potent precisely because the displacement of private affects from symbol to symbol is so easily accomplished.[25] It is thus concerned with managing collective attitudes by wielding significant symbols. "Propaganda in the broadest sense is the technique of influencing human action by the manipulation of representations." It utilizes the suggestibility of groups rather than coercing them outright. Intellectuals, therefore, could be defined as "those who live by manipulating contentious symbols."[26]

Equipped with data from the intensive study of individual personalities afforded by psychoanalysis, Lasswell could make some frank observations on other aspects of political behavior that were not customarily treated with an air of *Realpolitik*. Thus agitation marks the phase of political movements when a new system of symbols is propagated among and accepted by emotionally disposed malcontents, in defiance of authority. Bribery is a universal feature of politics because it gratifies universal drives, notably that against authority; unresolved Oedipus complexes harbor unconscious antiauthoritarian impulses which are expressed in compromising the powerful. Faction is nothing more than internecine power politics—the usual state of affairs anyway—reflecting contending forces within the individual; feuds, carrying this to extremes against prevalent mores, reactivate primitive impulses. Compromise is favored by a tendency to submit and subordinate oneself, in contrast to the more commonly met assertive drives. Even so harmless appearing an activity as fraternizing can be shown to be an implement in social struggle, akin to war, intrigue, the *Putsch,* the coup d'état, and the strike, but more subtle than they in the exploitation of the unconscious hatred of existing authority. And morale, far from being a spiritual quality with an idealistic flavor, is to Lasswell but the sustained subordination of individual to collective purposes that can be artificially induced and managed by the skilled direction of aggressive impulses and discharging of tensions.[27]

It might be thought from this much of our presentation that the dynamics of politics, as Lasswell conceives it, can be explained as no more than the unscrupulous manipulation of symbols by ruthless elites in a nightmare of vociferous appeals to the id. It might be thought that Lasswell merely gives a psychoanalytic twist to the Hobbesian state of nature, as it were, showing the superior efficacy of fraud over force on the battlefield of the unconscious, where all political issues are ultimately decided. But it is not as simple as that. True to his Freudian orientation, Lasswell employs the tripartite division of the psyche into id, ego, and superego, to account for succession and variation in politics. The meaning an individual attaches to a given symbol will depend on its relation to his complete personality structure. What Lasswell calls "the triple-appeal principle" can elucidate political change in a manner that a nonpsychoanalytic approach cannot. Institutions as social objects, he says, may appeal to human personalities in a specialized way, that is, to impulse, to reason, or to conscience, for one level of even the best integrated personality often predominates.[28] Thus it is the mores that appeal to the superego of most of the group's personalities, while it is counter-mores that appeal to the id and expediencies that appeal to the ego. In an institutional structure at equilibrium, economic, political, and technological institutions are particularly the area of play of the ego, religion that of the superego, and aesthetics that of the id.[29]

But political behavior is a disturbance of the equilibrium. Beginning in a moral crisis, political change ends in a new moral consensus. After a commencement in unrest and a public definition of alternatives, a readjustment takes place. Politics is no more than the transition between successive established consensuses.[30] During periods of rapid social change the readjustment is predictable. At times when "the prevalent body of authoritarian patterns"—law—is flouted, the resultant insecurities pave the way to new or formerly existing controls. And at times when discipline is rigid, the resultant insecurities pave the way for nonconformist behavior.[31] In other words, discipline on behalf of a common cause impels subsequent individualism, while periods of self-assertion culminate in a trend toward authoritarianism. Periods of crisis require "dictatorship, centralization, concentration, obedience, and bias." It is the season of the agitator. Between crises concessions can be made toward "democracy, decentralization, dispersion, originality, and objectivity." It is the season of the administrator.[32]

The manipulation of symbols by contending elites in order to activate the ungratified components of personalities whose equilibria are easily upset accounts for the dynamics of politics. "Political movements, then, derive their vitality from the displacement of private affects upon public objects, and political crises are complicated by the concurrent reactivation of specific primitive motives." War is the classic illustration of the overturning of psychic stability, releasing elementary motivations from the restraints of more complicated psychological structures. And like other crowd phenomena, chauvinism belongs to the kind of behavior where emotional processes overwhelm rational, the symbols of the state being employed to achieve the desired effect in mobilizing the community.[33]

Since at any given time the attention of the community is dispersed over various competing symbols, an elite must reinforce the competitive power of its symbol "by leading as many elements as possible in society to read their private meanings into it." The dethroning of an elite that constitutes a revolution requires the detachment of the affections of the mass from the existing symbols of authority and their transfer to the challenging symbols, the meanwhile concealing the counter-mores nature of revolutionary acts. With propaganda, "the conscience is quoted against the conscience" to assure reception of the novel, defiant symbol.[34] A "true" revolution is accomplished when symbols rooted in the conscience lose their grip. Movements for political independence, Lasswell thinks, are explicable, psychologically speaking, as the arrival at a consensus on a new symbol upon doing away with the old superego structure. After the conflict between id and superego precipitated by symbol action, the personality is stabilized on a fresh foundation. Violence is due to the release from constraint symbolically occasioned by the fall of an elite. When the orgy is done, identification and introjection of the new adjustment into the personalities of growing individuals preclude further controversy. "Once a part of the superego of the rising generation, the moral consensus is complete."[35]

If we construe propaganda as political platforms or promises, and the manipulation of symbols as political campaigning, then we can appreciate the telling indictment Lasswell's analysis delivers against the style of contemporary politics. This backing and filling of the political flux, the coming and going of symbols that serve the purposes of elites without appreciably diminishing the insecurities of those whom they so crassly sway, casts serious doubt on the efficacy of politics as a medium for the solution of social problems. One is reminded of nothing so much as Plato's allegory of the cave, wherein people respond to shadows of images that are themselves imitations of reality. But reality, whether it be Plato's ideal Forms or the substrates of personality, is but distantly related to the turmoil of daily political life. In Lasswell's memorable words,

> It is becoming something of a commonplace that politics is the arena of the irrational. But a more accurate description would be that politics is the process by which the irrational bases of society are brought out into the open.

When displacement is the elementary gambit of public life, political solutions are not likely to be those which are rationally the best but those which are emotionally satisfactory, and the psychological truth is that "the rational and dialectical phases of politics are subsidiary to the process of redefining an emotional consen-

sus."[36] With symbols merely the vehicles of emotional identifications, the repositories of displaced private motives, the political
demands they profess have slight relevance to actual social needs.
And when psychoanalysis reveals the probable remoteness of what
the individual demands from what he needs, then one may earnest-
ly question the utility of discussion as a technique of dealing with
social problems.[37] With more than a little justice Lasswell suggests a distrust of public debate as a method of relieving the strains
of adjusting to a changing environment. The premise of democratic politics that each man is the best judge of his own interests
is unsubstantiated by the disclosures of psychoanalytic research,
he maintains. To the contrary, it is disconnected from a plan of
life which yields happiness and adjustment. Therefore, consulta-
tion among all parties concerned with a view to the determination
of policy by bargaining and compromise is really beside the point.
"The individual who chooses a political policy as a symbol of his
wants is usually trying to relieve his own disorders by irrelevant
palliatives." Such adjustment as may be secured is more likely to
be symptomatic than reflective. If democracy vaunts dictatorship
by discussion, Lasswell could hardly be called cynical for remarking that propaganda is "the technique of dictating to the dic-
tators."[38]

It would be less intolerable to our political predispositions if
the behavior Lasswell depicts were transient occurrences. We
would not be too disturbed if the displacement of private affects
upon public objects, with the accompanying rationalization, were
occasional events, intermittent tempests in a prevailing calm. If
agitation nourishes discontent then all we would need do is remove
the discontent, using for that purpose social security at home or
economic assistance abroad. But we are not permitted to be so
naïve. The discontented we shall always have with us, for the private affects are instinctual. They are an ineradicable part of a biologically fixed human nature. The sexual- and death-instincts
can at best be mitigated, by repression or sublimation. In the per-
petual inquietude of politics, neither is likely to endure, if it

eventuates at all. The malady feeds upon itself. On these premises, there is no way out.

From a Neo-Freudian standpoint a political philosopher might utilize Lasswell's analysis to pass caustic judgment on some of the patterns of behavior of American political institutions. They present an environment that is hardly congenial to the discharge of the responsibilities expected of a citizen in a democratic society. They foment strain in interpersonal relations to an unconscionable extent and all but guarantee a chronic incidence of undesirable psychological conditions. No electorate can join in a rational consensus in public affairs when it operates in an atmosphere of parataxic distortion. But the Freudian approach Lasswell employed left little room for a constructive criticism of political behavior because it lacked a well-developed ego-psychology on which to base that criticism. When pathology is taken to be the usual state of affairs, there is no way to turn to find a system of political health.

This much of the discussion draws almost exclusively upon Lasswell's writings of the 1930's. It summarizes what may be called his destructive critique of political practices in general and of the politics of democracy in particular. As with Erich Fromm, an orthodox psychoanalytic approach to political institutions left Lasswell in something of a quandary when it came to excogitating a theory less censorious of democracy. Fromm, we saw, solved the problem in one way. Lasswell solved it in another, as we shall see in a moment.

In the ensuing decade Lasswell made one further return to the psychoanalytic-political fray with *Power and Personality*. There psychoanalytic data are used as auxiliaries to a conception of politics as power. *Homo politicus* is considered as one whose leading characteristic is the pursuit of power, the demand for deference, as the supreme value in a network of interpersonal relations that are one and all convertible into power relationships.[39] One would think that a political type oriented about power would be the result of an ego-psychology, in that power is sought as a means of self-realization in interpersonal relations. But the ego Lasswell predicates is always a debilitated one, an ego that has images of the interpersonal environment meaningful as extensions or compensations of degraded self-esteem stemming from the deprivations consistently applied in childhood. A political career—the quest for power—is embarked on as compensation for low estimates of the self generated in the family environment of infancy. And Lasswell speaks of everyone being born a politician (in this sense), with most of us outgrowing it, as though a political career were a regressive phenomenon that ought to be outgrown.[40] With the craving for power in the political type "intense and ungratified" it has definitely pathological denotations. Political success is still achieved by the use of the political formula as *homo politicus* performs in the arena of the irrational.[41] The emphasis is still upon the discouragement of normal sexual maturation and expression as the key to personality development and to the movement of political events, and, as one observer has noted, Lasswell considers the unconscious "not as a source of power but almost exclusively in terms of the impairment or loss of power."[42] Nevertheless, the book brings together many currents of Lasswell's thought, political and psychological, and can be regarded as a watershed in his intellectual career.

These were not Lasswell's last words on the subject by any means. A discerning critic of *Politics: Who Gets What, When, How* thought he saw Lasswell hint that all modern revolutions "represent the emergence of the . . . middle income skill group," more conventionally known as the middle class, and Lasswell himself interpreted the Russian Revolution as the emergence of a "party bureaucratic state" in place of the antecedent mixed state of landlords, official bureaucracy, and business. Since the propagandists and organizers of the Communist party exercise control, occupy financially lucrative positions, and have maximum deference attached to their political decisions, they enjoy the triple values of safety, income, and deference. In the long run, he suggested, the Russian Revolution may, like the French Revolution, enter history as a second bourgeois revolution, the old regime having been "liquidated for the benefit mainly of those who possess skills appropriate to an era of governmentalized social life."[43]

The concept of skills is one that seems to have been lost sight of in political analysis since the days of Aristotle. Lasswell must be credited with having revived a simple truth that is almost a truism, namely, that in any political society those who embody the values which that society esteems will have preferred access to the positions of greatest eminence or power. For Aristotle, men of wealth ruled in an oligarchical society, men of free birth in a democratic one, and men of genuine political talent or virtue in an aristocracy, for example. (Plato had followed much the same principle in his constitutional cycle.) For Lasswell, the utilization of skills by elites to secure values historically had brought power to different elites possessing various combinations of skills. In the feudal period fighting was the skill that had brought power; in the period of consolidation of national monarchies a premium had been placed on organizational ability; in the nineteenth and early twentieth centuries skill in bargaining had secured the hegemony of the private plutocrat. Today an elite skilled in propaganda is in the ascendancy; after that, who would rise? "The man of violence? the bargainer? the ceremonializer?" For a stable world order the best Lasswell could look forward to in the 1930's was

a universal body of symbols and practices sustaining an élite which propagates itself by peaceful methods and wields a monopoly of coercion which it is rarely necessary to apply to the uttermost. This means that the consensus on which order is based is necessarily nonrational; the world myth must be taken for granted by most of the population. The capacity of the generality of mankind to disembarrass themselves of the dominant legends of their early years is negligible, and if we pose the problem of unifying the world we must seek for the processes by which a nonrational consensus can be most expeditiously achieved. A sufficient concentration of motive around efficacious symbols must be elicited in order to inaugurate and stabilize this adjustment.[44]

Thus far and no further could an id-psychology go. Nor was Lasswell long in realizing that a nonrational consensus could endorse an odious regime. Lasswell believed that the rise of Nazism was due to the psychological impoverishment of a lower middle class whose emotional insecurity was fertile ground for movements of mass protest. In a society that accorded it small deference and limited economic opportunities, what that class looked for were symbols for both emotional attachment and destructiveness.[45] If, then, historical development had thrust the middle class to the fore as the mass of political movements, and if the possession of appropriate skills assured access to political power, then what was needed for the stability of a democracy was such a diffusion of skills as would virtually universalize the elite. This meant that for a purposive political analysis values would have to be redefined, the id-psychology would have to be laid aside, and political science would have to become a policy science.

In an essay written in the mid-thirties, Lasswell saw a world revolution in the rise of the middle class; it lacked only a unifying symbol to make it a political power to reckon with. Lasswell thought the necessary symbol could be found in its sacrifices in acquiring socially useful skills. And its claim on a reward in the struggle for social justice would come none too soon. A realization of its role in history, which would dispel its disunity and uncertainty, could, in America, enable the middle class to find a community of public interest that would avoid the disastrous fate of the European middle class.[46]

An intriguing essay of his of some six years later found that a balanced society achieved the democratization of power in what he called a commonwealth of mutual deference, "a community in which there is opportunity for the maturing of talent into socially useful skill." Deference means to be taken into consideration in the making of political decisions. Considering that political decisions are those backed by the strongest deprivational sanctions, up to and including violence, and considering that the most influential decisions are made by government, the democratization of power means "to maintain the practice of general participation in the making of influential decisions." Democracy is endangered by practices that disrupt relations of mutual respect and instead stir up impulses of destruction.[47] The opposition between democracy thus defined and destructiveness, which has perhaps more than a chance resemblance to Freud's dualism of Eros and the death-instinct, opened the way to a more subtle conception of democratic politics. The commonwealth of mutual deference curbs destructiveness by fostering creative interpersonal relations, culminating in the recruitment of leaders. Democratic leaders share the character structure consistent with such a community, and they are therefore widely recruited and enjoy communal support. If virtually every citizen is eligible to partake in decision making, with the assent of his fellow citizens, the elite can be universalized and power is not monopolized by a clique. "The elite of a democracy ('the ruling class') is society-wide."[48]

The concept of government as the most influential decision maker of a community is in reality the ultimate refinement of the means used by those who get what there is to get; it is influence in its most arrogant form. Lasswell could now once again try to join psychoanalysis and politics, this time with psychoanalysis in the diminuendo and this time with the bridge of power, a concept that has not yet left his thought. "Power is decision-making. A decision is a sanctioned choice, a choice which brings severe deprivations to bear against anyone who flouts it." The science of politics would be the science of power, and the importance of decisions is to be measured by their effect on the distribution of values.[49]

The schedule of values for the new science of politics to replace the triad of safety, income, and deference evolved into two larger groups containing subsidiary elements. Under welfare values are subsumed those required for the maintenance of one's security and psychic integrity, comprising well-being, wealth, skill, and enlightenment. Under deference values are subsumed those concerned with receiving notice or regard from others (or from oneself), comprising power, respect, rectitude, and affection. Again

Lasswell stipulates that these are representative and not exhaustive values, being those that are taken for granted in our civilization.[50]

These intellectual peregrinations amid value schemes and concepts of a democratic society indicate Lasswell's groping for a more traditional framework fit to contain a final (to date) psychoanalytic basis for a science of politics. A revised system of values and the recognition of the importance of a stable commonwealth of mutual deference imply a different type of character structure from that which orthodox Freudian psychology could yield. By 1951 Lasswell was leaning toward the ego-psychology of the Neo-Freudians, congruent with the newer value hierarchy. Character was to refer to "the self-system of a person" in conjunction with assistance or impediments to it given by the unconscious. The locus of the self-system is now to be found in the ego, and ideally the democratic character uses the energies of the unconscious as a source of support for the self-system.[51] As to its three main sets of patterns, the self-system of the democratic character maintains an open, rather than a closed, ego, in its identifications; that is, "the democratic attitude toward other human beings is warm rather than frigid, inclusive and expanding rather than exclusive and constricting." In its demands, the democratic character is multi-valued, disposed to share rather than to hoard values, and in particular attaching little weight—significantly—to the exercise of power. Finally, in its expectations, the democratic character has a deep confidence in man's benevolent potentialities, an affirmative trust rather than an apathetic endurance.[52]

After this refurbishment of theory Lasswell could look forward to a "drastic and continuing reconstruction" of our society by what seems to be a kind of behaviorism, in that it applies indulgences and deprivations to secure the desired results. Democratic behavior is to be rewarded by indulgences while deprivations are to be the lot of those who act contrarily.[53] If this technique appears somewhat primitive it is at least noteworthy that it contemplates nurturing an adult ego-structure—albeit an unsteady one —and does not regard the citizen as hopelessly irretrievable material once the forge of infantile experiences has wrought its work. To further assist in the maintenance of a democratic society, Lasswell advocates the development of policy sciences. These are to aid the development of democratic personality and amend the decision making process so as to fulfill the values of a democratic commonwealth.[54] This proposal accompanies the shift of ground Lasswell has made in the past decade, one which places power in the center of his conception of politics.[55] In reality it is less of a shift of ground than a more exacting redefinition of some older themes in an effort to systematize a science of politics that can comprehend the apparently contradictory ideas of power and democracy. Here the policy sciences take on heightened meaning. Their purpose is to abet and preserve a broad-based access to power and continuing accountability to a universal elite in order to sustain democratic values. Equality of opportunity in access to power makes the shadow of an elite of leadership the substance of democracy. The methods of accountability are nearly all of them the familiar American constitutional machinery.[56]

One may question the appellation "sciences," since they are not the objective scrutiny of events but investigations with a normative bias. The overriding value is now the dignity of man,[57] and the good society rests on the maximum sharing of all values, it being "right" to share them.[58] Thus by the 1950's Lasswell had boxed the compass of political science. From the cool reporting of hard and often unpleasant facts he had turned political science into an almost sentimental defense of a preferred set of values. A study of influence and the influential that had unmistakable anti-democratic implications had become a study of power that paradoxically rationalized an egalitarian society replete with individual rights. A science of political behavior that at one time swore by modern personality research—as Lasswell so often calls it—concluded by whispering one allusion to psychoanalysis in his most ambitious construction of political concepts.[59]

In the 1930's Lasswell the political scientist had pretty well painted himself into a corner with the psychoanalytic brush. Of what use is a science of politics if its basic proposition is a *reductio ad absurdum*, to wit, that a science to guide the rational ordering of public affairs is impossible in the face of psychological truths? A new tack had to be tried. This is not to say that professional or patriotic reasons caused Lasswell to moderate an uncompromising objectivity. His contact with newer modes of psychoanalytic thought (he joined the staff of Harry Stack Sullivan's Washington School of Psychiatry in 1938) and his further studies in political science proper brought to the fore latent and more constructive trends in his thought. If Lasswell's writings took him far afield from his initial application of psychoanalysis to politics, it is because he grew steadily disenchanted with orthodox psychoanalysis as a frame of reference for political philosophy. He realized before long some of the limitations of a Freudian approach to behavior; perhaps, on closer inspection, his utilization of psychoanalysis was in error to begin with too. The first possibility has already been suggested. The second must now be examined, together with Lasswell's positive contribution to social philosophy.

8

THE GOOD SOCIETY:
PREVENTION VERSUS
UTOPIA

PUTTING ASIDE for a moment Lasswell's later efforts to construct a science of politics, it must be admitted that his early theory of political dynamics looks promising as a key to the enigma of political fluctuations. Its clarification of the vexing topics of political crisis, revolution, and war is clearly an advance upon explanations that do not avail themselves of intensive personality research. Yet the very strength of his theory points to its greatest weakness. *Stasis* is a pathological political phenomenon, so to speak; it is not the only political condition we know of or are interested in. As we have seen, just as an id-psychology is predisposed to the study of psychic morbidity, so an adaptation of such a psychology to politics is apt to be unexpectedly precocious in dealing with its seamier aspects. It has been responsible in no small part for the unsavory reputation Lasswell's writings have earned in some quarters. What is missing from these writings for a more balanced view is a conception of human personality structure as a consistent, integrated entity that does more than respond erratically to random external stimuli. His sharp dichotomy between free association and logical thought, which was noted before, indicates a view of character that in turn reflects a perhaps faulty understanding of psychoanalysis.

There is evident in Lasswell's writings a tendency to reduce psychoanalysis to the technique of free association, or "free fantasy," in his phrase. In his canvassing of clinical material on which to build a social theory, Lasswell has inclined to utilize what he calls "the prolonged clinical interview." Further, he hopes the time is coming when the gap between the psychoanalyst and the "spot interpreter of behavior" will be closed.[1] Is a purely academic use of psychoanalysis valid for the excogitation of political theory? Is it not likely to become a superficial investigation of psychopathology employing the analytic technique to obtain such information as is of use to the interviewer? In Lasswell's hands psychoanalysis is a research technique and not a therapeutic one; the subject is to all intents and purposes ancillary to the whole process instead of being its central point. In such studies Lasswell would therefore encounter the action of the id as it brought about psychic incapacitation. At least two related difficulties ensue. On the one hand later stages in the subject's life that may have contributed to his illness are ignored; all adult aberrations are regarded as regressions to infantile deprivations; the relation of the growing citizen to social institutions is overlooked and the possibility of controlling or reforming the latter in the interests of shaping healthier character structures is forfeited. And on the other hand what Lasswell does learn of the mind by this method is its disordered state; its stabilizing and therapeutic powers are too easily glossed over in the desire to secure data for political science. At any rate, Lasswell does not pretend to speak as a practicing analyst, acknowledging that he has never practiced therapeutic psychoanalysis as such.[2]

Ernest Jones points out the vital necessity to have undergone the personal suffering of a didactic analysis as a requisite to exploring the deepest recesses of the mind. The desirability of refreshing and extending psychoanalytic knowledge, he adds, often induces students from allied fields to remain with psychoanalysis as lay—i.e., non-medically trained—analysts.[3] Although he did indeed undergo a didactic analysis,[4] Lasswell chose not to turn to the practice of lay analysis; in a country where the question of lay analysis has provoked considerable controversy the choice must not have been difficult to make, aside from the—to him—superior attraction of political science. Thus Lasswell's contact with clinical experience has been limited, for if full participation as well as observation constitutes a proper psychoanalytic interview (according to Neo-Freudian principles), then Lasswell's connection with analysis produces an insufficiently reliable source of data. What this source will yield is an incomplete comprehension of the personality, a view of it in its crippled condition. And a theory of political dynamics based on it, therefore, cannot help being similarly one-sided.

Nevertheless, with these qualifications in mind a good deal of wheat can be separated from the chaff of Lasswell's analysis of the political process that not only indicates the *via regia* of his own intellectual development but is consistent with Neo-Freudian social philosophy. Lasswell makes it plain that a recurrent resort to political activity in an effort to discharge emotional insecurities only perpetuates, if it does not aggravate, the psychic tension it is supposed to relieve. This peculiar brand of homeopathy simply will not work: no amount of indulgence of regressive tendencies will induce a conditioned corrective of them. To use technical terminology, outside the clinical situation a chronic activation of a transference yields only a *perpetuum mobile* of mental aberration. In another phrasing, parataxic distortion feeds upon itself when it runs rampant amidst the stresses of daily efforts to validate the self. The remedies proffered by political panaceas are so many futile purgatives that temporarily assuage the consequences of tension-fraught interpersonal relations without noticeably abating the sources of disturbance. It must be noted that Lasswell does not object to politics per se but to the style in which it is customarily carried on. The manipulation of symbols to effect the displacement of private affects upon public objects merits the reprobation of all who advocate sanity in politics. Maneuvers of this kind are a travesty of the good life, as Lasswell is well aware. However, a psychoanalytic view of politics is predicated on an outlook that can be more productive of beneficial results. It is in the very nature of a therapeutic science to esteem the value of prevention as compared with cure. The interception of unhealthy trends is more efficacious than their repair, and so Lasswell proposes what he calls "the politics of prevention" as an alternative to the deceptive attempts to heal psychic wounds that is conventional politics. The politics of prevention, he says, "draws attention squarely to the central problem of reducing the level of strain and maladaptation in society."[5]

Taking war and revolution to be the exacerbated upshots of emotional stress, Lasswell would apply the talents of the political psychiatrist to attacking personal insecurity in both cause and consequence. The problem of politics, he declares, is not to promote discussion, which often complicates social difficulties by awakening hostile attitudes that call forth "obstructive, fictitious, and irrelevant values." "The problem of politics is less to solve conflicts than to prevent them; less to serve as a safety valve for social protest than to apply social energy to the abolition of recurrent sources of strain in society."[6]

Changing the organization of government or reforming the social system, Lasswell believes, is outside the scope of preventive politics, for at best either merely serves as a kind of catharis for the participants in somewhat reducing their own tension levels.[7] The political demands they enunciate, however, "are of limited relevance to the changes which will produce permanent reductions in the tension level of society." At its most comprehensive, a program of democratic statesmanship will strike at the root of the evil not only by improving the practices of character formation, but also by organizing institutions so as to minimize the occurrence of provocative crises. A more practical suggestion is to anticipate and avert the intrapsychic causes of insecurity, which may require "the reconstruction of the individual's view of the world, and not [depend] upon belligerent crusades to change the world."[8] In particular, a more immediate program concerns those who engineer political maneuvers, those who have the unique talent of rationalizing in terms of public interests: the political leaders, the social scientists, the social administrators, the intellectuals. What is needed, Lasswell believes, is not reorganization but reorientation. The minds of these people have to be directed at the central problems of locating the chief factors affecting the tension level of the community, and ascertaining the relevance of a policy to the decrease of the level of tension. These are to be the proper criteria by which public policies are to be evaluated. Internationally, it requires "a continuing audit of the world level of insecurity."[9] Since free fantasy is as much a method as logic in adjusting to reality, and since free fantasy can be cultivated as much as logic, Lasswell implies—though he does not declare outright—that a didactic analysis can be an essential part of the training of public figures. It would provide them with the deepest comprehension of the meaning of insecurity as well as furnish them insight into their own private motives.[10]

Does a depreciation of the value of discussion and of the bargaining and compromise that are supposed to produce solutions to social problems necessarily raise the specter of dictatorship? Are the politics of democracy to be sacrificed for the politics of prevention? Lasswell rejoins that "the threadbare terminology of democracy versus dictatorship, of democracy versus aristocracy," only serves to lead us astray from the real issue. It is the truth about the conditions of harmonious human relationships that should reign, and that knowledge is not a monopoly of rulers as rulers.[11] Indeed, Lasswell's studies provide convincing enough evidence that dictatorship eventuates precisely when the conventional tactics of politics are relied upon to reach difficulties they cannot mitigate but only irritate. Once given a level of social tension that evokes a cry for reform, the snares and delusions that are the symbols of political programs act as vehicles of exploitation, and not of amelioration. When social tension is rife, rival elites capitalize on dependency demands of the mass with devalued selves. Any action is deemed better than the anguish of insecurity. "The flight into danger becomes an insecurity to end insecurity." Tyrants do not force themselves on masses, but quite the reverse. Lasswell emphasizes that *"Men can only be free when*

they are free of social anxiety." Thus the outlook for democracy
and stability is in any event unfavorable in a world whose ordinary insecurities are heightened by periodic economic crisis.[12]

It was with a good deal of courage, then, that Lasswell sought
to apply preventive politics to the atmosphere of an "expectation
of violence" that he foresaw would characterize the polarized
world of the postwar era. The liberalized, expanding economic
system that he recommended for America in *World Politics Faces
Economics* would, he hoped, be a practical demonstration that
"wars, though likely, are not inevitable if we continually practice
preventive politics."[13] Lasswell seems to be almost alone among
so-called foreign policy experts in affirming that "feelings of self-
respect," as well as considerations of power politics, will influence
developments in international politics. For example, rational
calculations of national interest may, in weak nations, be over-
ridden when pressing claims to recognition of international equality and expressing revulsion with colonialism.[14]

Turning from the opposing postures of the two great powers,
toward one or the other of whom all lesser powers will gravitate,
Lasswell finds the underdeveloped countries to be at the crux of
the problem of world security. It is very largely their self-respect
that is at issue. The irregular impact of American economic fluctuations on the economic, and consequently the political, structures of these nations jeopardizes the friendly relations with them
that are so desirable. The magnitude of their growth is staggering
enough; when it is erratic as well, the capacity of men to adjust
peacefully may be strained. Destructiveness can follow on the
frustrations fed by economic disorder. The importance of steady
economic growth in these nations cannot be overestimated, Lasswell feels, if international peace and domestic tranquillity are
to be safeguarded. The psychological foundations of both will be
substantially augmented by evenly paced expansion of productivity.[15] Toward this end, American investment policy, both
public and private, should encourage balanced industrialization
abroad. Furthermore, the modifications in the balance of power

wrought by the irregularities of the American economy point to the necessity of stabilizing the latter as well.[16]

In a later work Lasswell made a hurried allusion to the politics of prevention on the domestic scene. Perceiving a long-lasting period of crisis in store for us in a world of cold war, he surveyed the limitations on individual freedom that may have to be accepted in the name of national security in a "garrison-police state." Amid the shifts in power and institutional changes that were likely to come about, it would be necessary to avoid the mass hysteria of crowd behavior if the values of a democratic society were to be protected. Again the remedy is to lower the tension level—this time, however, "by a process of enlightenment in which future possibilities [of pandemonium] are discounted in advance." An understanding of the realities of the world situation and the factors involved in security and freedom would obviate the disasters of a crisis. Alerting the populace to prospective perils includes specifically the possibility of a "witch-hunting mentality." Opinion leaders could study the psychology of crowds as "a prophylactic against epidemics of the mind."[17]

While the psychology of these developments is scarcely touched upon in the book, it is evident that in the years intervening since his direct application of Freudian psychoanalysis to politics Lasswell had come to have a greater respect for an ego-oriented personality as the bulwark of a democratic society. And although one could wish for greater detail on the politics of prevention, in a sense all of National Security and Individual Freedom represents an embodiment of the precepts of the theory. Its unflinching realism in acknowledging the possibility of prolonged crisis, its recognition of the need to anticipate incursions on individual liberty resulting from that crisis, and the urgency with which it treats the necessity of taking preparatory measures, all reveal a determination to turn psychological (as well as political) studies to a constructive use one would not expect of a "new Machiavelli . . . offering no ideal to be realized."

The spirit is reminiscent of Freud's, but Lasswell had come a long way from the politics of psychopathology. Initially, the problem of Lasswell's intellectual career had been to locate an institutional fulcrum for the lever of the politics of prevention: hence the probing of the politics of democracy in the late 1930's and most of the 1940's. When the critical phase was over and when values had been redefined in accordance with a newer conception of human nature, the politics of power offered itself as the emissary best designed to recall from exile the prophet he could not at first honor, preventive politics. So we recognize that system behind the guise of the "policy sciences," again with the objective of overcoming obstacles to the realization of a "democratic personality and polity."[18] And in recent years the technique of anticipatory problem-solving has taken the form of "developmental construct" in Lasswell's writings.[19] By whatever name it appears, it is still the politics of prevention.

As Lasswell's view of human nature ripened into a greater appreciation of the importance of an ego-psychology, and as in later years he turned his attention increasingly to the traditional categories of political science, the politics of prevention took on a heuristic value for him. His explorations of the politics of democracy and the politics of power carried him far from the politics of psychopathology, but always the same goal remained in view: the delineation of a science of politics that would be of practical use in securing the institutions of a democratic society. At one time he may have appeared ruthless, at another time sentimental, yet he could truthfully claim not to have appreciably altered his essential values during his career.[20] The appellations "cynical" or "Machiavellian" are as misapplied to him as "pansexualist" was to Freud. Freud could hardly be said to have favored psychopathy in individuals. By the same token, Lasswell did not favor psychopathy in politics; he merely investigated it more systematically than had ever been done before. He has spent a lifetime trying to do something about it.

In summary, insofar as Lasswell's psychoanalytic writings are compatible with the Neo-Freudians' social theory, he fortifies the aversion of most of them to precipitate political action as the solution to the widespread mental illness that besets our society. The mere participation in movements for reform, he reveals, is itself apt to be a stimulant of pathological behavior. What optimism he displays for the benefits of contrived management of social institutions Lasswell reserves for its ability to prevent, rather than to remedy, the tension responsible for aberrant conduct. Though lacking the clinical experience to substantiate an unqualified statement, he intimates that the difficulties at the root of social problems are more likely to be encountered within the psyche than within the halls of the legislature. Thus for two reasons political crusading does not pay. In the first place, the psychological cost to the community at large of engaging in the political process is prohibitively high; the point of diminishing returns is met at the outset. And in the second place, an excursion into the arena of the irrational is a voyage up a blind alley; it can only terminate in a cul-de-sac.

The later Lasswell, the Lasswell that developed from the politics of prevention to the ardent exponent of democratic values, is in accord with the Neo-Freudians in a further regard. Except for Erich Fromm, all parties agree that a persistent application of human intelligence can go a long way toward solving the problems of a democratic society while still retaining the basic framework of present democratic institutions. In one respect Lasswell is on weaker ground than the Neo-Freudians. The interest in Freudian psychoanalysis of his younger years has left its mark on his subsequent thought. Too many orthodox elements survive in his writings after the 1930's. His later concordance with Neo-Freudian psychoanalytic principles, particularly from *Power and Personality* (1948) onward, appears to be less the result of clinical study than a revision stemming from broadened intellectual contacts. The diminished incisiveness of his observations on human psychology lends support to that opinion. Yet in another respect Lasswell is on firmer ground than the Neo-Freudians. Unlike them, he has had extensive training and experience in political science and is thus better prepared to explore the institutional ramifications of the Neo-Freudian view of human nature. When it comes to specifying concrete measures by which to implement the politics of prevention, Lasswell has the wherewithal to do so. What is to a large extent wishful thinking with the Neo-Freudians becomes, with him, a matter of political science. Knowledgeable in the ways of politics, he has not lost sight of their psychological origin. Wary of pitfalls, he is sophisticated enough to discern the psychological import of political programs. It remains to be seen whether the junction of the two disciplines he has effected will be carried forward by others.

While the majority of the Neo-Freudians would assent with varying degrees of willingness to the foregoing conclusions, Erich Fromm, for one, would enter a strong demurrer. Not for him are the timid precautions against raising the level of tension, nor will he play nursemaid to a valetudinarian psyche amidst the travails of life in a capitalist society. The remedy for a sick society to him is not to tinker with its manifold symptoms, patching a weakness here and ministering to a wound there. The basic cause of social pathology must be exorcised root and branch, and for that nothing less than a total reconstruction of capitalist society will suffice. Even reconstruction is too modest an undertaking. No matter that the realities of political reform present perplexing difficulties; Fromm simply ignores the problems of a transitional period. The complexities of a gradualist approach once out of mind, Fromm is at liberty to leap over intervening obstacles and carve the aspect of utopia with an inspired chisel. His program of rehabilitation, therefore, is more daring, or, if you like, more reckless, than any of his colleagues'. True, he can pause along the way to note that in the modern industrial system production of goods is no longer a problem, that mechanical energy has released enough human energy from producing goods for living to furnish a material basis for attacking the problem of social organization; and he suggests, for example, credits from state-owned banks and the socialization of "certain" (unnamed) enterprises. The implication is that the birth of the sane society will not be an especially painful one, the more so since Fromm eschews the midwifery of force that Marx predicted would be the instrument of such an occasion.[21] But it is pretty clear Fromm will not be detained with trifles. The matter is much too urgent for that. Likewise the extension of the principle of self-government from politics to economics, as a planned economy that exhibits the premeditated and joint effort of the whole society, which he once proposed, was, upon more mature reflection, seen to be insufficient. Because limited change spoils change as such, he maintains, an all-embracing socialism reorganizing the economic and social system *in toto* is the only solution answering to the need of a sane society that fashions sane men. By the criterion of sanity, one would have to surpass even Marx, and attain mental health with simultaneous alterations in religious and intellectual orientation, social character, and culture as well.[22]

What Fromm seeks to construct is a social framework that makes possible the living of the good life as he sees it. The object of his quest will be the circumstances congenial to the flourishing of men with productive orientations, in stark contrast to the alienated personalities who of necessity populate contemporary society. Fromm could not very well argue that piecemeal therapy of alienated individuals would sooner or later add up to a healthy social order—not, at any rate, without utterly repudiating the teaching of a lifetime to the contrary. Something more drastic is required, more drastic even than the Marxian system on which he could not, when all was said and done, pattern his most considered proposals. By broadening the concept of economic determinism that ran between the lines of his earlier writings in Germany to one of societal determinism, in the formation of social character, he emerges with a eudaemonistic, and no longer a materialistic, ethics. Taking his cue more from the humanistic philosophers than from either economic history or clinical psychoanalytic experience, he delineates a productive character structure that in a very large sense is an ideal. It can be actualized only by a projection into the future, and a society conducive to it will have to be tailored to fit. Hence the social and economic organization of the sane society is inevitably a myth, or, less charitably, a fantasy. If the construction would bring the contumely of the Marxist stigma, "utopian socialism," as it almost certainly would, it could be retorted that Fromm the Neo-Freudian has advanced beyond the comparatively limited conceptions of Marxist analysis. He is concerned less with the ownership of capital than with the possession of sanity, thereby showing a broader and more meaningful understanding of the human situation. Yet this has dangers of its own. For, while psychoanalysis does furnish some information about a productive character structure—though less than Fromm would be willing to admit—it furnishes no precise blueprint for the construction of an appropriate social system. Barring an extrapolation of the phylogeny-ontogeny recapitulation formula, which must yield weird results in any event, the picture of the good society must partake of the fictional. Fromm's portrayal of utopia will have to be scanned critically. It is a necessary, though perhaps not always proper, auxiliary apparatus to the vision that Fromm always kept in mind, the productive orientation.

> If society is concerned with making people virtuous, it must be concerned with making them productive and hence with creating the conditions for the development of productiveness. The first and foremost of these conditions is that the unfolding and growth of every person is the aim of all social and political activities, that man is the only purpose and end, and not a means for anybody or anything except himself.[23]

That Fromm envisions a totally new society, replete with ideology, is evident from his prescription for a guiding and stabilizing outlook that will there prevail. It involves him in questions of religion that his Neo-Freudian colleagues tended to avoid. By the standard of a productive character structure, the "religions" prevalent today are essentially negative, he says, serving to stunt the growth of human powers, especially of independence and integrity, while conducing to the loss of faith in oneself and others by projecting the better human qualities onto God.[24] Submissive worship of this kind is tantamount to alienation; comparable phenomena take place in voluntary obeisance to a political leader or a state. All of them require, in an authoritarian spirit, the surrender of the deepest human qualities for the sake of becoming a part of a protective power. Whether ancestor worship or fetishism, ritualism or totemism, they all compel exclusive devotion to an exterior criterion of value and truth; they are, as Freud had said, forms of neurosis.[25] Fromm reserves his severest strictures for nationalism. In common with other forms of quasi-religion, it is idolatrous and insane; its cult is patriotism. Nationalism may seem to be a rational system to its votaries, but in reality it is only a form of clan and totem worship. The standard of value and truth is outside the devotee, consisting of the interest of a state or a party; the flag is a holy object symbolizing the group. How else can we understand the phenomena of fascism and Stalinism, which moved millions to sacrifice integrity and reason, if not as "religious" movements?[26] Administrative or political arrangements to circumscribe national sovereignty and lower the barriers among nations, which other critics of rampant nationalism have advocated, clearly would be inadequate. One must fight fire with fire: a new religion must supplant the old. What is it to be?

At one time the psychoanalytic movement appeared to meet the need for a genuine religion, but as his removal from orthodox psychoanalysis widened through the years Fromm gained enough perspective to compare it too to a middle-class religious movement of the conventional kind. Since the 1930's members of the middle class, especially in America, have been without ideals of any kind to which to devote themselves, without a cause to inspire solidarity with others. The spiritual home provided by being part of the psychoanalytic movement often superseded therapeutic expectations, he avers. In this "surrogate for religion" the middle class found what it wanted: "a dogma, a ritual, a leader, a hierarchy, the feeling of possessing the truth, of being superior to the uninitiated," and with none of the effort or comprehension of human and social problems that would bring forth the characterological change required to restore contact with human reality.[27] The trouble with Freudian psychoanalysis is that it had become an inflexible, dogma-ridden, semi-pious movement, and a failure at that. It was a failure because it could not transcend the attitudes and thought patterns of a liberal middle-class society. Without a critical analysis of society from an absolute position neither repression as a social phenomenon nor the unconscious of the individual could be understood.[28] Thus a religion could not be earth-bound, as it were; it would have to have a universal, timeless quality coterminous and coeval with man and the human situation.

The problem seems to be impossible to solve, but on closer inspection it turns out to be in large part a verbal one. Is a religion necessary at all? It is, asserts Fromm, for everyone has a need for religion, if religion be defined as "any system of thought and action shared by a group which gives the individual a frame of orientation and an object of devotion."[29] Is this inconsistent with the opinion that theistic religion proper is on the wane, that the concept of God is merely one conditioned by historical development? It is not, according to Fromm, because this expression of man's "longing for truth and for unity" is soon to be overtaken by a new frame of orientation and object of devotion, a humanistic religion that places its faith in man.

> It is based on the idea that the potentialities of man are such that given the proper conditions he will be capable of building a social order governed by the principles of equality, justice and love. Man has not yet achieved the building of such an order, and therefore the conviction that he can do so requires faith.

Fromm is quick to add that such a faith is a rational one, relying on observation: of man, of child development, of changes among primitive peoples, and of the development of present civilizations.[30] This is entirely in keeping with the humanistic psychoanalysis Fromm also espouses, for both act to reveal man as man, peeling away the unproductive characteristics with which social living has clothed him, demonstrating the essential qualities of human beings that persist despite cultural camouflage. We perceive here an echo of the Ciceronian, or Stoic, doctrine of the natural equality of all men by virtue of their possession of right reason; regrettably, Fromm is no more successful than Cicero in specifying what the contents of right reason are. When Fromm avers that humanistic religion will be universalistic, will comprehend the humanistic teachings of all great religions, and will stress life rather than dogma,[31] he voices his conviction in the need for a return to the great humanistic tradition of Western society. He seems to believe that humanistic psychoanalysis leads to higher values that can only be called religious, that it paves the way for a return to a *Weltanschauung* which alone can provide the orientation and love to reintegrate man and give him the sense of purpose and unity with nature in which he can find at least his mortal salvation.

If this is what Fromm has in mind, then the term "religion" is ill-chosen. What is it that remains when one removes a supernatural being to whom obeisance is rendered, subtracts the adjuncts of dogma, ritual, and priestly hierarchy, and diminishes or eliminates the sense of being among the elect? There remains only a framework that is to be filled by evoking the humanistic ethics of the tradition of Aristotle and Spinoza, which is in actuality not a religion but a philosophy. And as for humanistic psychoanalysis, it is no longer a technique for individual psychotherapy but is a modern confirmation of the universal validity of natural law concepts, for it reveals what human nature really is and always and everywhere has been.

While these ramifications of his thought disclose Fromm to be a philosopher of no mean proportions (following in Freud's footsteps in at least this sense), it is clear that they cast doubt on his qualifications to speak as a scientist. One is left with the feeling that in the constructive parts of his writings he verbalizes more than he analyzes: the voice he speaks with is that of the prophet rather than that of the scientist, and his ardor is certainly a far cry from the cut-and-dried materialism of Freud. He would be hard put to portray his ideal in the concrete stock of words wrought from the materials of the analyst's laboratory, the consulting room. The reason is that the sane society and the productive orientation are for the most part ideals, largely the fruit of what may be called purposive speculation. In consequence, his portrayal of both will be vague where it should be precise, it will be idealistic where it should be realistic, it will be philosophical where it should be clinical, and it will be normative where it should be objective. At all events, it is unflaggingly single-minded in its dedication to the welfare of man as Fromm conceives that welfare to be. Of Fromm it can truly be said the beacon of his purpose generates more light than heat—perhaps too much light, for the perspicuity of his own vision.

We should not be surprised, therefore, if the emphasis in his formulations is on the emotional, if not the uncanny, aspect of personality, as the ratiocinative component fades into the background. He distinguishes between intelligence and reason, much as Kant had distinguished between understanding and reason. Intelligence, to Fromm, has practical value in dealing with concepts in daily living. The function of reason, by contrast, is to achieve a closer relationship to things by comprehending them with an intimate grasp. The object of reason is not felt to be apart from oneself; fruitful thought requires the subject to be "intensely interested in his object," to be emotionally responsive to it.[32] And Fromm describes the analyst as a "physician of the soul," expressly abnegating the words "psyche" and "mind"; the task of analytic therapy is to assist in the restoration of the patient's capacity to love.[33] Of love we shall have more to say presently. Here we may note that the borderline between reason, as Fromm uses the term, and intuition, as that word is commonly understood, practically disappears. There is, indeed, an almost mystical quality about some passages in his writings.[34] Fromm names Freud "the last great representative of rationalism" and simultaneously credits him with converting the reign of reason into a scientific reality whereby human suffering could be alleviated in combating mental disease. At the same time he censures him for confining reason only to thought while relegating feelings and emotions to an inferior position as the Enlightenment philosophers had done.[35] It is Fromm's aim to restore dignity to man's emotional life on an equal footing with his intellectual capacity for the scientific manipulation of the material world. Only the whole man can live a full life. Only a productive character structure can enjoy—or can merit—a sane society. Fromm may have gone to an extreme of his own, but it is not for petty reasons.

With the emphasis removed from the rational aspect of human nature, it is easy to understand why the idea that neurosis is due to mental conflict does not loom large in Fromm's thought. The individual is by nature a harmonious psychic unit, to him. Difficulties spring from extrapsychic sources, he believes, from the individual's continuous altercations with his social environment. These are the consequences of the inevitable rupture of the primary ties which once bound men together in their youth (both phylogenetically and ontogenetically speaking). Hence Fromm lays heavy and perhaps inordinate stress on the concept of relatedness, the replacement of primary ties by spontaneous human solidarity to answer to man's compelling need to be related to others so as to avoid aloneness, anxiety, and, ultimately, insanity. The need to unite with others, he feels, underlies the entire array of the closest human relations and is really a broad construction of the word "love." Human nature requires human relatedness and solidarity for its fulfillment.[36] There being no inner conflict to resolve, the equilibrium to be established will not be within the individual but between the individual and his social environment. Fromm seems to overlook the danger of the productively oriented individual losing himself altogether in the frantic search for relatedness with others. While this point will demand our attention again soon, a recollection of Fromm's distaste for the fraudulent interpersonal relations of today makes even more conclusive his argument for a total renovation of society.

It is time to detail the putative traits of the productive orientation and follow it with an outline of the proposed social order in which it will thrive. (This is consonant with Fromm's own order of emphasis, for—make no mistake about it—the new society is designed for its typical citizen, and not vice versa.) Since faith in man is the keynote of humanistic psychoanalysis and the social philosophy derived from it, all the leading characteristics of the productive orientation can be put in a nutshell: a productive personality is a man who is for himself. Life has no meaning, declares Fromm, "except the meaning man gives his life by the unfolding of his powers," the powers characteristic of man as man, realizing the potentialities implicit in human nature. This is so because of the "inherent tendency" of life to express itself, freedom being identical with self-realization.[37] Now, whereas Aristotle quickly separated out the vegetative and sensory aspects of human personality to find man's differentia to be a functioning of the soul under the guidance of reason, or at any rate not beyond the influence of reason (as we usually understand that word), Fromm has regard for the mental, emotional, and sensory capacities of man as elements of a total personality. And whereas to Aristotle the intellect is particularly and peculiarly the attribute of the human individual, to Fromm self-realization comprises the total personality—not thought alone but emotions as well, for these capacities are common to all men.[38] Fromm is also sure all men have the faculty for achieving a productive orientation unless "mentally and emotionally crippled."[39] Thus Fromm has considerably widened the concept of human nature beyond the scope allowed it by the Greeks, or, to speak more exactly, he has restored to full status those of its components the Greeks depreciated. His productive character structure is eudaemonistic, but Fromm gives the term a latitude Aristotle would not have contemplated. Perhaps a more accurate comparison would be with the Italian Renaissance conception of the *virtù* of the well-rounded man, who finds his self-realization in a versatile display of each of his capacities—artistic, literary, political, amatory, combative, and all. Spinoza's concept of virtue as power comes to mind, and Fromm quotes him with approval on just this point.[40] As a final item of comparison with Aristotle, Fromm postulates that the spontaneous activity of the self is not the mere doing of something in pursuit of the *ignis fatuus* of success but is present activity as an experience, exclusive of any material result. For Aristotle, pleasure is not an inherent condition of activity but something supererogative, the living of the virtuous life bringing happiness almost as an afterthought.[41]

The unlimited self-fulfillment stipulated by Fromm for the productive character can withstand the charge of unbounded hedonism, which it seems to imply. It is necessary, however, to differentiate between selfishness and self-love, which not only are not identical but are opposites. This is so because the care, respect, responsibility, and knowledge that love entails are the very reverse of selfishness. Mature self-love has in mind the embodiment of human qualities in the self, and it takes maturity to have the readiness and ability for such a self-affirmation. But once admit a valid assertion of the worth of one's life, happiness, growth, and freedom, then the self can be loved as much as any other person, and from this it follows that "love for one person implies love for man as such."[42] Much that is dubious in Fromm's idea of self-love can be explained by his aversion to the contemporary truncation of human personality. The taboo on selfishness that is characteristic of modern society is confused with that on self-love under the general ban "Don't be selfish." It springs from a regard of man as, in effect, an appurtenance of man as a socioeconomic unit, and only serves to suppress his spontaneity and the free development of his whole personality. What begins as individualism terminates, under the Protestant ethic, as asceticism, and points to a serious deficiency of present-day society. Modern culture has failed, Fromm claims, not because it has overvalued individualism but because it has denigrated the meaning of the term. And hence people err not because they pursue self-interest but because it is not the interest of the real self they pursue. We are not too selfish; we do not love ourselves.[43] Democracy too has failed in this respect, for it has not enabled the individual to be for himself affirmatively and emphatically in all his attributes. The problem of democracy, if it is to avoid an authoritarian regime, is to create the conditions where self-love, thus understood, can flourish in a total personality, thoroughly integrated and fully self-expressive.[44]

To eschew the capitalist view of man as exclusively a calculating economic unit, therefore, means to take into account his emotional capacities, and Fromm more than compensates for the one-sidedness of the former attitude with an emphasis on the latter that approaches an opposite extreme. To be productive one must express the untold potentialities for love inherent in human nature. Love alone, Fromm finds, can give man knowledge of his innermost being; the vital core cannot be reached by the knowledge supplied by mere cognition. Paradoxically, the act of loving, which is an act of giving oneself, is also a discovering of oneself, and, more generally, of discovering man.[45] To love, Fromm seems to be saying, is to divine the universal in the particular, while simultaneously gaining true insight into the particular itself. But love has not merely personal, pragmatic utility; it is of social value too, comparable to the Freudian concept of Eros. Hence Fromm can say that the urge for interpersonal union is not merely man's strongest impulse but "the force which keeps the human race together," from family to society. Its absence means insanity or destruction: "Without love, humanity could not exist for a day." The command "Love thy neighbor as thyself," therefore, is the prime rule of life, the infraction of which more than anything else underlies the unhappiness and mental illness repeatedly brought to the psychoanalyst's attention.[46] A bit less expansively, Fromm defines love as neither the loss of oneself in another person nor the outright possession of another person, but "as spontaneous affirmation of others, as the union of the individual with others on the basis of the preservation of the individual self." Having as its aim the well-being of its object, it is no illusion nor is it a pathological condition but a core-to-core relationship that yet preserves the integrity of both parties. Love, in brief, is intimate interpersonal union while maintaining the distinction and completeness of the self; it is participation in mutual self-realization.[47]

Fromm may be pardoned if his description of love is not entirely satisfactory, for communication of an emotional experience that is essentially beyond the means of rational, coherent explication has stymied better bards than he. His natural law view of human nature, his near-merger of the rational and emotional constituents of that nature, his reintroduction of religious, or quasi-religious, values into a system that has expanded well beyond the case material of clinical psychoanalytic experience, and the virtual impossibility of his locating tangible individual specimens of productively oriented people, have led him to depict a character structure that is extraordinarily difficult to describe concretely. Fromm is navigating unknown waters by night. One could desire a steadier, less zealous hand at the helm and greater assurance that the pilot is relying more on astronomy than on astrology. The productive character is so much more a creature of feeling than an agent of thought that a rational relationship with him is all but impossible of establishment even in retailing his essential attributes. It is clear, at any rate, that introspection is not his forte, and so it is not to be wondered that his search for self-fulfillment extends outside himself in the form of a need for transcendence.

Man, Fromm tells us, is not content to be only a creature; "he needs to feel as the creator, as one transcending the passive role of being created." A will to move beyond the limitations of mortality—to escape the confines of life, as it were—impels activity which, if it is not to transcend life by destroying it, must transcend it by such positive achievements as creating ideas and material objects. It is in productive work that man fulfills himself and secures a reunification with nature on equal terms. Work is an essential component of productivity, if it is work as spontaneous self-affirmation rather than as compulsion or as enslavement of

nature.[48] The need to devote one's talents to something significant, to labor purposively and not merely as the bearer of a skill
utilized as a commodity of the market, explains why the most
important incentive to work is not economic; nor are considerations of prestige, status, or power paramount. The true motives
of doing creative work for its own sake and of establishing economic independence, however, do not operate in twentieth-century capitalism. Today man is not the dominant element in the
productive process, with his own initiative, but only an instrument in the capitalist network, with his status and activity determined "by this quality of being a piece of equipment."[49] Thus
Fromm's is a psychological, rather than an economic, condemnation of capitalism; consequently the successor system is to be
premised on psychological, rather than on economic, efficiency.

The economic organization requisite to productive work is
one wherein all workers take part in their work actively and
responsibly and the work has an intrinsic significance; labor
employs capital instead of vice versa. This much Fromm admits
having in common with conventional schemes of socialism. In
addition, the worker must have full knowledge of his work and
of the relationship of that and the whole economy to the needs of
the community. Controversy over the ownership of the means
of production is beside the main point of "participation in management and decision making." The reform of the productive
process, in other words, is to be directed to the humanization of
work. Economic productivity is not the object; in the new social
order, social life is to take priority over it. And hence inequality
of income is not vicious provided it does not make for "differences
in the experience of life."[50]

The solution, Fromm suggests, lies in communitarian socialism, an organization of industry and of social life in small, highly
integrated communities the prototypes of which can be seen in
the communities of work that have sprung up in Europe in recent
years. They employ modern industry and do not rely on handi-
craft production. They provide for the active participation of

all members, economically and socially, and, by a complicated hierarchy presided over by a figure who in many respects resembles a politically responsible philosopher king, assure the centralization of leadership necessary to economic success. Conformity is avoided by "the emphasis on the practice of life as against ideological differences," allowing for the coexistence of men of the most varied beliefs and opinions. The nuclear unit is the Neighbor Group, consisting of half a dozen families who meet regularly under a Chief of Neighbor Groups to discuss contentious issues and forward the results of their deliberations to the head of the community. All aspects of life receive expression in a pervasive organizational system that channels individual interests into group activities.[51] The leading ideas in communitarian socialism are "concrete face-to-face groups, active responsible participation." In politics, too, a form of town meeting, having a maximum of about five hundred people, secures the complete discussion, concrete personal relations, knowledge of facts, and control over decisions that make for meaningful political activity.[52] With each man an end in himself, with economic and political activities taking second place to man's growth, with exploitation for material gain banished, with social affairs of enough importance to be of personal concern as public life blends with private, the conditions fostering the productive character structure will prevail. "A sane society," Fromm summarizes,

> is one which permits man to operate within manageable and observable dimensions, and to be an active and responsible participant in the life of society, as well as the master of his own life. It is one which furthers human solidarity and not only permits, but stimulates, its members to relate themselves to each other lovingly; a sane society furthers the productive activity of everybody in his work, stimulates the unfolding of reason and enables man to give expression to his inner needs in collective art and rituals.[53]

Fromm would be the last to say that communitarian socialism was beyond criticism,[54] and one or two remarks in that mood may be ventured here. We need not belabor the absence of economic realism which presumes that the far-flung industrial complex of twentieth-century capitalism can be fragmented into miniature communities while retaining some semblance of coordination and efficiency. The incredibly complicated activities of production, marketing, and research that large-scale interlocking enterprise makes possible could not conceivably be carried on in the communities of work Fromm describes. The ones now in existence are peripheral to the main body of industry, without which they could not subsist. For a scholar once familiar with the principles of historical materialism, Fromm is surprisingly naïve; considering the importance of economic organization even in the system of communitarian socialism, he could have been more critical on the subject.

Similarly, we may give short shrift to the idea that a relating of citizens to each other lovingly will dispense with the intricacies of government and administration. The state may wither away but *fonctionnaires* have a habit of persisting; not all relationships can be conducted face to face. Party machinery, intergovernmental relations, the execution of legal procedures, civil administration—none of these can be overlooked in even the best of all possible worlds no matter how superfluous they may be to the intrinsic qualities of a productive orientation. Again, some clear, hard thinking along the familiar lines of the social sciences is in order—here especially in political science and public administration—rather than the tacit assumption of these too withering away once paradise has been regained.

That much, perhaps, could be argued away with the rejoinder that the economic and political superstructures of contemporary society are just that: the inevitable consequences—and also contributory causes—of man's failure to relate himself spontaneously to his social environment. All the apparatus of modern capitalism forms a vicious circle with its capitalist characters, Fromm could well retort, which would vanish when the need for the former and the generation of the latter had given way to the halcyon circumstances of communitarian socialism. The issue may be waived, for our purposes. That is to say, the feasibility of his project is more or less a matter of speculation; it is the desirability of its results that is really in question, and some concern may be expressed on this score.

Is the productive orientation eudaemonia in its finest style? To move the argument to Fromm's own ground, is it not discrepant with the humanistic tradition? The productive character in the communitarian society is all social life and no private life. The extraordinary amount of public activity expected of a person, illustrated by the innumerable and omnipresent "teams" of the communities of work, saturates his existence. Can an individual find solitary quietude in the gamut of membership groups surrounding him? Fromm seems to underestimate the virtues of silent meditation. All the joys of life, however, do not accrue to *L'Allegro*; the ways of *Il Penseroso* are their own reward. One of the founders of a humanistic view of man and his vocation, in whose shadow Fromm likes to walk, conceded the active life to be the mark of eudaemonia, but to Aristotle activity in interpersonal relations was not the only variety of it. Thinking carried on for its own sake, he held, had a far superior claim to be called the life of action, for it expresses the quality unique to man, the rational principle.[55] It is pretty plain that Fromm has traveled a good distance from the traditional humanistic view of human nature. His attempt to restore the emotions to full standing, however commendable, has led him, willy-nilly, to detract from the unchallenged hegemony of reason.

This results in Fromm's divergence from Aristotle in yet another respect, for whereas to Fromm felicitous interpersonal relations are the cardinal virtue of the communities of work, to the Stagirite social life was not alone sufficient to justify political association. That was but a means to a higher end, the activity of the soul.[56] If Fromm is not in reality advocating resuscitation of the Greek *polis* as the proper form of society, which is at any rate suggested by the self-sufficiency of the communities of work and by the obliteration there of the distinction between private interest and public *esprit,* his ideas on social organization may be further canvassed to assess the import of his utopia. Under his scrutiny conventional society takes on sinister aspects. With human nature having "certain inherent mechanisms and laws," the individual is very much like Rousseau's noble savage born pristine pure only to be corrupted by social living. Civil society is virtually a conspiracy against the individual. The idea is not too far from Freud's view of civilization being tantamount to repression, and Fromm does not even share Freud's opinion of science as being the solitary creative force, the sole redeeming feature, of civilization. More moderately expressed, Fromm's position would echo the Cynic doctrine that man is by nature equipped with all the virtue he needs for a happy existence in this world, and social institutions, or conventions, are at best pleonastic, and rarely even that. But be it noted that the Cynic ideal was sufficient unto himself, whereas Fromm's ideal requires interpersonal relations and indeed is inconceivable without them.

The necessity for man to have interpersonal relations vitiates any theory of a state of nature Fromm may have had in mind. His conception of matriarchal society corresponds fairly closely to it, however, while patriarchal society is equated with our present civilization. Patriarchy features the state, hierarchy, and obedience to man-made laws. Matriarchy is characterized by equality, love, and an acceptance of nature.[57] Hence a return to man's primary bonds with nature and with himself is to be another form of matriarchy. Fromm calls this new form of matriarchy communitarian socialism, but what is this communitarian socialism if not a modern version of anarchistic communism? The form of social order Fromm advocates achieves economic, political, and social organization without the trappings of formal institutions. It is systematic and orderly, but it is voluntary and spontaneous. It relies on the natural sociability of men to bring into being the arrangements which social institutions could not. It is a form of collectivism that yet seeks individualism, utilizing the simple means of abolishing conventions. It being perfection itself, it tends, like all utopias, to be self-contained, fixed, and static; there is neither room nor need for change and development. It smacks also of the guild system of the Middle Ages, though without the monopolistic and restrictive practices of the guild system, and this, rather than the *polis*, appears to be what Fromm has before his eyes. If this is the case, it warrants a questioning of Fromm's political and social judgment. Is he as radical as he claims, or is his doctrine not in essence a reactionary one? The type of social organization he lauds is, one suspects, not an effort to deal with current problems but an attempt to escape from them. And the escape is through the back door, not the front, a flight to a period which, with all its charm (more fancied than real), is totally anachronistic for us. Under the impression that he is scanning ahead to tomorrow, Fromm is in reality turning the clock back to the day before yesterday. Likewise, the insistence on relatedness, on finding a sense of union with nature, on devotion to a transcendent cause—be it called humanistic psychoanalysis or religion—is evidence of a mistrust of reason. It is a renunciation of the integrity of reason unmixed with emotion; it could all too easily be considered a reversion toward irrationalism. Probably much against his desire, Fromm could be held to represent a reactionary trend among the Neo-Freudians which none of the rest of them share.

In the end, we have to return to psychoanalytic conceptions to find the root of the matter. Here we refer to a basic theorem of Fromm's view of personality, that its equilibrium, once disturbed by interpersonal difficulties, is to be restored by removing these outward sources of repression. The trouble may stem from Fromm's idea of the family as the psychological agent of society. As such, it neatly and dependably channels the influence of society to the growing child. The parents are passive agents of transmission, a smooth funnel to escort the influence of the society to the child with never a slip 'twixt cup and lip. This conception, however, does not take account of the internal conflicts among members of the family. In developing a not dissimilar theory, Franz Alexander, we recall, insisted that "the emotional relationships between members of the family are incomparably stronger determinants of character-formation of the child than the position of the family in a certain social group." And Abram Kardiner had made much the same point when he held the family to be less important in its formal organization than in the particular relations of its members to each other and the disciplines to which the child is subjected within it.[58] To put it another way, the Oedipus complex receives far too little attention from Fromm. He has not merely "desexualized" the Oedipus complex; he has—if the metaphor may be forgiven—nearly thrown baby out with bath.[59] It is one thing to chafe at the bit of orthodox psychoanalysis; it is another to expand the looser confines of Neo-Freudian psychoanalysis to daring extremes; it is still a third, however, to dispense with psychoanalytic principles altogether. Fromm's thought appears to have gone through all three stages, until a clinically derived psychoanalysis rooted in rationalistic principles can no longer contain his formulations at all. And so his system is essentially a sociological, or perhaps a philosophical, one, and not a psychological one. Social problems remain social problems with him, not individual problems, and for all his scathing descriptions of the unproductive character, for all his reprobation of alienation, for all his appeal to humanism, Fromm uses individual psychopathy to illustrate the evils of society.

Fromm is perhaps too adroit in employing psychopathology to animate his castigation of capitalist society. He thereby shifts the blame to society and is not troubled overmuch by problems of individual psychotherapy. As long as such a diagnosis of mental illness is retained, then the construction of the road to mental health is merely a matter of ingenuity in engineering the elements of social organization, and one need not be a psychoanalyst to play at that game. Fromm seems to have overreached himself in exploiting the social orientation of Neo-Freudian psychoanalysis. His colleagues insist, however, that mental illness festers in the psyche as what Karen Horney called a central inner conflict. Therefore the road to mental health is an arduous one, demanding that the individual slowly and painfully grapple with his conflict, reconstructing the personality so that psychic energy can be devoted to actualizing the real self. The microcosm must take priority over the macrocosm. The social environment can do little more than abate the interpersonal sources of tension. As Horney put it, "One must begin by facing and understanding and solving his own inner conflicts before trying to solve conflicts between self and mankind."[60] That requires a slower pace than Fromm's ambitious, if generous, vision contemplates, which may be regrettable from a humanistic standpoint. But as between prevention and utopia, the weight of theory and experience appears to lie in favor of the former.

On the whole, then, both Fromm's analysis and his proposals would not fulfill his expectations or ours. Practical considerations of economics or government aside, he misconstrues the function of interpersonal relations by placing them prior to the truer vocation of man—as humanists see it—of cultivating the active exercise of the intellect in guiding the good life. Furthermore, his neglect of the dynamic role of psychic conflict in impelling mental illness reveals the basic difficulty in his system. It is for the most part not derived from the empirical evidence of psychoanalysis but rather from a philosophical doctrine founded on a natural law theory of human nature. This critique of Fromm's ideas may appear to be harsh, and it must be apparent by now that the present author has a critical view of natural law theory also. Yet this assessment will not be the last word on either subject, and for those who prefer that wing of Neo-Freudian social philosophy, for those who desire a text on which to base a thoroughgoing impeachment of modern society, Fromm's application of natural law theory has much to offer. It is, in effect, a modernization of an ancient doctrine. All will acknowledge the good service done by that doctrine in furthering the development of modern political institutions under the rule of law; the Western intellectual

heritage would perhaps be unrecognizable without it. Very probably, however, it is insusceptible to validation by an empirical
investigation of human nature and its formation—although in a
sense Fromm's work can be interpreted as an effort at such validation—and it lends itself all too readily to the building of utopias
which may be wide of the mark. This is not to say that a natural
law theory is necessary for the theoretical construction of an ideal
social order; the second has operated independently of the first
on a number of occasions in the history of Western philosophy.
The pith of this critique is that Neo-Freudian psychoanalytic
principles proper do not justify the construction of visionary
commonwealths, and that a social science endeavoring to avail
itself of Neo-Freudian psychoanalysis to fortify a philosophy of
man and his works, or a program of action suitable thereto, should
rather turn to the writings of Fromm's colleagues.

That means calling upon the resources of disciplines which,
if they are not broad enough to comprehend Neo-Freudian psychoanalysis, may at least be flexible enough to profit by its revelations.
They would have to investigate ways of alleviating anxiety, of
enhancing personal security, of mitigating the atmosphere of
tension, especially in the domain of the formulation of public
policy, that presently constitutes a defamation of each citizen's
self-system. The type of action represented by preventive politics,
capitalizing on Neo-Freudian psychoanalytic principles, appears
to be a feasible as well as a desirable style of pragmatic endeavor
in the social sciences.

The Neo-Freudians themselves are neither deterministic by
philosophy nor defeatist by temperament. On the contrary, the
tenor of their writings is optimistic; they are confident their work
can be an instrument of great social utility. In Karen Horney's
words, "Psychoanalysis cannot solve the ills of the world, but it
can at least clarify some of the frictions and misunderstandings,
the hates, fears, hurts, and vulnerabilities, of which those ills are
at once cause and effect."[61] If the Neo-Freudians have been lax
in proposing ways of reducing social tension it is because they are,

on the whole, unsophisticated in the use of political concepts. Except for Erich Fromm, what they have to offer are suggestions, not answers; materials, not solutions. Social scientists proper will find it advantageous to bear in mind the fruits of their work when evaluating our social institutions. It must be remembered that institutions are not entities in their own right but are accepted patterns of behavior, and the behavior is carried on by human beings.

9

THE NEO-FREUDIAN
CONTRIBUTION:
AN ESTIMATE

IN CONCLUDING this study of the Neo-Freudians it might appear
to be superfluous to inquire into the ultimate value of their work.
Who would contend that we have been led astray by just another
interesting theory of psychology that has merely a vague and in-
substantial relation to social philosophy? If it were only a matter
of popularity, the perennially high sales of Neo-Freudian literature could be cited as evidence of success in propagating a new
dispensation in psychoanalytic psychology and philosophy. And
presumably, a survey of the influence of Neo-Freudian concepts
on the practice of psychotherapy, especially in the United States,
would yield a similarly happy verdict.[1] But we are concerned here
with the intrinsic merits of a body of ideas and their relevance
to pressing issues in social thought, over and above their applicability to clinical therapy and regardless of their familiarity to
the public at large. Our search for a fresh approach to visualizing
social problems, much less solving them, cannot be called completed until some attempt has been made to evaluate the Neo-
Freudian contribution.

While it would require a longer study than space permits to
discuss the scientific standing of the work of the Neo-Freudians,
at least a few words in passing must be said about this aspect of
the matter. Without descending into particulars, Neo-Freudian

social philosophy seems to be firmly enough grounded in data derived by the scientific method to make it worthy of serious consideration by students and practitioners of the social sciences. The knowledge these psychoanalysts employ is factual—as opposed to speculative, intuitive, or dogmatic—in the sense of resting on the empirical data obtained from the consulting room, which is their equivalent of the laboratory. For that reason it is subject to verification by skeptical investigators and it thereby fulfills the canons of communicability and publicity that are inseparable from scientific procedures. The resultant hypotheses concisely explain the phenomena encountered, as years of careful testing in clinical experience demonstrate. Neo-Freudian theories about the origin of anxiety and insecurity in interpersonal relations, for example, are not advanced to protect personal hunches; neither have the free associations emanating from the psychoanalytic couch been fitted to a Procrustean bed of preconceived notions. They are hypotheses which elucidate mental illnesses—and mental health—as we know them and they are in principle open to revision as the accumulation of further data warrants. To the foregoing an exception must be made of some of Erich Fromm's ideas, for, as the previous chapter argued, they appear to have been gathered largely from quasi-philosophical sources rather than from clinical psychoanalytic experience.

It might be rejoined that it would take a highly trained and specialized investigator indeed to confirm or disprove Neo-Freudian clinical findings—namely, a psychoanalyst, and preferably one of Neo-Freudian persuasion at that. Such a claim does not appear to detract seriously from the scientific validity of their premises. The identical problem is encountered, and usually in higher degree, in nearly every field of knowledge. Almost universally the unspecialized layman is debarred from questioning what he is asked to accept as truth. Yet, if anything, the advantage would lie with psychoanalysis—Neo-Freudian or other—because the nebulous distinction between normal and pathological psychic functioning lends a value to individual introspection that other disci-

plines seldom approach. To a not inconsiderable extent, therefore, the intelligent layman can verify the data of psychoanalysis
by his own efforts, and he will probably be more successful in
comprehending this type of knowledge than that reported by
other areas of learning. If the hypotheses suggested by Neo-
Freudian psychoanalysis are more convincing than those proffered
by other schools of psychoanalytic thought, it is probably less
because they have a firmer scientific grounding than because they
correspond more accurately to our own psychic wants and conflicts. These hypotheses have been sufficiently elaborated already.
It will be more profitable to us to investigate the substance of the
Neo-Freudian contribution to social philosophy than to linger
over questions of scientific method.[2]

Neo-Freudian social thought covers a wide area. It ranges
from an account of the molding of individual character to a survey
of the evolution of the social institutions influencing character
formation. It extends from a critical analysis of the action of
those institutions to an inventory of the more striking forms of
personal pathology in our own times. It comprises both an attempt to visualize an ideal society and recommendations for
coping with individual and social ills in more conventional ways
(accepting, for these purposes, Lasswell's positive contribution of
preventive politics and its later development as consistent with
Neo-Freudian ideas). Yet if there is a single unifying theme
permeating the writings of these analysts, one which could be
said to constitute the core of their observations on social affairs
and their leading contribution to social philosophy, it is that
mental health is a significant value, perhaps the supreme value,
both as a goal for individual living and as a guide for social study.
While the Neo-Freudians speak initially from the standpoint of
clinical psychotherapists, and their championship of mental
health is therefore something of a partisan one, they hold this
criterion to have a validity in its own right. It must be respected
in any segment of social thought and is indispensable to a proper
conception of man, they believe. It is not enough to ponder the

distribution of wealth or the status of civil liberties, for example, nor are the ultimate issues of human concern reached with estimates of interracial harmony or of the prospects for peace in our time. None of the Neo-Freudians would deny that these are important; all would affirm that they are secondary alongside the overriding value of the achievement of mental health. The proposition is neither as novel nor as iconoclastic as it may sound. Until the advent of psychoanalysis mental health was pretty much neglected as a value in ruminating on the human situation, this notwithstanding the concern of philosophers, ancient and modern, with what they called "the soul." In case there was any doubt about this wider import of Freudian psychoanalysis, the Neo-Freudians' insistence on the importance of the psychic well-being of the populace has laid them to rest.

It is this premise which chiefly accounts for the diversity and acumen of the Neo-Freudians' critique of modern Western civilization, particularly as exemplified by life in the United States. The younger analysts have weighed our social institutions in the balance of mental health and found them largely wanting. That they have worked well in many respects by affording a number of virtues deemed worthy by wise men cannot be gainsaid. Stability, unity, freedom, material opulence are all ours in greater or lesser measure. But our enjoyment of them is delusive and transient if they are not anchored in psychic harmony and the unhampered growth of personality, the Neo-Freudians claim. Viewing our society skeptically, they have shown its comparatively superficial values to be both mutually discrepant and in conflict with the opportunities for their realization. Individual achievement does not accord with Christian precepts of humility, for instance, nor does it join easily with the affectionate regard for family and friends with which we are supposed to be inculcated at the start. Again, the chances for individual success are steadily decreasing in view of the constant diminution of economic resources, and/or access to them, that the realities of existence unfold to men and women. The contradictions presented to the individual by this array of facts, whether or not he perceives them distinctly, make it nearly impossible for him to resolve on a course of life which will enable him to negotiate the hazards of ambiguous standards with unimpaired psychic integrity. These impairments are sufficiently numerous to make it evident that mental health has ranked all too low on our scale of social values. Neo-Freudian criticism has been especially withering on this point.

To put the matter more succinctly, these analysts essay to make it eminently clear not only that a society wedded to factitious values is an unsound one, but that a person cannot live the good life in a state of psychic dilapidation, outward appearances to the contrary notwithstanding. Anxiety, they argue, is utterly incompatible with eudaemonia. It is but a step further to contend that mental health is inseparable from any reasonable definition of man *qua* man. This step the Neo-Freudians take. It may well constitute their most enduring contribution to social philosophy.

Closely allied to the peerless premium placed on mental health is the conception of human nature the Neo-Freudians present. While it may be less momentous than the revision of values they urge, its potential significance for social studies ought not to be overlooked, of which more later. At present we must ascertain as nearly as can be done the view of man that gives coherence to these analysts' more positive observations on contemporary problems. Comparisons with Freud, though unfortunately much at his expense, occasionally will be useful in summarizing the topic. As a caution, however, it should be remembered that, with the exception of Erich Fromm, the Neo-Freudians refer to the human nature encountered in Western civilization only, especially in modern times and in the United States. The purported advantages of the natural law theory of man adopted by Fromm are abjured by his colleagues in their effort to fashion working hypotheses on the subject, even though Fromm's description of the typical character structure of our times accords with that of Horney, Sullivan, Kardiner, and Alexander.

Specifying exactly the Neo-Freudian conception of man is apt to be a difficult task, and it would be still more difficult to construct their counterpart to the ideal Freudian man that was attempted in Chapter 2. The reason is that—with the exception of Fromm—the younger analysts are less concerned with ordaining what human nature should be than with visualizing what it can become. They deal for the most part with possibilities, hardly at all with certainties. The accent is on the potential rather than on the actual. Nevertheless, all the members of the school—Fromm included this time—regard the capacity for psychic growth as inherent in human nature. The tendency toward psychic maturity, to them, is integral to the human estate. The origin of this view is plainly to be found in the experience of the psychoanalytic clinic. There they perceive, unmistakably and invariably, a drive toward mental health. The indigenous curative power of individuals not only evinces itself during psychoanalytic therapy but makes that therapy possible to begin with. In philosophical terminology, the Neo-Freudians would advance the opinion that man is a creature with a native inclination toward eudaemonia seen in its psychic aspect. They would scarcely concur in Freud's wry comment of man, "Taken all in all, his superiority over the other animals may come down to his capacity for neurosis."[3] The differentia of the human species lies rather in a forward movement that is interrupted—if it is at all—by provocations from the social environment.

With this in mind it is possible to specify at least two features of the Neo-Freudian conception of man. First, to them, any interruption or reversal of psychic development is tantamount to mental illness. An organism that is prevented from continuing its own way loses its distinctive character and assumes a pathological quality. Sullivan's elaboration of the six developmental epochs antecedent to adult maturity illustrates the matter. It is worth remarking again that the epochs refer to psychic progress, not to chronological position. And second, to the Neo-Freudians psychic growth is a lifelong process, continuing beyond infancy. The character of man takes some threescore years and ten to shape, they teach. The abandonment of the Freudian libido theory made possible for his successors a view of character formation free of the shackles of an all-controlling determinism that cramped an entire career into its first five years. Each individual is to work out the destiny of his own personality, and he is seen to have a lifetime in which to do it.

On these points it is important to recall that personality development is not regarded by these analysts as a phenomenon without rhyme or reason. It is seen to occur as a process of adapting to the environment, a conceptual approach especially prominent in the writings of Kardiner and Alexander. The first-named tends to dwell on the adaptive capacities of the individual as a social unit, with reference to his society's historical and institutional heritage and to his relations with others in promoting the total success of societal adaptation. Alexander, on the other hand, pays more attention to the adaptive capacities of an individual as an organism, with reference to both his inborn biological equipment and his anticipated psychic maturation. These approaches are not mutually exclusive but rather complementary: it is only a matter of which side of the glass one looks through. In the writings of both authors, moreover, there is a continual *sotto voce* reference to the ideas usually associated with a theory of adaptation: evolution, natural selection, and the survival of the fittest. Fitness to survive, however, is construed by them chiefly in terms of psychic welfare—again the criterion of mental health—and hence the selection of individuals to evolve to their fullest development, and consequently of societies to evolve to more advanced levels of civilization, is seen to depend upon the degree of success in liberating and shaping the dynamism of personality development. And both of these analysts, together with their colleagues, make it decidedly manifest that selection is not proceeding "naturally" but that factors amenable to human control are distorting individual and social development alike. As a school, the Neo-Freudians can therefore claim biological and historical bases for the social criticism they initially launch from clinical studies of personality. Their inquiries show the social conditions prevalent in our day to be inimical to the optimal expression of individual adaptive capacities. Too much of the human psychic potential, they assert, is being diverted into defensive measures aimed at protecting mental equilibrium and self-esteem—often unavailingly—and not enough is being channeled into abetting mutual psychic growth.

One further point here: we have nearly overlooked a feature vital to the Neo-Freudians' employment of these ideas. The phrase "adaptation to the environment" should read "adaptation to the social environment." Institutions operate by means of people; individuals also operate with reference to other individuals (including, of course, unconscious images of selves and others). The method of operation—the style of adaptation—is a factor of the nature of interpersonal relations regnant at a particular time and place, in the Neo-Freudian scheme of things. We have seen the concept of interpersonal relations as much as anything else to be what differentiates the younger analysts from Freud. The most obvious advantage for social philosophy of this newer orientation, as has been noted more than once in this volume, is that it encourages selective and constructive social criticism instead of impotent, if eloquent, lamentations over somatic and instinctual inevitabilities. Seizing the advantage, the Neo-Freudians repeatedly point to the inadequacy and inappropriateness of interpersonal relations in our society as the cause par excellence of disruption of personality development. The native human predisposition toward mental health, they believe, is warped or stunted by the necessity of adapting to a network of interpersonal relations that implicitly substitutes a neurotic for a healthy norm of psychic maturation. In the vanguard of this trend of thought, Fromm perhaps would paraphrase Rousseau with the charge that men are born healthy but they are nearly everywhere in thralldom to pathological influences.

Other aspects of the view of modern Western man reviewed in this book are not so easy to retail in their particulars. The very spirit of Neo-Freudian writings on the subject is contrary to a neat cataloging of the variegated manifestation of the human potential. Still, one is struck by the encomiums to the value of emotional experience that punctuate nearly all the major writings of the school. More secure than Freud was in their appreciation of a viable, healthy ego, they are likewise better prepared to accept the full value of emotional life. They do not visualize the intellect as perpetually dogged by unruly feelings whose eruption means psychic catastrophe. Where Freud saw a state of probable tension, the newer school sees a condition of possible harmony. The concern of the Neo-Freudians, in fact, is whether emotions are genuine, instead of the counterfeits that so often pass for them in Western society today. Much of Neo-Freudian social criticism is directed against the numbness of feelings, the insensitivity to one's own emotional disposition—alienation, in the technical term—that they perceive to be a typical feature of mental illness in our times.

Among the entire gamut of the emotions, the Neo-Freudians focus on love as the most important. Erich Fromm may exaggerate the value of love, to the detriment of intellectual faculties exercised in solitude, but his error, if any, is one of emphasis, not of direction. With the younger analysts, love, in a context of interpersonal relations, is regarded as an expression of a mature personality under the guidance of a self-system, and not, as with Freud, as a quasi-neurotic phenomenon with regressive implications. Emotional fulfillment of the most intimate kind is now seen as a healthy, normal activity, an indispensable one, rather than as a backstairs affair in which the id outwits the ego. The Neo-Freudian concept of love, as a mutual concern for the security and maturation of self-systems, is more than an adequate replacement for that questionable entity, libido, in explaining social cohesion. Moreover, it postulates a rational rather than a sexual basis for that cohesion. It could well be argued that the Neo-Freudian understanding of love, bereft of a theory of libido, paradoxically comes closer to the broad Freudian concept of Eros than does Eros plus sexuality. This is not to say that the Neo-Freudians depreciate the value of sexuality. Far from it: they give it due proportion and remove much of the irrational and illegitimate aura with which the work and influence of Freud had surrounded it. At the same time, it is a terrible indictment to level against contemporary Western society to declare, as the Neo-Freudians do, that love is an absolute necessity for the good life and yet simultaneously to demonstrate that the conditions of life in the modern world make it next to impossible to find love.

While the attention the Neo-Freudians give to emotions is in a sense a reaction to Freud's great esteem for ratiocinative processes, they accept his high valuation of rational faculties but not the emphasis he placed on their all but isolated integrity. To them, reason is not a mere by-product of the essentially "instinctual" nature of man, the accidental residue of an encounter of the pleasure principle with the environment. The reality principle is inherent in human nature too, in other words. The intellect has an intrinsic worth of its own; the rational activity of the psyche is not supplementary but autochthonous. It is thus possible, they believe, for man to live a life largely under his own direction. Fromm speaks for his colleagues in this respect when he conceives of life as a liberating experience comprising "the spontaneous activity of the total, integrated personality."[4] Man, to them, is at least potentially a dynamic entity with a positive career of self-realization. With excessive trepidation the Freudian man walked the razor's edge of his unconscious, in their view, and reason exerted a desperate, rigid domination in maintaining psychic equilibrium instead of a comfortable hegemony in guiding man to his fulfillment.

Taking these characteristics in the large, the Neo-Freudian conception of human nature is a balanced, integrated, and not unattractive one. The question is what to do with it. It is an ambiguous conception available for contradictory uses. On the one hand, it tends toward the utopian, if not the impossible, in that it slips too easily from an expected maximum to a demanded minimum. As we saw before, Fromm seized that horn of the dilemma with some unhappy consequences. On the other hand, the conception tends toward the sentimental, if not the maudlin, in that it is prone to revere a standard of personality that has tantalized us in one form or another since Aristotle, until it is now eminently acceptable as the self-image of a complacent and still mediocre middle class. Most of the Neo-Freudians have seized this horn of the dilemma, and the most they have made of it is to use it as a bastion from which to shower a fusillade of critical barbs at a style of interpersonal relations to all appearances calculated to menace the cherished ideal, the meanwhile being singularly deficient in concrete proposals for reform. Perhaps the two uses are not contradictory after all, and perhaps the differences between Fromm and his confreres have been unduly stressed in this book. In either case, implicit in the conception is an expectation of social conditions permissive of the unfettered growth and expression of personality. It is hard to see how the potential for the maturation of human nature could be realized in a society predicated on unmitigated discipline, monolithic conformity, or the extinction of individual opportunity. A marked preference for liberalism, the open society, free institutions—call it what you will—pervades their writings and at the same time stamps Neo-Freudian literature as a collective protest against constrictive interpersonal relations and a life geared to repressive influences. That this is a liability as well as an asset will be noted later. At any rate it is safe to state that their view of human nature places the Neo-Freudians firmly in the humanistic, individualistic, libertarian tradition of Western thought.

So much for a summary of the substantive Neo-Freudian contribution to social philosophy. There is another kind of contribution they have made to the field that is worthy of discussion here. This is more methodological, or procedural, in nature, insofar as it can be distinguished from matters of substance. Suppose we put the matter this way. Any of the areas of social study finds it convenient to have certain elements, or categories, into which its data are classified or through which they are filtered. This is not the place to ordain the proper methodology for such studies, but it seems likely that these categories would include at least a conception of human nature, a theory of historical change, a reliable source of knowledge from which its hypotheses are derived, and some idea, however vague, of the scope of the discipline in question. Plato, for example, viewed man as fundamentally an unruly, materialistic, pleasure-seeking animal whose saving grace was his occasional susceptibility to the guidance of reason; he envisioned historical change as degeneration which could at best be retarded by men or regenerated by God; he placed his entire confidence in dialectic, leading to apprehension of the Form of the Good, as the only dependable source of knowledge; and he regarded political science as virtually coterminous with the study of the ethical relations among Greeks living in a *polis*. That there may be other categories is not denied. That these are minimal and useful can be asserted with some assurance. The Neo-Freudians have materials to offer for all of them, materials which, with varying degrees of adjustment, can be turned to advantage in perhaps any area of social studies.

Enough has been said of the Neo-Freudian conception of human nature to make a review unnecessary now. It only remains to state that since personality is, by their showing, to a great extent molded by the social environment, the conception is in principle flexible in being able to take account of changes in institutional patterns or historical trends. It is thus a working conception, as the anthropological investigations directed by Abram Kardiner demonstrate. Its salient features—the proclivity for growth, the tendency toward mental health, the variety and depth of emotional experience, the capacity for affective relations, the security of reason, and the harmonious integration of them all—are serviceable as touchstones for comparing the human condition of one society with another, of one society at different stages in its history, or, with greater hazard, as a collective standard for the evaluation of a culture from an "objective" position. The use of this Neo-

Freudian contribution to the resources of social research appears to be limited only by the ingenuity of those who employ it.

Of the Neo-Freudian conception of historical change, and the materials it offers for cognate studies, somewhat more has to be said. Speaking as psychoanalysts, Kardiner, Fromm, and Alexander—who have made the chief contributions of the school to historical studies—incline to view long-term cultural development (or retrogression) in its relation to individual personality. Social institutions and their evolution, in other words, are seen as functions of men's psychic needs, and not merely as responses to their material requirements. The march of events and the cultural footprints they leave behind cannot be properly understood, in their opinion, until the human component is given its position as the focal point of historiography. Thus they perceive the historical trend of Western civilization since the Renaissance to have individualism as its hallmark: the emergence of the individual human being as the vital unit of social and philosophical considerations and of his self-validation as the central feature of a way of life and a system of values. They apprehend modern Western society as providing an institutional framework that until recent times afforded both psychological and practical satisfactions to its members. Scientific and technological methods of manipulating the external environment placed terrestrial (instead of celestial) happiness within the reach of all who sought to relieve psychological pressures by means of individual achievement here and now, the theory runs. The temporal value of material success surpassed the spiritual value of eternal felicity when once the anonymous security of medieval days was overshadowed by the attraction of individual identity and attainment. Here is their explanation for the alterations in the configuration of Western culture that have given it its distinctive character for some five centuries. The school makes it plain, however, that the intricate, dynamic, competitive society of our own day is not adequately furnishing the conditions of life needed for the psychic well-being of large numbers of people, despite the pecuniary

success we boast. It is, on the contrary, threatened by semifratri-
cidal interpersonal relations that may be more than the cohesiveness and stability of a social order can tolerate over any long
period of time. The studies of individual and social pathology
produced by these analysts seem to be ample evidence that this is
so, and is their explanation for the erratic course of cultural development within our own lifetimes.

The accuracy of this vista is not the issue here, though there
is much to argue for it. As a type of framework for understanding
and evaluating historical change, its utility for social studies appears to be great. This method dispenses with appeals to metaphysical or theological causation for the explanation of historical
change. Such dubious factors as the forces of economic production, the divine spirit, the inevitability of progress, the law of
decay, are found to be inadequate or irrelevant, for they leave out
of account the simple fact that history is concerned with men. It
is the record of their successive efforts to come to terms with what
they believe to be their problems, and these problems are visualized most realistically as questions of devising institutional satisfactions for psychic necessities. As psychic necessities are trans-
formed, so must the cultural answers to them be altered, and historical change is to be accounted for chiefly, if not exclusively, in
these terms. The Neo-Freudian contribution to historiography
seems to be a substantial one.

There is another side to the coin of Neo-Freudian historical
interpretation too. We are familiar with the conviction of the
group that the leading influence on the formation of character is
the system of values of a society as they are channeled to the individual by interpersonal relations, especially in his early experiences in the family. Magnification of this character into social
character, or basic personality (in Fromm's phrase and Kardiner's,
respectively), and its affinity to the values on which the society is
predicated, explain the coherence and durability of a civilization,
they maintain. The theory is not unfamiliar to students of social
thought, reaching as it does far back into Western intellectual

history. Two of the founding fathers of political philosophy, if
not of the entire body of Western thought, were so impressed with
its importance as not to be above including lengthy tracts on
pedagogy and character formation in their most profound writings. For Plato perceived that legislative regulation of daily behavior was distinctly inferior to the systematic cultivation of
character by carefully preserved educational practices as the means
of perpetuating a well-founded social order or for meeting the
needs of inferior societies. And Aristotle was equally aware that
the soundest way of preserving a constitution, or way of life, was
to habituate citizens to the appropriate temper from childhood
onward: the firmest support of a constitution, he tells us, is the
character of its citizen-body.[5] Although the theme subsequently
suffered an almost total eclipse in Western intellectual currents,[6]
modern psychoanalytic testimony can do much to reinvigorate it
as a tool for social inquiry. We reproduce ourselves, character-
ologically speaking, according to a pattern that can no longer
be put aside as inscrutable.

To depreciate Neo-Freudian ideas on the subject as a mere
refurbishment of the concept of national character is to ignore
the nationalistic and racist implications with which the latter
term has been invested, a stigma that could not be attached to the
newer approach. The main obstacle to employing it seems to be
that of spatially and temporally delimiting the population to
which it is to be applied. And should this difficulty be met, the
validity of the resulting generalizations would in all likelihood
be inversely proportional to the magnitude of the group under
study. Furthermore, we are faced with a problem of another
sort. Do we have two sides to the historical coin or do we have
another version of the chicken-and-the-egg riddle? Do men make
culture or does culture make men? Unless we dispense with the
notion of causation altogether, the best solution to the puzzle is
probably to regard it as a process of mutual and cumulative causation of which the component elements can only be tentatively
separated for purposes of study but hardly at all for purposes of

ascertaining chronological sequence. On balance, the contribution of the Neo-Freudians here appears to be more suggestive than conclusive.

What is to be a reliable and fruitful source of knowledge for the social philosopher? To this next topic to engage our attention the Neo-Freudians have materials to offer also. Previous pages of this book have shown that members of the group secure their data from investigations in anthropology, sociology, and history as well as from sources more directly relevant to their profession, clinical psychoanalysis and, on a broader scale, studies in psychopathology. The two last-named are particularly deserving of further discussion because they suggest an amendment to procedures currently in vogue in the social sciences.

Having particular reference to Kardiner's concept of basic personality and his and Ovesey's employment of it in their study of the American Negro, the question arises whether qualitative data can claim par with quantitative data in social studies. No anthropological inquiry, with or without psychodynamic biography, can hope to survey the behavior patterns—much less the unconscious motivations—of an entire society by a complete census. But social scientists might well reserve approval of the analysts' audacity in generalizing for a population of some fifteen million people on the basis of a sample of a mere twenty-five. Is a study so grounded not an affront to the accepted methodology of the social sciences today? We are accustomed to having our path to truth illuminated by frequency distributions as we travel the highway of induction. We are used to accepting enlightenment only if resplendent in the regalia of statistics. What is nonquantifiable is nonmeasurable, and hence nonmaterial and so of no scientific or other value. The discussion of the basic personality of the American Negro rests on an inadequate and necessarily unrepresentative sample, the objection might run, and therefore it ought not to be taken too seriously.

But the fact is it was not intended to be a sample as the statistician understands the term. The Kardiner study, and for that matter other Neo-Freudian investigations employing the concept of basic personality (or social character), are an implicit challenge to the hegemony of induction outside the area of the pure or natural sciences. They advance the possibility of restoring the validity and utility of generalizing from a small but solid foundation of qualitative data. Single-minded fascination with the authority of quantitative evidence can easily mean a denigration of the value of qualitative contributions to our knowledge. Exclusive reliance on induction represents a would-be ostracizing of deductive thinking—even of philosophy, it may be—from the social sciences. Without abandoning induction *in toto,* the procedural orientation of the Neo-Freudians suggests this other approach. There is good reason behind their position. The ultimate subject matter of social studies consists of human beings. Since the essential realities of people are qualitative and intangible, we have to capitalize on deduction sooner or later and make the best use of tools which provide us with facts that are at bottom so resistant to induction. Psychodynamic biography appears to be one such technique, basic personality the allied concept. This is perhaps the boldest of the methodological innovations contained in Neo-Freudian writings. In addition, its feasibility pretty clearly rests upon the validity of their concept of basic personality, and that, in turn, depends largely upon their view of human nature. One need not follow them in this chain of reasoning point for point, however, to appreciate the potential value of their contribution here.

Coming to possible amendments to the final category noted above, the scope of inquiry legitimately occupying the student of social problems, the Neo-Freudians declare with one voice that it is to be interpersonal relations. The functioning of social institutions, the organization of associations, group behavior patterns, the attitudes and opinions of individuals, these and other topics that customarily engage the observer of the human condition must resolve themselves in the end into the study of interpersonal relations, they affirm. The implication is that unless this eventual issue is reached, social inquiry is superficial, if not meaningless.

At first glance this answer does not tell us much because by definition all social relations are interpersonal relations anyway. If anything, it tells us too much because of the very size of the task it would impose. It involves a multitude of data so staggering in extent that even the most gifted investigator cannot hope to master it, even with the aid of psychodynamic biographies or other newfangled psychoanalytic techniques. It is only reasonable to expect the scope of research to be delimited in the first instance by the conventional divisions of subject matter in the social sciences, in the next instance by the student's own area of interest, and in the last instance by the feasibility of gathering material on a particular question. Furthermore, the Neo-Freudian position would relegate political science, economics, and so on to the status of mere handmaidens of psychoanalytic psychology, a prospect no investigator bred in time-honored ways would face with relish. Is this not demanding too much?

It is demanding too much, and no Neo-Freudian, except perhaps Harry Stack Sullivan, would do so. It would be more accurate to interpret the group as advocating interdisciplinary research —"transdisciplinary" might be a better word—rather than the abolition of the customary disciplines themselves. Since a human being is not exclusively a political unit or an economic agent, for example, he cannot be understood fully or properly until all aspects of his intercourse with others have been considered (not forgetting, either, his intrapersonal relations with his unconscious). But there is no need to argue at this late date that many parts do not always make a whole, or that the additive approach has irremediable deficiencies. It is not so much interdisciplinary or transdisciplinary research that the Neo-Freudians call for as a shift in the focus of any social research. The essential import of their message here is that regardless of the special disciplinary tack the real data to be studied, the only data from which significant conclusions can be drawn, are the kind and quality of relations carried on between people and—as we already know—the connection between these relations and the psychic functioning of the participants. Societies and their inhabitants are to be understood most lucidly, this group of analysts maintains, from the style of contact current among people, as conducing to authority or equality, subordination or independence, distrust or love, fear or self-esteem, dissimulation or spontaneity, and so on. It is in interpersonal relations that the nature of a human being reveals itself, and it does so, incidentally, in a form particularly suitable for investigation. Once more we see the Neo-Freudian insistence on human beings as the ultimate subject matter of inquiry in the social sciences, once more we see their belief that a thorough comprehension of human nature must underlie a social philosophy. When their emphasis on interpersonal relations is construed in this way, as keeping the attention of research into social problems firmly to its fundamental material, it can only be considered a beneficial amendment to methodology.

A final assessment of the value of the Neo-Freudian contribution to social thought would be premature now. Aside from the insoluble difficulty of segregating the influence of Neo-Freudian from other schools of psychoanalysis, we lack an adequate historical perspective in which to place their ideas. Moreover, some of the Neo-Freudians are still alive and writing, and we may expect further development or modification of what they have already said. What follows is intended to be tentative, not definitive.

The sum total of the Neo-Freudian impact upon our culture is likely to be less than massive. It is probable that except for their testimonials to the importance of mental health, their methodological innovations will outlast their substantive contributions to our ways of thought. The fault is not entirely theirs. Partly it lies with the zeal with which early proponents of psychoanalysis assaulted the traditional breastworks of the social sciences, giving to psychoanalysis a revolutionary flavor that made it at once fashionable and disreputable. Partly also it lies with the unreceptive attitude of many social scientists toward what they not unnaturally regarded as presumptuous intrusions by an unorthodox and unproved body of ideas.[7] When the Neo-Freudians arrived upon the scene the temper of the times had changed. The social philosophy they had to offer could more readily be assimilated by American intellectuals, and for that matter, being more easily digestible, it is likely to leave less of an impression on Western, or even American, culture.

The assault on traditional ways of thinking about social problems and acting upon them by the political process was led by Harold D. Lasswell. In the United States, at least, he was a general without an army; the attack was beaten by the simple tactic of virtually ignoring it. The substance of Lasswell's writings in the first decade of his career must have been repulsive to the bulk of American political scientists. What he uncovered about politics then could give slight comfort to students who desired above all to shore up the theoretical foundations of American democracy at a time when it was threatened from abroad. Insofar as American political scientists were interested in psychology, it was as an aid to such comparatively innocuous pastimes as the gauging of public opinion, the content analysis of media of mass communications, and the study of voting behavior. For as Lasswell himself observed, they cared for psychology only if it could give support to the belief in individual dignity that underlies a democratic society or if it could strengthen the functioning of its institutions.[8] When a psychoanalytic psychology could not comport with these goals, its reception was bound to be a cold one. It is significant that by the time Lasswell had gained sufficient respectability in his profession to be elected president of the American Political Science Association, in 1955, he was no longer irreverently revamping the basic presuppositions of democratic political theory with rude incursions from Freudian psychology. By the end of the 1930's Lasswell had shifted his attention to the politics of democracy and was busy exploring the scope and method needed to effectuate the politics of prevention, which seemed safe and sane enough. So long as he did not act the *enfant terrible,* so long as the revelations of a psychoanalytic psychology could be adapted to the more venerable preconceptions of the political science of a democracy, Lasswell could be a member of the fraternity in good standing.

Admittedly no champion of democracy likes to be advised that its statesmen are typically, if not invariably, more eligible for a prolonged stay in a psychiatric ward than for dignified residence in an executive mansion. It is just as sure that no dyed-in-the-wool democrat enjoys any suggestion of the inherent inability of the ordinary citizen to make a rational selection of a policy genuinely calculated to secure his best interests, especially when those interests are held to be unconscious, instinctual, and offensive. And there are few votaries of democratic political institutions who can imperturbably accept the suggestion that the political process— parties, pressure groups, campaigns, the legislative contest, the administrative technique—is merely so much legerdemain with ambiguous symbols in a game with neither purpose nor end. Admittedly too Lasswell was premature in advancing so boldly and in such unaccustomed language the provocative proposals he did when they rested on theories of personality whose limitations he himself was soon to see. But by the time Lasswell gave up his sally on the strongholds of political orthodoxy, psychoanalysis had pretty well shot its bolt in politics. The area in which public policy is determined, the most formalized and presumably the most efficacious of the processes by which men deliberately bring their collective judgment to bear on solving social problems, was then foreclosed to the influence of any psychoanalytic doctrine with antidemocratic implications. Henceforth only contributions of a more conventional kind from this comparatively brash discipline, contributions not so seemingly subversive of established principles or not pressed so vigorously, could be acceptable there. The Neo-Freudians stepped into the breach.

The analysis of modern Western man and his predicament in his society offered by the Neo-Freudians was such as to commend itself favorably to American intellectuals and, in a somewhat diluted form, to the American public. The Neo-Freudians are conspicuously the intellectual children of their time, answering to its problems and reflecting its needs. Most of their major writings, and the experience and teaching on which they rest, date from the middle or late 1930's and the 1940's.[9] These were years of stress for American society, faced as it was by the twin threats of economic depression at home and totalitarianism abroad. The injury to individual security and self-respect implicit in the competitive atmosphere of the former, and the insult to individual liberty and the full expression of personality made explicit in the policies of the latter, combined to throw into jeopardy values of which Americans had regarded themselves as the foremost exemplars. Uncertainty, fear, conflict, hostility—in a word, anxiety—were corroding the psychic vitals of a generation. That generation seemed to yearn for a sympathetic portrait of itself and at the same time to crave a sturdy reaffirmation of traditional, humane principles. Neo-Freudian theories of personality in its social environment were handsomely appropriate to the spirit of the era. In large measure they gave their public—professional and lay alike—pretty much what it wanted and received in return a considerably more hospitable welcome than was accorded more radical censors of the status quo. But to paraphrase the ancient adage, nothing fails like success. The immediate appeal of their message constitutes at once a great strength and a great weakness of the school. This is not to say their work is merely topical, for their contention that pandemic insecurity has been years in the making—some five centuries, in fact, if not more—lends their social analysis a depth in time bordering on historical determinism. To their credit their vindication of older ideals alternates with well-aimed thrusts at the faultier features of Western society, and this is the aspect of their work that has been emphasized in the present volume. Yet on the whole, theirs is a conservative voice, advocating the conservation of a heritage to which practically all devotees of the sanctity of the individual and his free development can subscribe with little or no reservation.

Even the substantial amendments to our social institutions

the Neo-Freudians believe to be desirable are so doubtful of implementation as scarcely to imperil the cherished ideal—again
with the exception of Fromm. Their deficiency in specifying concrete measures of reform has been noted before, coupled with the
apology that it was due not to willful negligence but to an inexperi-
ence and an unfamiliarity with the political processes used to
realize social goals. In any case, large-scale social engineering appears to be completely incompatible with their disinclination to
foment stress in interpersonal relations by rapid and pervasive
social change and with their aversion toward any danger it could
present to the diversified expression of individual personality.
Neo-Freudian shortcomings here are compensated for by Lasswell's idea of preventive politics. It would turn the skills of
social scientists toward evaluating the operation of current institutions by their effects on the tension level of the community. It
would judge the probable consequences of proposed programs
and their initiation by the same criterion. As a resource for planning it permits the forestalling of experience in the parataxic
mode (in Harry Stack Sullivan's phrase) by anticipating the reactivation of latent insecurities. More positively, it is an attitude
permissive of the deliberate selection of communal courses of
action designed to foster psychic integrity—mental health—among
the body politic.

Nevertheless, the self-imposed limitation of this method of
operation almost completely precludes addressing itself to what
is by the Neo-Freudian account the most virulent source of social
and individual ills: the spawning of anxiety in the interpersonal
relations of family life. For better or for worse, the institution of
the family has proved to be beyond the reach of all but the most
radical reforms or profound historical changes. Plans to "rationalize" the family, from Plato to Hitler, have met with universal
revulsion from those who believe in the inviolability of this most
intimate type of interpersonal relation. And the influence of such
longer-term changes as the industrial revolution, urbanization,
and feminism have scarcely been susceptible to forethought by

would-be social engineers. The Neo-Freudians implicitly choose the course of moderation, patience, tolerance, and education in improving character formation in the family. As Abram Kardiner has said, the institution of the family, as it has developed and as it now functions in our society, may be imperfect in some respects, but experience shows it to produce the type of individual most capable of sustaining a stable and creative civilization.[10] Considering the importance the Neo-Freudians attach to the origin and initial development of the Oedipus complex, their antipathy for tampering directly with the family is alone sufficient evidence of the fundamentally conservative orientation of their teaching. If their findings about the critical role of the family in character formation are correct, we may expect only a very gradual, almost imperceptible, modification of our culture to result from their attitude and work, and meanwhile the evils they elucidate remain with us. In a certain and very painful sense the Neo-Freudians are hoist by their own petard.

Against this background the comparatively revolutionary proposals of Erich Fromm appear not so unreasonable after all. The objections made to them in the last chapter point to their faults as depending, in theory, on a natural law philosophy of human nature and as failing, in fact, to bring about the type of society either consistent with his own principles or palatable to any large number of citizens of the twentieth century. Given his basic proposition, however, that the social institutions of capitalist society are irremediably opposed to living the productive life—and the evidence he adduces is cogent, if not completely convincing—his indictment of contemporary Western culture is strong justification for commencing a second march on shaping our social organization. The repeated, remorseless, all but systematic depredations committed upon human personality, the seemingly contrived thwarting of creative inclinations and amicable relationships that he believes to be undermining a civilization, are enough to exasperate any conscientious humanist and goad him into raising the banner of revolt. Fromm does so with zeal, if not passion, and a sympathetic follower can only regret that the ensuing march bids fair to bog down on its first step even if its direction be accepted. His vision of a sane society composed of sane citizens, therefore, stands as a distant ideal and will probably affect us no more than distant ideals usually do. Outside religious affairs, that does not appear to be surpassingly great, and hence the influence of this branch of Neo-Freudian social philosophy is not likely to be very large either.

In summary, the Neo-Freudians' diagnoses of our social and individual ills are provocative, in many instances undeniably accurate, and in virtually all aspects in harmony with the outlook of our times. Their recommendations for dealing with these problems are less than original where they exist at all, or, in the case of Fromm, too original. Their basic principles deepen and illuminate a venerable philosophical tradition of our civilization in a way that should be welcomed by all adherents of humanism. The conceptual innovations they offer for further research and study are highly suggestive and recommend themselves for fuller exploitation. The ultimate success of the work of the Neo-Freudians, outside the clinic, therefore depends less on them than on those who may avail themselves of the materials they have put forward.

BIOGRAPHICAL SKETCHES

FRANZ ALEXANDER (b. 1891)

A career that appeared headed for the obscurity of bacteriological research was thrust on a new course of development by chance observation of inmates in the Neuropsychiatric Clinic of the University of Budapest and the gratifying results reached with them by a colleague familiar with Freudian psychology. Previously Alexander, who was born in Budapest and received his M.D. at that city's University in 1913, had been a research associate in physiology and then in bacteriology at the University and had served with a field laboratory and malaria station in the Austro-Hungarian Army during World War I. After a year of postgraduate work at the Psychiatric Clinic of the University of Berlin, he became the first training candidate at the Berlin Institute for Psychoanalysis, newly founded by Max Eitingon, one of the "Committee" of intimate adherents of Freud. Alexander remained there as Clinical Associate and lecturer in psychoanalysis from 1921 to 1930. In the latter year he was invited to become a visiting professor of psychoanalysis—perhaps the first such title ever held in the United States—at the University of Chicago. A year as research associate in criminology at the Judge Baker Foundation in Boston, which yielded *Roots of Crime,* preceded the foundation of the Chicago Institute for Psychoanalysis in 1932, of which he was named Director. From 1938 onward he was first associate and then full professor of psychiatry at the University of Illinois, as well as being attending physician at the Cook County Psychopathic Hospital for a like period. From 1947 to 1949 Alexander served as consultant to the National Advisory Mental Health Council, a body auxiliary to the Office of the Surgeon General of the United States; he was then appointed to full membership for a three-year term. His attention over the last quarter-century, however, has centered on activities connected with the Chicago Institute. A new post, as head of the Psychiatric Department and

Director of the Psychiatric and Psychosomatic Research Institute at Mt. Sinai Hospital, Los Angeles, may lead to new discoveries in fields in which he is pre-eminent.

ERICH FROMM (b. 1900)

Alone among the Neo-Freudians Erich Fromm has not had a medical background for his psychoanalytic work. His studies at Frankfurt/Main, Munich, and Heidelberg (from which last-named University he received his Ph.D. in 1922) were in sociology and psychology. It was not until 1923–24 that this Frankfurt-born social scientist took training at the Berlin Institute for Psychoanalysis. The years from 1929 to 1932 were spent as a lecturer in the Psychoanalytic Institute of Frankfurt while he doubled in that capacity at the University's Institute for Social Research, the meantime producing a number of writings marked for their interdisciplinary orientation. When, in 1933, he was invited to lecture at the Chicago Institute for Psychoanalysis, he elected to settle in the United States and became a member of the International Institute of Social Research at Columbia University, where he remained until 1939. After lecturing at Columbia for two years further, Fromm's talents became much in demand. Thus in 1941–42 he served with Karen Horney's American Institute of Psychoanalysis, has conducted courses at the New School for Social Research since that date, and from 1943 onward was a leading member of the staffs of the Washington School of Psychiatry and the William Alanson White Institute of Psychiatry in New York (both of these being under the guiding spirit of Harry Stack Sullivan). Bennington College, Vermont, had Fromm on its faculty from 1942 to 1951, when he became a professor at the National University of Mexico. Among his other honors are a fellowship in the New York Academy of Science, the delivery of the Terry Foundation Lectures at Yale University in 1950 (published as *Psychoanalysis and Religion*), and participation in the Fourth International Congress on Mental Health, Mexico City, in 1951.

KAREN HORNEY (1885–1952)

It is the feminine member of the Neo-Freudians who has had the most controversial career. Born in Berlin and educated at the Universities of Freiburg, Göttingen, and Berlin, she received her M.D. degree in 1913. A promising career in orthodox psychoanalysis was then begun with two years of study under Karl Abraham, the "Committeeman" whose abilities Freud esteemed most. Following four years of service as resident physician at the Lankwitz Psychiatric Hospital, Berlin, and a year on the staff of the Berlin Neurological Out-Patient Clinic, she became an instructor at the Berlin Institute for Psychoanalysis, a position she held from 1920 to 1932. Her emigration to America took place in 1932, when Franz Alexander invited her to be Associate Director of his Chicago Institute for Psychoanalysis. Largely theoretical differences led to her departure to New York in 1934, where she joined the staff of the orthodox Freudian New York Psychoanalytic Institute, in the following year taking on additional labors as a lecturer at the New School for Social Research. By 1941 her widening divergence from Freudian tenets resulted in her disqualification by the Institute as training analyst and instructor. It was the upshot of a rancorous dispute whose issue Horney framed as one of dogmatism in classical psychoanalytic education that drove out deviating ideas, which she felt a young experimental science could ill afford. She resigned her affiliations with orthodox societies and, with a few analysts of like mind, founded the Association for the Advancement of Psychoanalysis. She acceded to and retained to her death the post of Dean of the companion American Institute for Psychoanalysis, editing, from 1948 onward, the Association's periodical, *The American Journal of Psychoanalysis*.

ABRAM KARDINER (b. 1891)

Of the Neo-Freudians, only Kardiner can claim the distinction of having undergone a didactic (training) analysis with Freud himself. It took place in 1921–22, some four years after this New York–born graduate of the City College (1912) had taken his M.D. at Cornell University. Upon his return to the United States he became a member of the faculty of the New York Psychoanalytic Institute (the orthodox Freudian school for training analysts), where he remained until 1944. His energies were divided between that and an instructorship in psychiatry at Cornell, from 1923 to 1929, after which he served as associate in psychiatry at Columbia University until 1932. The relationship with Columbia has been his most enduring, academically, for in 1939 Kardiner began a fourteen-year tenure in its Department of Anthropology and Sociology. His regular psychoanalytic practice was fortified by duties as assistant clinical professor of psychiatry at Columbia beginning in 1944, and he advanced in rank to full professor in 1949 and was made director of Columbia's Psychoanalytic Clinic in 1955, a post he still holds.

HAROLD D. LASSWELL (b. 1902)

There is nothing in Lasswell's academic career to betray the interest in psychoanalysis that made him almost unique in his profession, although that career has been distinguished in other respects. Coming from a small town in Illinois, Lasswell took a Ph.B. and a Ph.D. at the University of Chicago in 1922 and 1926, successively. Considering that he acted as an assistant in the Department of Political Science during his graduate studies and then rose in the University's Political Science Department through 1938, his background seems parochial indeed. But summer studies during 1923–25 at the Universities of London, Geneva, Paris, and Berlin brought him into touch with the psychoanalytic movement. Thus by 1938 he could spend two years as a political scientist on the staff of the Washington School of Psychiatry, and from 1939 to 1945 could serve as Director of War Communications Research of the Library of Congress, where he was largely engaged in content analysis of communications media. From 1938 to 1945 Lasswell was Visiting Sterling Lecturer at the Yale Law School, and he joined the Yale faculty as Professor of Law in 1946; since 1952 he has been Professor of Law and Political Science there. A busy scholarly career has included lecturing at the New School for Social Research (1939–46), at the New York Academy of Medicine (where he delivered the 1948 Salmon Lectures in Psychiatry, published as *Power and Personality*), and visiting professorships over the years at several universities. He has managed to find time to act as consultant to various departments of the federal government and the Research Advisory Board of the Committee for Economic Development, to maintain active membership in many professional societies (serving as President of the American Political Science Association in 1955–56), and to be advisory editor to a number of journals prominent in the social sciences. Since 1954 Lasswell has also been a fellow of the Center for Advanced Study in the Behavioral Sciences at Stanford University.

HARRY STACK SULLIVAN (1892–1949)

Sullivan's acquaintance with psychoanalysis came about mainly through his contact with William Alanson White, an early and zealous American advocate of the new science. An interest in schizophrenia dating from before his medical training—Sullivan, from Norwich, N.Y., completed his M.D. at the Chicago College of Medicine and Surgery in 1917—led him through a series of military, governmental, and civil posts in a few short years until he began his real career in 1922 as a Veterans Bureau Liaison Officer at St. Elizabeth's Hospital, Washington, D.C. It was there that he met White, and, although his tenure on White's staff lasted but a year, the relationship continued after Sullivan's transfer to the nearby Sheppard and Enoch Pratt Hospital (also a psychiatric institution), where Sullivan was quickly promoted from Assistant Physician to Director of Clinical Research. Meanwhile he became an instructor (1924) and then Associate Professor (1925) of Psychiatry at the University of Maryland School of Medicine. Sullivan temporarily transferred his activities to New York in 1931, where he commenced and retained a private psychiatric practice until 1939. Nevertheless he was able to become a trustee of the William Alanson White Psychiatric Foundation in Washington in 1933 and to remain its President from then until 1943, and to serve as Director of the affiliated Washington School of Psychiatry from 1936 and as its President from then until 1947. In addition to taking part over the years in a number of conferences dealing with problems of mental health, Sullivan acted as Professor and Head of the Department of Psychiatry of Georgetown University Medical School from 1939 onward and served as consultant in psychiatry to the Director of the Selective Service System in 1940–41. From 1938 to 1945 he held the co-editorship of the journal he helped found, *Psychiatry,* and in 1945 took over full editorship. The better part of his efforts since 1941, however, was devoted to teaching and research at the Washington School of Psychiatry.

NOTES

Complete authors' names, titles, and publication data
will be found in the Bibliography, pp. 267–78.

CHAPTER 1

1. Quoted in Gervais, p. 294.
2. *Rendezvous with Destiny*, p. 311. On the currency of pseudo-psychoanalytic ideas in the 1920's and 1930's see Zilboorg, *Sigmund Freud*, pp. 72–74.
3. *The History of the Psychoanalytic Movement* (first published in 1914), p. 933. Cf. *The Future of an Illusion* (1927), p. 64.
4. Freud modestly shrank from accepting the sobriquet for his own ideas. *New Introductory Lectures on Psychoanalysis*, pp. 216, 248.
5. *A General Introduction to Psycho-Analysis* (1920) (by permission of Liveright Publishers, N.Y., copyright 1948 R. S. Hoch), pp. 22, 23, 252; *Wit and Its Relation to the Unconscious* (1905), in *Basic Writings*, p. 748. As Franz Alexander put it, "In attacking Freud, every one defended his own repressions" ("Sigmund Freud, 1856–1939," p. 577).
6. "Psycho-Analysis" (reprinted from a 1923 encyclopedia article), p. 102; *The Ego and the Id* (1923), p. 9. On Adler, see Thompson, p. 59, and *The History of the Psychoanalytic Movement*, pp. 965 ff.
7. *The Interpretation of Dreams* (1899), pp. 542, 548.
8. Freud, *An Outline of Psychoanalysis* (1940), p. 83; *General Introduction*, pp. 376–78, 395.
9. See Laski, *A Grammar of Politics* (first published in 1925), pp. 39, 57, 91, and T. H. Green, *Lectures on the Principles of Political Obligation* (first published in 1882), pp. 29–48. Green used the phrase "moral self," but it is almost unquestionably the same in content, if different in form, from Laski's concept. Both of them, of course, go back to ancient Greek ideas.
10. *Outline*, pp. 81, 104; Lasswell, "The Study of the Ill as a Method of Research into Political Personalities," p. 1001; Jones, I, 269.
11. *The Interpretation of Dreams*, pp. 381–82, 500ff. Cf. *General Introduction*, pp. 75, 397; *Wit and Its Relation to the Unconscious*, p. 697.
12. "The Moses of Michelangelo" (1914), p. 271. The artist knew this long before the scientist discovered it. "For you must know, Sancho," advises Don Quixote, "if you do not know already, that between lovers the outward actions and movements they reveal when their loves are under discussion are most certain messengers, bearing news of what is going on in their innermost souls." (From the J. M. Cohen translation [Penguin Books, 1954], II, 525; quoted by permission.) In his most lucid work, Freud introduces psychoanalysis by way of the parapraxes (*General Introduction*, Lectures 2–4).

13. *The Interpretation of Dreams,* p. 540, emphasis removed.
14. *Ibid.,* pp. 319, 206–7.
15. *Outline,* p. 53.
16. *Three Contributions to the Theory of Sex* (1905), p. 577; "The Libido Theory" (1923), p. 132.
17. *Civilization and Its Discontents* (1930), p. 95; *General Introduction,* pp. 306ff, 311.
18. *General Introduction,* p. 311; *New Introductory Lectures,* p. 133; *Three Contributions,* p. 577. Is it a coincidence that the opening sentences of Freud's *Beyond the Pleasure Principle* are almost a paraphrase of the famous opening sentences of Bentham's *Introduction to the Principles of Morals and Legislation?*
19. *Three Contributions,* p. 604. "The theory of repression is the pillar upon which the edifice of psychoanalysis rests" (*The History of the Psychoanalytic Movement,* p. 939).
20. *General Introduction,* p. 24; *The Interpretation of Dreams,* p. 391.
21. *Three Contributions,* p. 608; *General Introduction,* p. 272, emphasis removed. See *Outline,* pp. 28–30, and *Three Contributions,* pp. 620–22, for summaries.
22. *Three Contributions,* p. 602; *The History of the Psychoanalytic Movement,* pp. 936–37.
23. E.g., in *Group Psychology and the Analysis of the Ego* (1922), pp. 37–38; and in "Why War?" (1933), p. 280. The reference seems singularly ill-chosen, inasmuch as Plato concludes his dialogue with a conception of love which is not only nonsexual but contemptuous of all activities not conducive to contemplation of the Form of beauty. Freud noted, however, that the love of man for man that results from work in common is "desexualized, sublimated homosexual love" (*Group Psychology,* p. 57 [by permission of Liveright, Publishers, N.Y., copyright 1951]).
24. *General Introduction,* pp. 23–24, 311–12, 273, 306. Cf. *Beyond the Pleasure Principle,* pp. 5–6.
25. Kardiner, *Sex and Morality,* pp. 50, 57; Fromm, "The Humanistic Implications of Instinctivistic 'Radicalism,'" pp. 343–44; *General Introduction,* pp. 376–77.
26. *New Introductory Lectures,* pp. 205–6; Schoenwald, p. 238.
27. Thompson, pp. 12, 47ff; Jones, III, 267; Franz Alexander, "Development of the Fundamental Concepts of Psychoanalysis," p. 16. Freud states the problem succinctly, though technically, in "The Libido Theory," p. 133.
28. With regard to the revised instinct theory, Jones observes that "Freud was an obstinate dualist" (III, 266–67). Freud himself had earlier held the mind to be the arena of dualisms (*General Introduction,* p. 68), and reiterated his dualistic views subsequently in *Beyond the Pleasure Principle,* p. 72.
29. *Outline,* p. 20; *Beyond the Pleasure Principle,* pp. 47, 53–54 (by permission of Liveright, Publishers, N.Y., copyright 1950); *Civilization and Its Discontents,* pp. 97, 102. Cf. *The Ego and the Id,* pp. 55–56, and "The Libido Theory," pp. 134–35.
30. *Beyond the Pleasure Principle,* pp. 49–50, 51.

31. *Civilization and Its Discontents,* pp. 85, 86, 102–3; "Why War?" p. 281; *Civilization and Its Discontents,* p. 97.

32. *Group Psychology,* p. 37; *Outline,* p. 24; *Three Contributions,* pp. 553n, 611.

33. *Outline,* pp. 24, 22; *Three Contributions,* p. 612. See also Jones, II, 143, 283, and *The History of the Psychoanalytic Movement,* p. 974.

34. Jones (II, 283) says the theory dates as far back as 1894, though the term is mentioned only in passing in *The Interpretation of Dreams* (see p. 236), despite Freud's continual updating of his masterpiece.

35. *Group Psychology,* p. 57.

36. *Group Psychology,* p. 51; "Why War?" pp. 283–84; *Civilization and Its Discontents,* pp. 73, 135–36, 144. The last quotation, not in this edition, was added by Freud in the 1933 revision. See Jones, III, 348.

37. A. A. Brill, "Reminiscences of Freud," p. 182.

38. *Outline,* p. 21. Freud also noted that fate ruled over the Greek gods. *The Future of an Illusion,* p. 28.

39. *Outline,* pp. 14, 19, 43, 109; *New Introductory Lectures,* pp. 104, 105.

40. *Outline,* pp. 15, 110–11, 19; *The Ego and the Id,* pp. 29–30; *New Introductory Lectures,* p. 106; *Civilization and Its Discontents,* p. 10.

41. *Outline,* pp. 121, 17; *The Ego and the Id,* p. 49; *Civilization and Its Discontents,* pp. 127, 105; *New Introductory Lectures,* pp. 94, 92.

42. *New Introductory Lectures,* pp. 108–10; *The Ego and the Id,* pp. 82–83; *Outline,* p. 83.

43. *New Introductory Lectures,* pp. 118–19. The difficult paper is *The Problem of Anxiety* (1926), q.v., pp. 69–84, especially p. 80, for a summary.

44. *Three Contributions,* p. 617n. The theory of the Oedipus complex stirred a furor. For Freud's wry comment on the public's ingratitude for the discovery and its retreat from its implications, see *General Introduction,* p. 184.

45. *The Interpretation of Dreams,* pp. 303–9. On infantile behavior, see, e.g., *General Introduction,* pp. 291, 293. Jones states that it was his self-analysis, one of Freud's two major achievements (the other being the refinement of the method of free association), that enabled him to explore the Oedipus complex (I, 241).

46. The Oedipal relationship is elaborated from the masculine standpoint. For feminine psychology, which is, as it were, a by-product of the masculine, see *New Introductory Lectures,* pp. 153–85. "Complexes" are defined by Freud as "Circles of thought and interests of strong affective value." *General Introduction,* p. 98.

47. *The Interpretation of Dreams,* pp. 306–7, 391, 492; *Three Contributions,* p. 617n. For an account of the workings of the family situation, see *General Introduction,* pp. 184, 291–94.

48. *The Interpretation of Dreams,* p. 308; *General Introduction,* p. 290, emphasis supplied.

49. *Beyond the Pleasure Principle,* p. 48.

50. *Moses and Monotheism,* pp. 157, 209. Freud summoned proof for the theory by likening the psychology of primitive races to the psychology of the neurotic, each being archaic in its way. See *Totem and Taboo* (1913), pp. 807, 834.

51. Jones, II, 195; III, 311, 313. For Freud's not very clear exposition of "the omnipotence of thoughts," see *Totem and Taboo*, pp. 873–77.
52. *Moses and Monotheism*, p. 209.
53. Jones, III, 322.
54. *The Interpretation of Dreams*, p. 308; *Totem and Taboo*, p. 927; *The Future of an Illusion*, p. 77.
55. Jones, III, 435. Jones gives no reason for selecting these time periods.
56. *Outline*, pp. 66, 70; *General Introduction*, p. 257.
57. *Civilization and Its Discontents*, p. 74.
58. *Ibid.*, pp. 86, 63.
59. *Outline*, pp. 29–30, The resultant castration complex, in the male, and penis envy, in the female, are of scant interest in this volume. For further data see, e.g., *id.*, and *New Introductory Lectures*, p. 170.
60. *Totem and Taboo*, pp. 915–17, 908.
61. *Ibid.*, pp. 928–29.
62. *Ibid.*, pp. 919, 922.

CHAPTER 2

1. The best-known refutations of *Totem and Taboo* are A. L. Kroeber, "Totem and Taboo: An Ethnologic Psychoanalysis"; Bronislaw Malinowski, *Sex and Repression in Savage Society*; and Edward Westermarck, *Three Essays on Sex and Marriage*, pp. 3–123.
2. Jones, *The Life and Work of Sigmund Freud*, III, p. 331. On the contributions of anthropology see Thompson, *Psychoanalysis: Evolution and Development*, pp. 194, 38–39, and Edward Sapir, "Why Cultural Anthropology Needs the Psychiatrist."
3. "A Hypothesis Rooted in the Preconceptions of a Single Civilization Tested by Bronislaw Malinowski," esp. pp. 482–84.
4. *Fundamentals of Psychoanalysis*, p. 152. Cf. Helen V. McLean, "A Few Comments on 'Moses and Monotheism,'" p. 211, for a similar view.
5. *General Introduction*, pp. 321, 141. See *ibid.*, pp. 143–47, for illustrations. As may be expected, all the symbols are sexual. Cf. *New Introductory Lectures*, p. 15, where Freud reaffirms the significance of his discovery.
6. *Group Psychology*, pp. 40, 100.
7. *Ibid.*, pp. 92, 91, 33, 99. See Saul Scheidlinger, *Psychoanalysis and Group Behavior*, for an application of Freudian crowd psychology to education and group psychotherapy, aside from its lucid restatement, pp. 136–45, of the gist of *Group Psychology* bereft of the theories of the primal horde and the archaic heritage.
8. *Totem and Taboo*, pp. 927, 915; *Civilization and Its Discontents*, pp. 120–22, 90.
9. *Group Psychology*, pp. 93, 89.
10. *Moses and Monotheism*, pp. 172–73.
11. *Group Psychology*, p. 1n.
12. *Ibid.*, p. 57.
13. *Moses and Monotheism*, pp. 162–64.
14. *The Future of an Illusion*, pp. 6, 7.

15. "The Themes of Work and Play in the Structure of Freud's Thought," p. 311. We can well believe Jones's remark that Freud "had no more than the average interest in politics and modes of government" (I, 5).

16. *New Introductory Lectures,* p. 230.

17. *The Future of an Illusion,* pp. 24ff; *Civilization and Its Discontents,* p. 21. Cf. *Moses and Monotheism,* p. 89, and *New Introductory Lectures,* pp. 221–23.

18. *The Future of an Illusion,* pp. 26–27, 77–78; *Totem and Taboo,* pp. 826, 919–20; *New Introductory Lectures,* p. 229.

19. *New Introductory Lectures,* p. 230; *The Future of an Illusion,* p. 77; *Civilization and Its Discontents,* pp. 141–42.

20. *The Future of an Illusion,* pp. 54, 48, 78, 99–100.

21. *Ibid.,* pp. 57, 74, 79. Cf. *Civilization and Its Discontents,* p. 23.

22. *The Future of an Illusion,* pp. 56, 48, 85, 102, 89 (emphasis removed), 96–97, 98; *New Introductory Lectures,* pp. 219, 232–33, 238, 239. Franz Alexander observes that in deposing formal religion, Freud was enthroning his own nineteenth-century religion, science ("A Review of Two Decades," p. 24).

23. As, e.g., in Henry Steele Commager, *The American Mind,* pp. 120–28.

24. *New Introductory Lectures,* pp. 234–35.

25. "The Moses of Michelangelo," pp. 279, 283.

26. *Psychoanalysis and Religion* (first published in 1950), p. 6.

27. Erich Fromm, *Sigmund Freud's Mission,* pp. 28, 33. The illustrations of obscene jokes Freud gave in *Wit and Its Relation to the Unconscious* would disappoint anyone with a prurient interest.

28. John Stuart Mill, *Autobiography* (1873), esp. Chaps. I and II. The quotation is from p. 34. The well-known crisis in Mill's mental history is nothing more than a belated (at age 20) resolution of the Oedipus complex; see *ibid.,* pp. 99ff. On Freud's Oedipus complex, see Fromm, *Sigmund Freud's Mission,* pp. 53, 16, 59–60.

29. See Freud's *tour de force* in so doing in *A General Introduction to Psycho-Analysis,* pp. 136ff.

30. "Why War?" p. 284.

31. *Totem and Taboo,* pp. 916, 917; *Civilization and Its Discontents,* pp. 91–92.

32. *Civilization and Its Discontents,* pp. 63, 74–76; *The Future of an Illusion,* pp. 84, 87.

33. *Civilization and Its Discontents,* p. 59; *The Future of an Illusion,* pp. 5–6, 11. Cf. pp. 21–22 of the latter work and "Why War?" pp. 275–76, for further remarks on the transition from the state of nature to civil society.

34. *The Future of an Illusion,* pp. 77, 79.

35. *Ibid.,* pp. 3, 22; *Civilization and Its Discontents,* pp. 53ff.

36. *The Future of an Illusion,* pp. 84–85; *Civilization and Its Discontents,* pp. 102–3.

37. "Why War?" pp. 276, 280.

38. *The Future of an Illusion,* p. 14; *Civilization and Its Discontents,* pp. 116, 120.

39. Quoted in Jones, I, 176.

40. *Civilization and Its Discontents,* pp. 74–75.
41. *The Future of an Illusion,* pp. 79, 89.
42. *Civilization and Its Discontents,* pp. 88–89. That Freud did not think much of communism, pure or applied, is further exemplified by remarks in "Why War?" pp. 280, 283, and *New Introductory Lectures,* pp. 245–47.
43. "Why War?" pp. 282–83.
44. *The Future of an Illusion,* pp. 13–14; *Civilization and Its Discontents,* p. 41; "Why War?" p. 284.

CHAPTER 3

1. On the possible causes, see, respectively, Thompson, *Psychoanalysis: Evolution and Development,* p. 13; C. P. Oberndorf, *A History of Psychoanalysis in America,* pp. 2, 247; and Franz Alexander, *Our Age of Unreason* (1942), p. 8, and Karen Horney, *Our Inner Conflicts,* p. 12.
2. Karen Horney, *New Ways in Psychoanalysis,* pp. 8, 80.
3. Karen Horney, *The Neurotic Personality of Our Time,* pp. 82–83, 160–61, 285; *New Ways,* p. 84.
4. *The Neurotic Personality,* pp. 160, 285.
5. *New Ways,* pp. 81, 8, 87; *The Neurotic Personality,* pp. 19–20.
6. *The Neurotic Personality,* p. 157; *New Ways,* pp. 83, 10.
7. Erich Fromm, "Individual and Social Origins of Neurosis," pp. 381–82; *Psychoanalysis and Religion,* pp. 79, 82. Cf. *Escape from Freedom,* pp. 177–78, and *Man for Himself,* p. 157.
8. Erich Fromm, *The Sane Society,* p. 42, emphasis removed.
9. *Ibid.,* pp. 43–44; *The Forgotten Language* (copyright 1951 by Erich Fromm), pp. 205–8. Fromm relies on the anthropological work of Bachofen and Morgan to substantiate his thesis. *The Forgotten Language,* pp. 205, 209.
10. *Escape from Freedom,* pp. 24–39. The phrase "ambiguous gift" is on p. 32.
11. *The Forgotten Language,* p. 212.
12. *Ibid.,* pp. 196, 201–2, 204–5.
13. Abram Kardiner, *Sex and Morality,* pp. 134, 59, 198–99, 132.
14. *Ibid.,* pp. 31, 32, 134; cf. pp. 199–200. All quotations from *Sex and Morality,* copyright 1954 by Abram Kardiner, are used by special permission of the publishers, the Bobbs-Merrill Company, Inc.
15. Abram Kardiner, *The Individual and His Society* (first published in 1939), pp. 386–87, 99–100, 481; Abram Kardiner and Lionel Ovesey, *The Mark of Oppression,* p. 25.
16. *The Individual and His Society,* pp. 385, 100.
17. Kardiner and Ovesey, *The Mark of Oppression,* p. 26; *The Individual and His Society,* pp. 479, 480. The latter book and *The Psychological Frontiers of Society* (first published in 1945) were collaborative works that successively refined the integration of anthropology with psychodynamic biography; the most fruitful product of that development has been *The Mark of Oppression,* "A Psychosocial Study of the American Negro."
18. *The Individual and His Society,* pp. 402, 62. See *ibid.,* pp. 17–18,

for Kardiner's critique of the related theory of sublimation. When Kardiner makes occasional loose references to a "sexual instinct" in his expositional writings it is as a highly educable biological drive. See, e.g., *Sex and Morality,* pp. 102, 130, and "New Attitudes Toward Sex," pp. 123, 127–28.

19. *The Interpersonal Theory of Psychiatry,* pp. 285, 21.
20. Karen Horney, *Neurosis and Human Growth,* p. 373.
21. *New Ways,* pp. 127–29.
22. *Ibid.,* pp. 131, 130.
23. "The Cultural Revolution to End War," p. 86. Sullivan rejects the death-instinct abruptly in *Conceptions of Modern Psychiatry,* p. 48n.
24. "Aggressiveness—Individual and Collective," pp. 86, 91, 85.
25. The fine points of these distinctions do not concern us here. For a sampling of the not very satisfactory literature on this topic see Nathan Freeman, "Concepts of Adler and Horney"; Walter T. James, "Karen Horney and Erich Fromm in Relation to Alfred Adler"; and Thompson, pp. 159, 171, 197, 199.
26. *International Journal of Psychoanalysis,* XXI, 240–41; *ibid.,* pp. 360–63, by Adolph Stern.
27. "Der Kampf in der Kultur," p. 115, tr. supplied. For a brief discussion of "Der Kampf in der Kultur" and other of Horney's early writings that omened the break with orthodoxy, see Frederick A. Weiss, "Karen Horney—Her Early Papers," pp. 55–64.
28. "Tenth Anniversary," p. 3. Cf. Thompson, pp. 13, 54, and esp. 58, for an expanded exposition of the theme.
29. *New Ways,* pp. 24, 8–9, 189, 191. Cf. Thompson, pp. 9–10, 27, where a similar view is expressed.
30. Kardiner, *Sex and Morality,* p. 102; Horney, *New Ways,* pp. 48, 168ff; Fromm, "Psychoanalytic Characterology and Its Application to the Understanding of Culture," p. 2; Kardiner, *The Individual and His Society,* pp. 390–93.
31. For a short delineation of one such character type by Freud, see his "Character and Anal Erotism" (1908). Karl Abraham gives a classic Freudian exposition of several types of libidinally determined character in *Selected Papers of Karl Abraham,* pp. 370–417; and note the rationale for the theory on pp. 248–79. Cf. Thompson's summary, pp. 64ff.
32. *New Ways,* pp. 58, 65, 52.
33. *Ibid.,* pp. 62, 73, 24, 9, 76.
34. *Ibid.,* pp. 58–59; *The Neurotic Personality,* pp. vii, viii.
35. *New Ways,* pp. 78, 9.
36. *Conceptions,* pp. 31ff. Thompson elucidates in *Psychoanalysis,* p. 42. So rigorous is Sullivan's exclusion of the libido theory from his own work that this writer found the term but once in all the Sullivaniana examined: *The Interpersonal Theory,* p. 295, where it is quickly disposed of.
37. *The Individual and His Society,* pp. 250, 400–403.
38. Abram Kardiner, "Adaptational Theory: The Cross Cultural Point of View," pp. 59, 60.
39. *The Individual and His Society,* p. 107. On Freud, see *supra,* p. 20.
40. "Adaptational Theory," p. 61. For a critical evaluation of Kar-

diner's innovations in Freudian theory on this point, see Read Bain's review of *The Individual and His Society*. A rebuttal by a Freudian-oriented anthropologist is in Géza Róheim, "Society and the Individual."

41. Horney, *New Ways*, pp. 188–91; Kardiner, "New Attitudes Toward Sex," p. 128.

42. *Conceptions*, p. 48n.

43. *The Interpersonal Theory of Psychiatry*, *The Psychiatric Interview*, and *Clinical Studies in Psychiatry*.

44. *Conceptions*, p. v. Sullivan emphatically asserted the importance of the theory of anxiety in *The Interpersonal Theory*, p. 8. The careful study by Dorothy R. Blitsten, "The Significance of Harry Stack Sullivan's Theories for Social Science," is regrettably deficient in this respect because of its date.

45. Thompson, p. 195. How much weight shall we attach to Sullivan's passing remark, "I grew up in the psychoanalytic school . . ."? *The Psychiatric Interview*, p. 35.

46. Patrick Mullahy, "The Theories of H. S. Sullivan," p. 54; Alfred H. Stanton, "Sullivan's Conceptions," p. 61; Thompson, pp. 219, 221; and Mabel Blake Cohen's Introduction to Sullivan, *The Interpersonal Theory*, p. xii. A beginner's lexicon may be had by consulting such works as the anonymous review of *Conceptions* in *Psychiatric Quarterly*, XXI, 494–99; Edith Jacobson's review of *Conceptions* in *Psychoanalytic Quarterly*, XVII, 393–95; Thompson, p. 110; and William F. Murphy's review of *The Interpersonal Theory* in *Psychoanalytic Quarterly*, XXII, 446–50. Cf. Sullivan, *The Interpersonal Theory*, pp. 167n, 193.

47. A. A. Brill's Introduction to *The Basic Writings of Sigmund Freud*, p. 12, emphasis removed.

48. *The Interpersonal Theory*, p. 313.

49. See "Psychiatry: Introduction to the Study of Interpersonal Relations," p. 121.

50. Blitsten, p. 58; *Conceptions*, p. 4; *The Interpersonal Theory*, pp. 19–20. Thompson compares this approach favorably with Freud's view of man as an isolated product of his sexual development (p. 115).

51. "Socio-Psychiatric Research," p. 978; *Conceptions*, p. 88.

52. *The New York Times*, October 15, 1951, p. 28. Cf. Sullivan's obituary in *ibid.*, January 16, 1949. See Sullivan's comprehensive understanding of "mental disorders" in the article by that title which he wrote for the *Encyclopedia of the Social Sciences*. On the extensive influence of psychoanalysis on psychiatry in the United States, see Franz Alexander, "A Review of Two Decades," pp. 18, 26, and Zilboorg, *Sigmund Freud*, p. 16.

53. "A Note on the Implications of Psychiatry," p. 849; *The Interpersonal Theory*, p. 32.

54. Blitsten, p. 17. See also Sullivan, "The Training of the General Medical Student in Psychiatry," p. 376, for a more complicated affirmation.

55. Sullivan, "A Note on Formulating the Relationship of the Individual and the Group," p. 934. For a clearer statement of the matter see Thompson, pp. 215–16; cf. Mullahy, "The Theories of H. S. Sullivan," pp. 18–19, and Mullahy's Introduction to *A Study of Interpersonal Re-*

lations, p. xxvii. For Sullivan on "dissociation," see *Conceptions,* pp. 10, 22. For Sullivan on dreams as a route to the dissociated, see *The Interpersonal Theory,* pp. 330–32, and *Conceptions,* pp. 33–34.

56. "Towards a Psychiatry of Peoples," p. 105, reprinted in *The Interpersonal Theory,* p. 368. See other favorable references to Bridgman on pp. 14–15, 19, of the latter volume.

57. Catherine Harris, "Sullivan's Concept of Scientific Method as Applied to Psychiatry," p. 41.

58. Sullivan's definition of "group" is in "A Note on the Implications of Psychiatry," pp. 858–59. The criticisms are in Catherine Harris, p. 34, and Gardner Murphy and Elizabeth Cattell, p. 175.

59. "The Illusion of Personal Individuality," pp. 317–32; "Socio-Psychiatric Research," pp. 990 (emphasis removed), 978.

60. "Psychiatry: Introduction to the Study of Interpersonal Relations," p. 121; *The Interpersonal Theory,* pp. 110–11, emphasis removed. See p. 103 of that book for a more technical rephrasing.

61. *Conceptions,* pp. vii, vi, 10.

62. *The Interpersonal Theory,* p. 165; *Conceptions,* p. 10; "Psychiatry: Introduction to the Study of Interpersonal Relations," p. 123n; Blitsten, pp. 62, 58.

63. Murphy and Cattell, p. 162.

64. "Socio-Psychiatric Research," pp. 990–91. Sullivan repudiates a genetic basis for mental illness ("I have a very simple attitude there: not proved") in *Clinical Studies,* p. 359.

65. "Psychiatry," in *Encyclopedia of the Social Sciences,* p. 580; "Towards a Psychiatry of Peoples," p. 105. Cf. *Clinical Studies,* p. 146, and Mullahy, "Introduction" to *A Study of Interpersonal Relations,* p. xxxi.

66. *The Psychiatric Interview,* p. 3. For further remarks on Sullivan's technique, see *ibid.,* p. 50.

67. *New Ways,* pp. 166–67; "On Difficulties in Dealing with the Transference," pp. 1–2.

68. Karen Horney, *Self-Analysis,* p. 145. Horney gives a more extended narration of her transference technique in "What Does the Analyst Do?" pp. 187–209.

69. "The Social Philosophy of 'Will Therapy,'" p. 232.

70. "Remarks on the Problem of Free Association," pp. 1–6; the longer quotation is from p. 6. Cf. *The Sane Society,* pp. 166–69.

71. Franz Alexander, *Psychoanalysis and Psychotherapy, q.v.* esp. pp. 130–38, 39–44. Cf. "Development of the Fundamental Concepts of Psychoanalysis," pp. 31–33, for another statement.

72. See "Man Is Not a Thing," p. 11.

73. On parataxic distortion, see Sullivan, *The Psychiatric Interview,* p. 26, *Clinical Studies,* p. 200, and the necessary clarification in Thompson, pp. 111–12, 216. A useful explanation for the layman on the differences between the old and the new methods of clinical psychoanalysis is Rioch, pp. 80–97. On a more sophisticated and technical level, consult Franz Alexander, "Analysis of the Therapeutic Factors in Psychoanalytic Treatment," pp. 436–54.

74. "Environmental Factors in Etiology and Course Under Treatment of Schizophrenia," p. 20.

75. *Escape from Freedom*, p. 287, emphasis removed; *Man for Himself*, p. 60.

76. "Psychoanalysis and Social Disorganization," p. 794; "Psychoanalytic Aspect of Mental Hygiene and the Environment," pp. 189–90; Franz Alexander and Hugo Staub, *The Criminal, the Judge, and the Public*, (first published in 1931) p. 34.

77. *Our Age of Unreason* (1942), pp. 236–37; "Psychoanalysis and Social Disorganization," p. 794 (copyright 1937 by the University of Chicago); "Psychoanalytic Aspect," pp. 190–91. The theme is put more forcefully in Franz Alexander, "Educative Influence of Personality Factors in the Environment," pp. 41–42.

78. *Our Age of Unreason* (1942), p. 241.

79. "Psychoanalysis Revised," pp. 22–23.

80. *Ibid.*, p. 5; "Educative Influence," p. 39. The latter work reiterates Alexander's distaste for what he calls the "ethnological bias" on pp. 35–36, 41–42, 45–46, apparently overlooking Horney's explicit and implicit contention of the basic anxiety being generated in the child by his family environment and not by "culture" in general.

81. "A Tentative Analysis of the Variables in Personality Development," pp. 589–90; "Development of the Fundamental Concepts of Psychoanalysis," p. 23 (copyright 1952 by the University of Chicago); "The Sociological and Biological Orientation of Psychoanalysis," pp. 240, 249.

82. "Psychoanalytic Aspect," p. 189; *Our Age of Unreason* (1942), pp. 228–29; "Sociological and Biological Orientation," p. 245; "Development of the Fundamental Concepts of Psychoanalysis," p. 31.

83. *Fundamentals of Psychoanalysis*, p. 150; "Psychoanalysis and Social Disorganization," pp. 791, 796, 799.

84. "Psychoanalysis and Social Disorganization," pp. 802, 791–92, 799.

85. Franz Alexander and William Healy, *Roots of Crime*, p. 280; Franz Alexander, "The Dynamics of Personality Development," pp. 139, 140.

86. Horney, *New Ways*, p. 153.

CHAPTER 4

1. "Tenth Anniversary," p. 3. For a concentrated venting of traditionalist grievances against Neo-Freudian tendencies see Otto Fenichel's review of Horney's *New Ways in Psychoanalysis* in *Psychoanalytic Quarterly*, esp. pp. 114–15.

2. Abram Kardiner, "Psychoanalysis and Psychology," p. 238.

3. "The Relation of Culture to Mental Disorders," p. 173; *The Psychological Frontiers of Society*, p. 415; *The Individual and His Society*, p. 428; "Security, Cultural Restraints, Intrasocial Dependencies, and Hostilities," p. 184.

4. *Sex and Morality*, pp. 58, 61, 82.

5. "Psychodynamics and the Social Sciences," p. 317; *The Individual and His Society*, pp. 18, 90, 109. For the principles of psychodynamics, too lengthy to be quoted here, see *Psychological Frontiers*, pp. 21–22.

6. "Psychodynamics and the Social Sciences," p. 317, emphasis re-

moved; *The Individual and His Society,* p. 120; Kardiner and Ovesey, *The Mark of Oppression,* pp. 77–78. Cf. *Psychological Frontiers,* pp. 23–24, for a more comprehensive statement.

7. *Psychological Frontiers,* p. 23; *The Individual and His Society,* pp. 345, 471, 31, 204–5.

8. *The Individual and His Society,* p. 471; "Adaptational Theory," p. 65; *Sex and Morality,* p. 28; "Cultural Factors in Prophylaxis," p. 234.

9. Kardiner and Ovesey, p. 381; *The Individual and His Society,* p. 25; *Sex and Morality,* p. 253.

10. *The Individual and His Society,* p. 237; Kardiner and Ovesey, p. 8; "Psychodynamics and the Social Sciences," p. 317; *Psychological Frontiers,* pp. 20–21. Ralph Linton's Foreword to *The Individual and His Society,* esp. pp. vi–viii, can be of assistance in understanding the concept of basic personality, as can Linton's "The Concept of National Character," pp. 133–50.

11. *The Individual and His Society,* pp. 132, 238; Kardiner and Ovesey, p. 371, emphasis removed.

12. "The Concept of National Character," pp. 138, 139. See also Devereux, p. 15. In both these writings Linton expresses his doubts about equating basic personality with national character. (The Devereux volume is by Linton, lightly edited by Devereux.)

13. *The Individual and His Society,* pp. 430, 462, 78, 484, 110.

14. *The Individual and His Society,* pp. 132, 471; *Psychological Frontiers,* pp. 234, 39; Kardiner and Ovesey, p. 15.

15. *Psychological Frontiers,* pp. 361, 29, 426; Kardiner and Ovesey, p. 339.

16. For Freud's not-too-clear exposition of the theme see *Totem and Taboo,* pp. 873–77.

17. When Erich Fromm takes Kardiner to task for, in effect, utilizing Freudian concepts in disguise he appears to miss the point of Kardiner's reformulations. See Fromm's "Psychoanalytic Characterology and Its Application to the Understanding of Culture," pp. 3–4.

18. *The Individual and His Society,* p. 404.

19. *Escape from Freedom,* pp. 14–15.

20. "Politik und Psychoanalyse," pp. 440–44; "Über Methode und Aufgabe einer analytischen Sozialpsychologie," pp. 48–49.

21. "Die Entwicklung des Christusdogmas," pp. 312, 209.

22. "Politik und Psychoanalyse," p. 444; Über Methode und Aufgabe," p. 31, emphasis removed. Here as elsewhere when Fromm's German works are quoted, the translation is supplied by the present author.

23. "Politik und Psychoanalyse," pp. 441–42.

24. "Die Entwicklung des Christusdogmas," pp. 308–9; "Politik und Psychoanalyse," p. 444; "Über Methode und Aufgabe," p. 34, emphasis removed.

25. "Politik und Psychoanalyse," p. 445; "Über Methode und Aufgabe," pp. 50, 53; "Die psychoanalytische Charakterologie und ihre Bedeutung für die Sozialpsychologie," pp. 267–68.

26. "Über Methode und Aufgabe," pp. 35 (emphasis removed), 40; "Politik und Psychoanalyse," pp. 445, 446–47.

27. "Über Methode und Aufgabe," pp. 47–48.
28. The allusions are, of course, to the first section of *The Communist Manifesto,* "Bourgeois and Proletarians," and Max Weber, *The Protestant Ethic and the Spirit of Capitalism* (first published in 1904–5), respectively.
29. *Escape from Freedom,* pp. 18, 102. Kardiner expresses the same idea in *Sex and Morality,* pp. 94–95.
30. *Man for Himself,* pp. 78–79; "What Shall We Do with Germany?" p. 10; *Psychoanalysis and Religion,* p. 52; "Psychoanalytic Characterology," p. 12. Fromm affirms the concept of social character to be crucial to his thought (and summarizes it) in "The Humanistic Implications of Instinctivistic 'Radicalism,' " p. 347.
31. *Escape from Freedom,* p. 287; *Man for Himself,* p. 60; "Selfishness and Self-Love," p. 515; "Psychoanalytic Characterology," p. 10, emphasis removed. Cf. "Psychoanalytic Characterology," pp. 6–7, and *The Sane Society,* p. 82 (*inter alia*), for reiterations of the theme.
32. "Selfishness and Self-Love," p. 515. Cf. *Escape from Freedom,* p. 277, for a rephrasing.
33. *The Sane Society,* pp. 78–79; "Individual and Social Origins of Neurosis," p. 381; *Escape from Freedom,* p. 284, emphasis removed. Cf. *Man for Himself,* p. 59, for a restatement.
34. *Escape from Freedom,* pp. 281, 65; *Man for Himself,* p. 60.
35. *Man for Himself,* p. 196; "Sex and Character: The Kinsey Report Viewed from the Standpoint of Psychoanalysis," pp. 309–10.
36. For Fromm's allusions to natural rights theory, see the phraseology in *The Forgotten Language,* p. 222, *Escape from Freedom,* pp. 279, 289, and *The Sane Society,* p. 57.
37. *Psychoanalysis and Religion,* p. 74; *Man for Himself,* p. 23.
38. *The Forgotten Language,* pp. 18, 7, 17.
39. *Ibid.,* pp. 33, 47, 147; cf. *Escape from Freedom,* p. 206n, and *Psychoanalysis and Religion,* p. 97.
40. *Man for Himself,* pp. 34–35. For Freud on the amorality of the instincts, see *supra,* p. 14.
41. This line of criticism is taken in a forceful rebuttal of *The Sane Society* by Patrick Mullahy in "Philosophical Anthropology versus Empirical Science," pp. 399–409. Fromm's substitution of philosophy for empiricism is also taken to task in another review of the same book by Alan Gewirth in *Ethics,* pp. 289–92. On Fromm's qualifications to speak as a psychoanalyst, see the unkind remarks by Karl Menninger in "Loneliness in the Modern World," p. 317.
42. *The Sane Society,* pp. 12, 14; *Escape from Freedom,* pp. 138–39; *Psychoanalysis and Religion,* p. 74. Cf. "The Contribution of the Social Sciences to Mental Hygiene," p. 38, for a pithy summary of this theme. Franz Alexander also objects to adjustment as the standard of normality, preferring, instead, individual self-realization, both in and out of the clinic. See *The Western Mind in Transition,* pp. 203–5.
43. *Man for Himself,* pp. 12, 13; *The Sane Society,* pp. 20, 12–15, 72. For an intriguing essay that likewise turns the tables and treats society—and not its aberrant individuals—as sick, see Frank.

44. In *Man for Himself* Fromm announced (p. 84n) that "productiveness" in that book was an expansion of the "spontaneity" of *Escape from Freedom*. Kariel, "The Normative Pattern of Erich Fromm's Escape from Freedom," sadly misconstrues Fromm by imputing self-preservation as his *summum bonum*, adding a charge of psychological determinism that is quite obviously the opposite of what Fromm has in mind.

45. *Man for Himself*, pp. 218–20; *Escape from Freedom*, pp. 269, 183; "Individual and Social Origins of Neurosis," p. 382.

46. *Escape from Freedom*, pp. 25, 290; *The Art of Loving*, p. 9; *Man for Himself*, pp. 14, 58; "Sex and Character: The Kinsey Report," p. 305.

47. *Escape from Freedom*, pp. 287–88; *The Sane Society*, pp. 71–72, 49ff, 28, 27.

48. Freud, *Three Contributions to the Theory of Sex*, pp. 616–17.

49. *The Sane Society*, pp. 40–41; *Psychoanalysis and Religion*, pp. 81–82.

50. *The Sane Society*, pp. 274, 275; *Man for Himself*, pp. x, 223.

51. *Psychoanalysis: Evolution and Development*, p. 201.

52. Abstract of Horney's contribution to Kelman, "Human Nature Can Change," p. 68. Cf. "What Does the Analyst Do?" pp. 207–8, for a reiteration based on clinical practice.

53. A. D. Harris, "Let Your Soul Alone," p. 288.

54. "Der Kampf in der Kultur," pp. 112–13, 117.

55. "The Flight from Womanhood" and "The Problem of Feminine Masochism." Two other Neo-Freudians echo Horney's criticism of the derivative status (vis-à-vis male psychology) Freud assigned to feminine psychology. See Abram Kardiner, *Sex and Morality*, pp. 48–49, and Erich Fromm, *Sigmund Freud's Mission*, p. 22. Fromm stresses socioeconomic role in explaining female sexuality in "Sex and Character," in Anshen, p. 390.

56. See *New Ways in Psychoanalysis*, p. 41.

57. *The Neurotic Personality of Our Time*, p. 28.

58. *Ibid.*, p. 105. All the conflicts to be mentioned are, of course, unconscious. See *Our Inner Conflicts*, pp. 29–31.

59. See *The Neurotic Personality*, pp. 62, 76, 147ff.

60. "Culture and Neurosis," pp. 230, 221–22; *The Neurotic Personality*, pp. 19, 18.

61. *The Neurotic Personality*, pp. 288, 290, 23. The pervasiveness of competition to all aspects of life in our culture is cited in "Culture and Neurosis," p. 227. Thompson calls attention to Horney's pathfinding view of the need for love as a neurotic operation in *Psychoanalysis*, p. 198.

62. *New Ways*, pp. 73, 194, 175–79. Cf. "What Is a Neurosis?" pp. 426–32, esp. pp. 428, 431, where a clinical definition of neuroses reiterates this view.

63. *Our Inner Conflicts*, pp. 12, 18, 56–57, 95.

64. *Ibid.*, p. 189.

65. *Neurosis and Human Growth*, p. 113, reiterated p. 368.

66. *Ibid.*, pp. 15, 13; abstract of Horney's contribution to Kelman, "Psychoanalysis and Moral Values," p. 64.

67. Horney, "Maturity and the Individual," p. 85; Portnoy, p. 64.

68. *Neurosis and Human Growth*, pp. 18, 22, 367–68, 17. For an en-

lightening discussion of the "idealized self," and, indeed, of Horney's
final formulation in all its aspects, see the Portnoy review, pp. 63–71.

69. *Neurosis and Human Growth*, pp. 173–74, 18, 308. Horney cites
the unhealthy effects of a totalitarian regime on a self-reliant person in
"Can You Take a Stand?" p. 132. Cf. Portnoy, p. 70.

70. "A Note on the Implications of Psychiatry, the Study of Interpersonal Relations, for Investigations in the Social Sciences," p. 859; *The
Interpersonal Theory of Psychiatry*, p. 21. At the latter citation Sullivan
calls the conventional biological view of instincts "completely preposter-
ous."

71. *Conceptions of Modern Psychiatry*, pp. 49, 48; Mullahy, "The
Theories of H. S. Sullivan," p. 35. Blitsten rephrases the concept in
"The Significance of Harry Stack Sullivan's Theories for Social Science,"
p. 67.

72. *Conceptions*, p. 48; *The Psychiatric Interview*, p. 106, emphasis
removed; "The Cultural Revolution to End War," p. 86. Blitsten adds
that growth is irreversible, regression leading to pathology and, ultimately, death (p. 70).

73. *Conceptions*, p. 24, 31. See Mullahy, "The Theories of H. S.
Sullivan," pp. 22–23, for some clarifying remarks.

74. *The Interpersonal Theory of Psychiatry* is almost entirely devoted
to describing the developmental epochs, though a summary can be found
on pp. 290–91. See also *Conceptions*, pp. 14–27.

75. "Mental-Health Potentialities of the World Health Organization," p. 32; "Towards a Psychiatry of Peoples," p. 106 (reprinted in
The Interpersonal Theory, p. 368).

76. "Towards a Psychiatry of Peoples," p. 107 (reprinted in *The
Interpersonal Theory*, pp. 369–70); *Conceptions*, pp. 43, 6.

77. "Towards a Psychiatry of Peoples," pp. 107, 109 (reprinted in
The Interpersonal Theory, pp. 370–71, 373); *Conceptions*, pp. 6–7.

78. "The Cultural Revolution to End War," p. 82; *Conceptions*, pp.
111–12.

79. A provocative article by Kingsley Davis, however, does take up
the matter, with particular reference to the American Negro. See his
"Mental Hygiene and the Class Structure."

80. See Strupp for a discussion of the topic.

81. *The Interpersonal Theory*, p. 267: "I use those words inter-
changeably." For Freud's explicit distinction between the two, see *An
Outline of Psychoanalysis*, p. 26. On one occasion Sullivan referred—
perhaps too hastily—to infantile sexuality, the Oedipal relationship, and
the transference as all being comprehended in the concept of parataxic
distortion: "Notes on Investigation, Therapy, and Education in Psychiatry and Their Relations to Schizophrenia," p. 280.

CHAPTER 5

1. "Tensions Interpersonal and International: A Psychiatrist's View,"
p. 109; *The Psychiatric Interview*, p. 218; *The Interpersonal Theory of
Psychiatry*, p. 113.

2. As in "A Note on the Implications of Psychiatry, the Study of Inter-

personal Relations, for Investigations in the Social Sciences," p. 850, and *The Interpersonal Theory*, pp. 42, 59.

3. *Clinical Studies in Psychiatry*, p. 365; *The Interpersonal Theory*, pp. 55–56.

4. *Clinical Studies*, p. 305; *The Interpersonal Theory*, pp. 8, 151–52, 165–66; *The Psychiatric Interview*, p. 102. Thompson elaborates in *Psychoanalysis*, p. 113, as does Mullahy in "The Theories of H. S. Sullivan," pp. 39–41.

5. *The Interpersonal Theory*, pp. 102, 103.

6. *The Psychiatric Interview*, p. 102; *The Interpersonal Theory*, p. 120; "Tensions Interpersonal and International," p. 95; "The Meaning of Anxiety in Psychiatry and in Life," pp. 9, 10.

7. *The Interpersonal Theory*, pp. 9, 115; "The Meaning of Anxiety," p. 5, reiterated p. 10. The induction takes place by an as yet undefined process called "empathy." See *The Interpersonal Theory*, p. 41.

8. *The Interpersonal Theory*, pp. 160, 95; "The Meaning of Anxiety," p. 4. Cf. Mabel Blake Cohen's Introduction to *The Interpersonal Theory*, p. xv, for additional remarks.

9. "Tensions Interpersonal and International," p. 105; *Conceptions*, p. 87; *The Psychiatric Interview*, p. 18.

10. *Clinical Studies*, p. 134; *The Interpersonal Theory*, p. 168.

11. "The Cultural Revolution to End War," p. 85. Abram Kardiner expresses a similar estimate of the psychiatrist's task in *Sex and Morality*, pp. 265–66.

12. "Tensions Interpersonal and International," pp. 133, 134.

13. *New Ways in Psychoanalysis*, pp. 172–73. We must keep in mind Horney's later amendment to the effect that the conflict between healthy and neurotic trends may also constitute the core of neurosis.

14. *Our Inner Conflicts*, pp. 220, 241.

15. Patrick Mullahy, "Philosophical Anthropology versus Empirical Science," p. 409.

16. *The Neurotic Personality of Our Time*, pp. 284–85, 80; *New Ways*, p. 173.

17. *New Ways*, p. 174; "Culture and Neurosis," p. 228.

18. *Neurosis and Human Growth*, pp. 187, 160, 368, 157; *Our Inner Conflicts*, p. 74.

19. *Neurosis and Human Growth*, p. 21; *Our Inner Conflicts*, p. 111. Portnoy elaborates in his review of the first-named book, pp. 67–68.

20. *New Ways*, pp. 305, 11; *Neurosis and Human Growth*, pp. 334, 341, 348.

21. *Our Inner Conflicts*, pp. 23–24, 26, 134.

22. *The Neurotic Personality*, pp. 288, 289; *New Ways*, p. 173. See p. 177 of the last-named book for Horney's agenda for a relevant sociological analysis of culture.

23. In addition to the previously mentioned "Psychoanalysis Revised," there are direct denials in the second (1951) edition of *Our Age of Unreason* (e.g., p. 192) as well as additions to and deletions from the first (1942) edition that are intended to accomplish the same thing. (Cf. pp. 228–30 of the earlier edition with pp. 191–92 and 200–201 of the

later.) He had previously admitted to being grouped with the newer school. *Our Age of Unreason* (1942), pp. 230, 12.

24. *Fundamentals of Psychoanalysis*, pp. 17–18, 34; cf. "Psychoanalysis and Medicine," esp. pp. 66, 67.

25. *Fundamentals*, pp. 35–36, recapitulated in *Psychoanalysis and Psychotherapy*, p. 17.

26. *Fundamentals*, pp. 41–43; *Our Age of Unreason* (1942), pp. 206–7, 202, 204. For a more extended consideration of play as surplus energy, and its inhibition as a danger to civilization, see *The Western Mind in Transition*, pp. 241–66.

27. *Psychoanalysis and Psychotherapy*, p. 30; *The Western Mind in Transition*, p. 204. With the theory of surplus energy, an emotion like altruism would have a "biological foundation." "The Dynamics of Personality Development," p. 141.

28. *Fundamentals*, pp. 37–38; *Our Age of Unreason* (1942), pp. 209, 200; cf. "Psychoanalytic Aspect of Mental Hygiene and the Environment," pp. 193–94, for a rephrasing.

29. *Fundamentals*, p. 38.

30. At one time Alexander equated lifelong anabolic processes with Eros and lifelong catabolic processes with the death-instinct. *The Psychoanalysis of the Total Personality* (first published in 1927), p. 158.

31. "Adventure and Security in a Changing World," pp. 3, 16–17.

32. "The Psychoanalyst Looks at Contemporary Art," pp. 139–54; the quotation is from p. 148. With a few changes this essay is reprinted in *The Western Mind in Transition*, pp. 165–91.

33. *Fundamentals*, pp. 87–89.

34. "The Sociological and Biological Orientation of Psychoanalysis," pp. 236, 238.

35. See Franz Alexander, *Psychosomatic Medicine*, esp. pp. 12, 36–38, and his "Fundamental Concepts of Psychosomatic Research," esp. pp. 205–6.

36. *Current Biography*, p. 10; cf. "Psychoanalysis and Medicine," p. 64.

37. *The Psychoanalysis of the Total Personality*, p. 15.

38. *Our Age of Unreason* (1942), p. 209.

39. *Fundamentals*, p. 72; *Psychoanalysis and Psychotherapy*, pp. 163–65.

40. *Our Age of Unreason* (1942), p. 288.

41. *Ibid.*, p. 319.

42. *Fundamentals*, p. 204; *Our Age of Unreason* (1942), pp. 10, 302.

43. *Our Age of Unreason* (1942), pp. 133–35. One is tempted to compare this with Harold J. Laski's theory of revolution being due to the discrepancy between economic relations and the economic forces on which they rest. See *The State in Theory and Practice*, esp. pp. 104, 242–43. Or again, there is E. H. Carr's theory that crises in international relations proceed from the challenge of a realistic distribution of power to the hegemony of a utopian but feckless morality (*The Twenty Years' Crisis*). Other theories of why the times are out of joint can doubtless suggest themselves.

44. *Our Age of Unreason* (1942), p. 137; "Educative Influence of Personality Factors in the Environment," p. 46.

45. *Psychoanalysis and Psychotherapy*, p. 19; *Our Age of Unreason* (1942), p. 138.

46. *Our Age of Unreason* (1942), pp. 137, 309.

47. *Ibid.*, pp. 307–8; "Aggressiveness—Individual and Collective," esp. pp. 92–93. Cf. Kardiner, *Sex and Morality*, pp. 180–81, on the connection between insecurity and aggressiveness.

48. *Our Age of Unreason* (1942), p. 167; *Fundamentals*, p. 72. Horney relates anxiety and hostility in a not dissimilar manner in *The Neurotic Personality of Our Time*, pp. 60–78.

49. *The Neurotic Personality*, p. 289.

50. *Ibid.*, pp. 174ff, 173.

51. *Our Age of Unreason* (1942), pp. 289, 290, 277; *Fundamentals*, p. 194.

52. *Our Age of Unreason* (1942), pp. 249–50, 252, 257; "Hostility and Fear in Social Life," pp. 27–29; "The Dynamics of Personality Development," p. 142.

53. *Our Age of Unreason* (1942), 291–92, 317.

54. *Our Age of Unreason* (1951), pp. 262–71. See *The Western Mind in Transition*, pp. 224–25, for a later and equally emphatic condemnation of this aspect of modern life.

55. *Our Age of Unreason* (1951), pp. 228, 226–27. Thus, p. 313 of the revised edition deletes "planning" from among the economic requirements specified on p. 262 of the original edition, while an unfavorable reference to economic freedom and a criticism of economic competition (1942, p. 340) also go by the board nine years later (1951, p. 316).

56. *Our Age of Unreason* (1951), p. 204. This passage was not in the original text.

57. *The Western Mind in Transition*, pp. 44, 71, 237–38, 234–35, 276.

58. *Sex and Morality*, pp. 108, 48.

59. *The Psychological Frontiers of Society*, pp. 256, 414–15.

60. *Ibid.*, pp. 340, 361, 347; *Sex and Morality*, p. 199.

61. *Psychological Frontiers*, pp. 347, 373–75, 407–8.

62. *Ibid.*, pp. 376, 430–31, 446. A lamentably short appreciation of Kardiner's work, Delmore Schwartz, "The Sick City and the Family Romance," can be of some assistance in understanding the foregoing. Schwartz observes facetiously (p. 47) that "In America Mother's Day is the national celebration of the Oedipus Complex."

63. *Psychological Frontiers*, p. 449; "Security, Cultural Restraints, Intrasocial Dependencies, and Hostilities," p. 184.

64. Kardiner and Ovesey, *The Mark of Oppression*, p. 15; *Psychological Frontiers*, pp. 423, 417, 424; "Cultural Factors in Prophylaxis," pp. 233, 234. Cf. Kardiner, "New Attitudes Toward Sex," p. 134, on the importance of the family in cultivating the social emotions.

65. *Psychological Frontiers*, pp. 442, 407, 406.

66. *Ibid.*, pp. 442, 406; *Sex and Morality*, pp. 215, 116.

67. *Psychological Frontiers*, pp. 409, 406, 410. Cf. *Sex and Morality*, pp. 37–38. Erich Fromm treats this far-reaching revolution similarly in *Escape from Freedom*, pp. 40–63.

68. *Psychological Frontiers*, pp. 376, 342, 412; *Sex and Morality*, pp. 231, 254–55, 168. In Schwartz's words, "The chief ideal of Western culture is the possession of one million dollars" (p. 47).

69. *Psychological Frontiers,* pp. 255, 425; *The Individual and His Society,* p. 237.
70. *Sex and Morality,* pp. 20, 159, 61. Cf. Erich Fromm, "Sex and Character: The Kinsey Report," pp. 305–6, for another Neo-Freudian critique of sex morality.
71. *The Individual and His Society,* p. 340; *Sex and Morality,* p. 60.
72. *Sex and Morality,* pp. 60, 31–33, 237–38. Cf. Sullivan, *The Interpersonal Theory,* p. 266, on the conflict between sexuality and security.
73. *Psychological Frontiers,* p. 412; *Sex and Morality,* pp. 228–29, 259; "Cultural Factors in Prophylaxis," p. 236.

CHAPTER 6

1. Freud, *A General Introduction to Psycho-Analysis,* pp. 263, 264, 319. Horney, *Our Inner Conflicts,* pp. 11, 13; *New Ways in Psychoanalysis,* pp. 9, 152–53, 279; "What Is a Neurosis?" p. 427.
2. "Neurosis and the Whole Personality," esp. p. 348.
3. *The Psychoanalysis of the Total Personality,* pp. 16, 17, 105.
4. *Ibid.,* p. 39. A quarter of a century later Alexander still saw the basic purpose of psychotherapy to be to increase the patient's self-confidence by fortifying his ego, all aspects of the process to be managed with this in mind. See "Analysis of the Therapeutic Factors in Psychoanalytic Treatment."
5. *The Psychoanalysis of the Total Personality,* pp. 50ff.
6. *Fundamentals of Psychoanalysis,* p. 83.
7. *The Psychoanalysis of the Total Personality,* pp. 95–96, 64.
8. Jones, III, 438; Freud, *Civilization and Its Discontents,* p. 142.
9. Alexander and Staub, *The Criminal, the Judge, and the Public,* pp. 81–82, 8, 9, 40. These and other major themes of the book are reviewed in Alexander's "Mental Hygiene and Criminology."
10. Alexander and Staub, p. 45. For further differentiation between the two types see *ibid.,* p. 81.
11. "The Neurotic Character," esp. p. 308; Alexander and Staub, pp. 42, 106, 210.
12. Alexander and Staub, pp. 38–39, 54; *Fundamentals,* pp. 118, 239; "Neurosis and the Whole Personality," p. 348. Freud expressed a similar view on the sense of guilt in "Some Character-Types Met With in Psycho-Analytic Work" (first published in 1915–16), p. 342; cf. *New Introductory Lectures on Psycho-Analysis,* pp. 149–50, for further remarks.
13. Alexander and Staub, pp. 54, 107, 231. On this point see also Alexander and Healy, *Roots of Crime,* p. 293.
14. Alexander and Staub, pp. 214–15, 222, 226. Gregory Zilboorg, who until his recent death was one of the leading exponents of a psychoanalytic understanding of social pathology, names as one of the major contributions of psychoanalysis to the subject the perception of the part played by the revenge motive in criminology and penology and the influence of human emotions permeating the supposed objectivity of criminal processes. "The Contribution of Psycho-Analysis to Forensic Psychiatry," pp. 319, 322. A like view is given in Roche, "Criminal Responsibility."
15. Alexander and Staub, pp. 16, 226. Zilboorg has gone so far as to say that "the greatest contribution of psycho-analysis to criminal

thought" was to center upon the actor, and not, as the machinery of justice does, upon the act. "The Contribution of Psycho-Analysis," p. 322.

16. Alexander and Staub, pp. xii, 23, 69, 68. For indications of the present ferment on the controversial M'Naghten rule, stirred partly by the uncertain role of the psychiatrist in clarifying the vague concept of criminal insanity, see Soboloff, pp. 783–86, 877–79; Hall (for a more traditional view); and the symposium on "Insanity and the Criminal Law." The contribution of Philip Q. Roche to the last-named, "Criminality and Mental Illness—Two Facets of the Same Coin," pp. 320–24, agrees precisely with the analysis of Alexander and Staub.

17. Alexander and Staub, pp. 65, 62 (emphasis removed). Cf. Harold D. Lasswell, "Impact of Psychoanalytic Thinking on the Social Sciences," p. 105, for an identical proposal.

18. Alexander and Staub, p. 62. Cf. Roche, "Criminal Responsibility," pp. 113–14, where criminal responsibility is separated from guilt-finding altogether.

19. Alexander and Staub, pp. 63, 210, 106–7.

20. *Ibid.*, pp. 233, 234, 237–38. The views of a jurist who would employ psychiatry as a remedial measure, but not as a preventive one, are cogently expressed in Bok, pp. 186–228.

21. Alexander and Healy, *Roots of Crime,* pp. 303–4, 296–97.

22. "Contribution to Psychological Factors in Anti-Social Behavior." This article repeats many themes (some verbatim) of the earlier and later studies of aberrant behavior and is useful for noting the transition in Alexander's approach.

23. Alexander and Healy, pp. 288, 276, 277. It may or may not be significant that nearly all the delinquents studied were petty larcenists.

24. *Ibid.*, pp. 278–79.

25. *Ibid.,* pp. 288, 291.

26. *Ibid.,* pp. 4–5.

27. *Ibid.,* pp. 282–83, 284.

28. *Our Age of Unreason* (1942), pp. 302–3, 305. The Freudian interpretation would be that capital punishment is a symbolic reenactment of the primal crime of slaying the great man, with all that it entails for preserving moral standards and social stability.

29. *Ibid.,* p. 306.

30. *Roots of Crime,* p. 4. See also "Contribution to Psychological Factors," p. 143. For a study of the causes and patterns of juvenile delinquency that gives the lie to conventional explanations for its incidence—low economic status, absence of recreational facilities, substandard housing—see *Juvenile Delinquency* (Senate Report), esp. pp. 100–104, 129, 134–37, 153, 155.

31. *Roots of Crime,* pp. 277–78, 279, 276.

32. As a means of action Alexander at one time suggested the diffusion of knowledge and extension of research concerning the factors in childhood which create the fear and hostility that so formidably impede social solidarity. However difficult of application, it was better than awaiting the miracle of the advent of a utopia. See "Psychoanalytic Aspect of Mental Hygiene and the Environment," p. 197.

33. Kardiner and Ovesey, *The Mark of Oppression,* pp. 302, xvi, v.

34. *Ibid.*, pp. 11, 36–37, 302, 364.

35. *Ibid.*, pp. 20, 364, 81, 61, 317.

36. *Ibid.*, pp. 32, 385, 377, 302–3.

37. *Ibid.*, pp. 296–97, 81. The first citation is to Ovesey's contribution to the book; all others in the present volume are to Kardiner's.

38. *Ibid.*, pp. xiv, 386, xv, xiv.

39. *Ibid.*, p. 37.

40. *Ibid.*, pp. 381, 54, 65, 382; Kardiner, *Sex and Morality*, p. 213.

41. Kardiner and Ovesey, p. 366.

42. *Ibid.*, pp. 60, 346–49, 69–70.

43. *Ibid.*, pp. 81, 316, 337–38, 387.

44. *Man for Himself*, p. 67, 81.

45. See *Escape from Freedom*, pp. 63–104, esp. pp. 83, 91, 93.

46. *The Sane Society*, p. 110. Fromm enlarges, with some repetition, in *The Art of Loving*, p. 85.

47. *Man for Himself*, p. 57; *Psychoanalysis and Religion*, p. 63.

48. *The Sane Society*, pp. 111n, 141n. Incidentally, there are four types of "unproductive" orientations depicted in *Man for Himself*, the receptive, exploitative, hoarding, and marketing, of which only the last receives extensive treatment.

49. *Man for Himself*, pp. 61, 112, 113.

50. *Ibid.*, p. 58; *The Sane Society*, p. vii. Cf. Thompson, pp. 72ff, for some doubts about the completeness of the transformation. Another critic of *Man for Himself* also is not so sure that Fromm has discarded the libido theory entirely. See Bernard Zuger in *American Journal of Psychoanalysis*. Occasional references to the canalization of energy in molding social character (e.g., *The Sane Society*, p. 79, *Escape from Freedom*, p. 284, *Man for Himself*, p. 59), wherein "energy" could be taken as a euphemism for "libido," strengthen these doubts.

51. *Escape from Freedom*, pp. 185–86, 206, 253, 200; *The Sane Society*, p. 152 . Cf. "Faith as a Character Trait," p. 319, for a recapitulation, and see Franz Alexander, *The Western Mind in Transition*, p. 236, for a like reaction to the pressure of public opinion.

52. *Man for Himself*, pp. 87, 73, 74; *The Art of Loving*, p. 15; *Escape from Freedom*, p. 264.

53. *The Sane Society*, pp. 158, 155, 161; *Escape from Freedom*, pp. 254–55; "The Contribution of the Social Sciences to Mental Hygiene," p. 41.

54. *The Sane Society*, p. 146; *Escape from Freedom*, pp. 118–19; *Man for Himself*, pp. 77–78; *Psychoanalysis and Religion*, p. 75.

55. *Man for Himself*, pp. 69, 68, 136. On the trend toward enhancing one's sexual desirability as a manifestation of anxiety over sexual insecurity, see Kardiner, *Sex and Morality*, p. 34.

56. *Man for Himself*, pp. 73, 112, 76; *The Art of Loving*, pp. 4, 132. On the paucity of love, see the latter work, p. 83, for a more expansive damnation.

57. *The Sane Society*, pp. 186–87, 185, 340, 341. The theme is summarized in "The Contribution of the Social Sciences to Mental Hygiene," p. 40.

58. *Sex and Morality*, p. 229.

59. *The Sane Society*, pp. 110, 124, emphasis removed. "He has be-

come, one might say, estranged from himself" (p. 120). In this respect, Fromm's concept of alienation appears to be identical with Horney's.

60. *Ibid.,* pp. 120, 155, 196–97; *Psychoanalysis and Religion,* p. 54.

61. *The Sane Society,* p. 124; *Psychoanalysis and Religion,* pp. 32–33; "The Contribution of the Social Sciences to Mental Hygiene," p. 39. One commentator has suggested a similarity to Durkheim's concept of *anomie;* see Louis Wirth in Hadley, ed., "Escape from Freedom: a Synoptic Series of Reviews," p. 130.

62. *Escape from Freedom,* pp. 244–47. See "The Contribution of the Social Sciences to Mental Hygiene," pp. 39–40, for Fromm's condemnation of time-killing entertainment; cf. Kardiner, *Sex and Morality,* p. 249, for an identical view of mass culture, and Alexander, *The Western Mind in Transition,* pp. 270–71, 239, for a prospect of leisure as a problem of mental health.

63. *The Sane Society,* pp. 134–37; *Sigmund Freud's Mission,* p. 113. In "The Humanistic Implications of Instinctivistic 'Radicalism,' " p. 346, Fromm castigates unlimited sexual gratification for its use as a binding force of modern capitalism.

CHAPTER 7

1. Inevitably, "Professor Lasswell appears almost the new Machiavelli for his appallingly penetrating analysis of the bad features of human nature. He differs, however, radically from the Florentine in offering no ideal to be realized." Jászi's review of *World Politics and Personal Insecurity,* in *International Journal of Ethics,* p. 448 (copyright 1935 by the University of Chicago).

2. See Lasswell, "Psychology and Political Science in the U.S.A."

3. In separating Lasswell's career into these periods, I am aware of taking issue with so keen a student of political thought as David Easton. (See his "Harold Lasswell: Policy Scientist for a Democratic Society.") Easton divides Lasswell's writings into an early elitist (amoral) and a later decisionalist (moralist) phase, relating the change in his attitude to a change in his frame of reference, from a Paretan influence to the decision-making approach, coinciding with the outbreak of World War II. I think, however, that Easton is in error in finding a Paretan source for ideas that coincided with Freudian psychology; if anything, it would be the other way around. And while Easton could not have foreseen *Democratic Character* (1951), he could have avoided excessive reliance on the comparatively slight *Democracy Through Public Opinion.* These matters may become clearer as the discussion proceeds.

4. *Psychopathology and Politics,* pp. 31, 37, 191.

5. *Ibid.,* pp. 28, 8–10, 173 (copyright 1931 by the University of Chicago).

6. *Ibid.,* p. 174. Cf. *World Politics and Personal Insecurity,* pp. 34–35, for a restatement.

7. *Psychopathology and Politics,* pp. 74–75, 262, 76; *Politics: Who Gets What, When, How,* pp. 182–83.

8. *Psychopathology and Politics,* pp. 75, 173; *Politics: Who Gets What, When, How,* pp. 16, 17. Cf. *Power and Personality,* pp. 38–40, for

the political type in terms of the development of motives, and pp. 52–53 and 156–57 for the operation of the family in activating the low estimates of the self that yield the political personality. Lasswell and Blumenstock, *World Revolutionary Propaganda*, p. 296, summarizes the matter compendiously.

9. *Psychopathology and Politics*, pp. 262, 102–3, 255.

10. *Ibid.*, p. 125; *Power and Personality*, pp. 88–89.

11. *Psychopathology and Politics*, p. 263; *Power and Personality*, pp. 59, 90.

12. *Politics: Who Gets What, When, How*, pp. 203, 205.

13. "What Psychiatrists and Social Scientists Can Learn from One Another," p. 37. They are also found in combinations. *Psychopathology and Politics*, p. 262.

14. *Politics: Who Gets What, When, How*, p. 204.

15. *Psychopathology and Politics*, p. 184; *Politics: Who Gets What, When, How*, p. 3.

16. *Politics: Who Gets What, When, How*, p. 24.

17. *World Politics and Personal Insecurity*, p. 3.

18. *Politics: Who Gets What, When, How*, pp. 3, 6; *Psychopathology and Politics*, p. 201. A decade after enunciating the triad of safety, income, and deference as typical values, Lasswell confessed his indebtedness to Hobbes for them ("The Data of Psychoanalysis and the Social Sciences," p. 26). Lasswell made the values almost meaningless when he defined them to include "life, bodily soundness, goods, reputation, intimacy, freedom of movement" ("A Provisional Classification of Symbol Data," p. 203). By that date, however, his psychoanalytic period was nearly over and a revision of values for the second period may have been in progress.

19. *Politics: Who Gets What, When, How*, p. 26; *World Politics and Personal Insecurity*, p. 207.

20. *World Politics and Personal Insecurity*, p. 143; "The Strategy of Revolutionary and War Propaganda," p. 193; *Politics: Who Gets What, When, How*, p. 29.

21. *Psychopathology and Politics*, pp. 256, 192; *World Politics and Personal Insecurity*, pp. 35–36.

22. *Psychopathology and Politics*, p. 184; "The Study and Practice of Propaganda," p. 13 (copyright 1935 by the University of Minnesota).

23. *Psychopathology and Politics*, pp. 185–86; *World Politics and Personal Insecurity*, p. 39.

24. "The Person: Subject and Object of Propaganda," p. 187; *World Politics and Personal Insecurity*, p. 44.

25. *World Politics and Personal Insecurity*, p. 45; *Psychopathology and Politics*, p. 189.

26. "The Theory of Political Propaganda," p. 627; "Propaganda," in *Encyclopedia of the Social Sciences*, p. 521 (used by permission of the Macmillan Company); *Propaganda Technique in the World War*, p. 9; "The Person: Subject and Object of Propaganda," p. 189.

27. Some of the articles authored by Lasswell for the *Encyclopedia of the Social Sciences* are "Agitation," "Bribery," "Compromise," "Faction," "Feuds," "Fraternizing," "Morale."

28. *World Politics and Personal Insecurity,* p. 62; "The Triple-Appeal Principle: A Contribution of Psychoanalysis to Political and Social Science," pp. 523–24, 532, 528.

29. *World Politics and Personal Insecurity,* p. 64; "The Triple-Appeal Principle," pp. 532–33.

30. "Types of Political Personalities," p. 164; *Psychopathology and Politics,* pp. 184–85.

31. *World Politics and Personal Insecurity,* pp. 65–66. The technical phrasing is "Prolonged ego and superego indulgence produces redefinitions in directions gratifying to the id; prolonged ego and id indulgence produces redefinitions in directions relative to the superego." "The Triple-Appeal Principle," p. 538 (copyright 1932 by the University of Chicago).

32. *Politics: Who Gets What, When, How,* pp. 39, 111, 15. In view of Lasswell's psychoanalytic orientation, the scheme must be said to coincide with, rather than receive its derivation from, Machiavelli's theory of lions and foxes, and Pareto's of combinations and group-persistences.

33. *Psychopathology and Politics,* pp. 183, 179; "Chauvinism."

34. *World Politics and Personal Insecurity,* p. 8; *Psychopathology and Politics,* p. 189; "The Strategy of Revolutionary and War Propaganda," p. 199; Lasswell and Blumenstock, p. 123.

35. "The Strategy of Revolutionary and War Propaganda," pp. 199–200; *World Politics and Personal Insecurity,* pp. 98–99, 194; *Psychopathology and Politics,* pp. 179–80, 193.

36. *Psychopathology and Politics,* pp. 184–85. Plato put it another way: "All goes wrong when, starved for lack of anything good in their own lives, men turn to public affairs hoping to snatch from thence the happiness they hunger for." *Rep.* 521B (*The Republic of Plato,* tr. Cornford, p. 235).

37. *Psychopathology and Politics,* pp. 193–94.

38. *Ibid.,* p. 194; "The Theory of Political Propaganda," p. 631.

39. *Power and Personality,* pp. 21–22, 10, 16.

40. *Ibid.,* pp. 52–53, 39, 40, 160.

41. *Ibid.,* pp. 38, 152.

42. *Ibid.,* pp. 167, 165–66; Percy Winner's review in *Psychoanalytic Quarterly,* p. 242.

43. Lasswell and Blumenstock, p. 340. The critic was Max Ascoli.

44. *Politics: Who Gets What, When, How,* p. 153; *World Politics and Personal Insecurity,* p. 237.

45. "The Psychology of Hitlerism as a Response of the Lower Middle Classes to Continuing Insecurity" (first published in 1933), p. 236. In *Our Age of Unreason* (1942), p. 125, Franz Alexander also ascribes the rise of German totalitarianism to the insecurity of that country's middle class during the Weimar Republic. Erich Fromm returns a similar verdict in *Escape from Freedom,* pp. 211ff. The theory has been taken to task by some critics. See Stamps, *Why Democracies Fail,* pp. 77–83, for a good summary. The controversy seems to turn on whether support of Nazism can be measured only by membership in the party or electoral returns for it. The main theme of *World Politics and Personal Insecurity* was

the improbability of creating a unifying formula to receive the bourgeois insecurities engendered by the symbols of Marxism, with special reference to Germany (see pp. 257–65).

46. "The Moral Vocation of the Middle-Income Skill Group," pp. 127–37. In places this rather unusual article has a hortatory ring not unlike the *Communist Manifesto,* appealing, however, to a decidedly different audience.

47. "Psychology Looks at Morals and Politics," pp. 329, 332, 333, 330 (copyright 1941 by the University of Chicago). The theme survived in an article written fourteen years later: "In a democratic system of public order the overriding purpose is to maintain a decision process in which the opinions and convictions of the community are taken into account." "Current Studies of the Decision Process," p. 395.

48. *Power and Personality,* pp. 110, 146, 152, 109.

49. Lasswell, Leites, *et al.,* p. 8; "The Developing Science of Democracy," p. 31.

50. "The Data of Psychoanalysis and the Social Sciences," p. 26. For attributes of each of the values see *The World Revolution of Our Time,* pp. 41–44, and for their application to the analytic interview see "Impact of Psychoanalytic Thinking on the Social Sciences," pp. 108–11. An essay of 1943 reveals Lasswell's value system in a state of flux: Lasswell and McDougal, esp. pp. 36, 67–68, 95.

51. *Democratic Character,* pp. 482 (emphasis removed), 481, 503. The book contains a sprinkling of references to Harry Stack Sullivan. *Power and Personality,* p. 39, vaguely foreshadows this new formulation, while in "Impact of Psychoanalytic Thinking," pp. 90–91, Lasswell acknowledges the influences of infancy to be open to modification by adult experiences.

52. *Democratic Character,* pp. 481, 495, 497–98, 502. On p. 498 Lasswell repudiates *homo politicus* defined as the seeker after power as "out of harmony with our basic concept of human dignity."

53. *Ibid.,* p. 513. For an earlier example of how the deprivation-indulgence method would work see the Instant Reply Plan outlined in *Democracy Through Public Opinion,* pp. 96–116, where antidemocratic propaganda is quickly identified and systematically rebutted.

54. *Power and Personality,* p. 120; cf. *ibid.,* pp. 118ff and 146, for a delineation of a science of social psychiatry as the medical counterpart to the policy sciences.

55. See, e.g., Lasswell and Kaplan, pp. xvii, 74–77, 82, 240.

56. *Ibid.,* pp. 202, 227, 226; "The Elite Concept," pp. 7, 11. Further remarks on the policy sciences may be found in *The World Revolution of Our Time* and "The Political Science of Science."

57. "The highest social ideal of European tradition" ("The Normative Impact of the Behavioral Sciences," p. 3; copyright 1957 by the University of Chicago). "The overriding goal of policy in our body politic" ("The Political Science of Science," p. 961). "No amount of empirical research can be expected to alter our basic preference for human dignity, rather than the indignity of man" (*The World Revolution of Our Time,* p. 12).

58. *The World Revolution of Our Time,* p. 22. See Easton, p. 468, for a sympathetic explanation of Lasswell's unwonted normative bent.

59. See *Power and Society,* pp. 49–50.

CHAPTER 8

1. *Politics: Who Gets What, When, How,* p. 191; "The Study and Practice of Propaganda," p. 12; *Power and Personality,* p. 198. Some of the cases summarized in *Psychopathology and Politics,* he admits, "were described on the basis of many hours of interviewing by a procedure of free association closely resembling orthodox psychoanalysis" ("The Developing Science of Democracy," p. 38; copyright 1942 by the University of Chicago). Cf. pp. 13 and 204–20 of *Psychopathology and Politics* for further details, and see the similar remarks on pp. 273–74 of the "Afterthoughts" appended to the 1960 reprint of the book.

2. Letter to the author dated June 2, 1959, publicly confirmed in "Afterthoughts," pp. 271–72. The passivity of the interviewer using such a technique can be discerned from his "Veränderungen an einer Versuchperson während einer kurzen Folge von psychoanalytischen Interviews," esp. p. 377. It is a far cry from participant observation.

3. *The Life and Work of Sigmund Freud,* III, 288–89.

4. Mandelstam, p. 172n, citing a personal communication from Lasswell; see also "Afterthoughts," p. 272.

5. *Psychopathology and Politics,* p. 197.

6. *World Politics and Personal Insecurity,* p. 26; *Psychopathology and Politics,* pp. 196–97.

7. *Psychopathology and Politics,* p. 198; *Power and Personality,* p. 129.

8. *Psychopathology and Politics,* pp. 203, 194; *Power and Personality,* p. 174.

9. *Psychopathology and Politics,* p. 198; *World Politics and Personal Insecurity,* p. 26. In *Power and Personality,* pp. 168–71, Lasswell proposes a world survey of personality formation to determine which environmental and predispositional factors foster or inhibit the making of a democratic character structure.

10. See *Power and Personality,* p. 196. In *ibid.,* p. 187, Lasswell suggests the creation of a board to evaluate the democratic trends in the personalities of prominent political figures, based upon data disclosed in investigations voluntarily submitted to.

11. *Psychopathology and Politics,* p. 197.

12. *World Politics and Personal Insecurity,* pp. 8, 46, 75; *Power and Personality,* p. 163; *Politics: Who Gets What, When, How,* p. 206.

13. *World Politics Faces Economics,* p. 8 (used by permission of the McGraw-Hill Book Company, Inc.; copyright 1945).

14. *Ibid.,* p. 29.

15. *Ibid.,* pp. 44, 36–37.

16. *Ibid.,* pp. 67, 89–90. For a moving report on insecurity and neurosis in underdeveloped countries that confirms Lasswell's warning, see Esfandiary.

17. *National Security and Individual Freedom,* pp. 180–82 (used by permission of the McGraw-Hill Book Company, Inc.; copyright 1950). For aspects of the garrison-police state see *ibid.,* pp. 23–49, and "Propaganda and Mass Insecurity."

18. *Power and Personality,* p. 148.

19. See, e.g., "The World Revolutionary Situation" and "Political Power and Democratic Values." It was adumbrated earlier in *World*

Politics and Personal Insecurity, pp. 4–5, and *Power and Personality,* pp. 207–8.

20. Mandelstam, p. 201n, citing a personal communication from Lasswell.

21. *Escape from Freedom,* p. 238; *Man for Himself,* p. 140; *The Sane Society,* pp. 333, 361.

22. *Escape from Freedom,* pp. 273, 272; *The Sane Society,* pp. 361, 277, 272, 271. One observer likened Fromm's socialism to Owen's and Fourier's, rather than to the present British type of economic reform only. See Asa Briggs' review in *New Statesman and Nation.*

23. *Man for Himself,* p. 229. See Arnold W. Green, "Sociological Analysis of Horney and Fromm," p. 537, for an appreciation. Plato's construction of an ideal *polis* on the basis of the ideal, or just, individual, in the *Republic,* was a not dissimilar precedent for Fromm's attempt.

24. *Psychoanalysis and Religion,* pp. 26, 35, 49–51.

25. *The Sane Society,* p. 123; *Psychoanalysis and Religion,* pp. 35, 29, 27.

26. *The Sane Society,* p. 58; *Psychoanalysis and Religion,* pp. 31–32.

27. *Sigmund Freud's Mission,* pp. 105–6, 108, 111–12.

28. *Ibid.,* pp. 110, 3–4.

29. *The Sane Society,* p. 175; *Psychoanalysis and Religion,* pp. 26, 21 (emphasis removed). Thompson elaborates in *Psychoanalysis,* p. 145.

30. *The Sane Society,* p. 352; *The Art of Loving,* pp. 72, 125; "Faith as a Character Trait," p. 315. Cf. *Man for Himself,* p. 208, for a restatement.

31. *The Sane Society,* pp. 351, 352. Cf. *Psychoanalysis and Religion,* p. 37. A strong consciousness of the Judaic-Christian religious tradition is also evident in his works. It may not be beside the point that his dissertation was entitled "Soziologie des jüdischen Gesetzes" ("Die Entwicklung des Christusdogmas," p. 371n).

32. *The Sane Society,* pp. 169–70; *Man for Himself,* pp. 102–4.

33. *Psychoanalysis and Religion,* pp. 7, 6, 87.

34. His formula for concentration as a method of discovering oneself is rather distant from a psychoanalytic view of the matter. "It would be helpful to practice a few very simple exercises, as, for instance, to sit in a relaxed position (neither slouching, nor rigid), to close one's eyes, and to try to see a white screen in front of one's eyes, and to try to remove all interfering pictures and thoughts, then to try to follow one's breathing; not to think about it, nor force it, but to follow it—and in doing so to sense it; furthermore to try to have a sense of 'I'; I = myself, as the center of my powers, as the creator of my world. One should, at least, do such a concentration exercise every morning for twenty minutes (and if possible longer) and every evening before going to bed." *The Art of Loving,* pp. 112–13. Fromm derived the technique from Augusta Slesinger ("Remarks on the Problem of Free Association," pp. 4–5).

35. *Sigmund Freud's Mission,* pp. 114, 112, 2, 7; cf. *Psychoanalysis and Religion,* pp. 6–7.

36. *Escape from Freedom,* pp. 36, 19; *The Sane Society,* p. 30; *Man for Himself,* p. 14. At one point Fromm makes reference to a "herd instinct" to account for group solidarity (*Psychoanalysis and Religion,*

p. 58), an obvious throwback to Freudian group psychology that he did not pursue further.

37. *Man for Himself,* pp. 45 (emphasis removed), 87, 84; *Escape from Freedom,* pp. 269–70.

38. *Man for Himself,* p. 84; *Escape from Freedom,* p. 258. Aristotle, *Nic. Eth.* 1098a and 1169a, respectively.

39. *Man for Himself,* p. 85, emphasis removed. Aristotle too excludes those whose capacity for achieving human excellence, or virtue, has not been impaired, on the ground, however, that virtue can be learned by practice and not only expressed spontaneously from within (*Nic. Eth.* 1099b).

40. *Man for Himself,* pp. 26–27.

41. *Escape from Freedom,* pp. 258, 262. *Nic. Eth.* 1174b, 1100b.

42. *Man for Himself,* pp. 131, 130; *Escape from Freedom,* p. 115. "The love for my own self is inseparably connected with the love for any other self." *Man for Himself,* p. 129. Fromm follows Aristotle on self-love too; see *Nic. Eth.* 1169a.

43. *Man for Himself,* pp. 126–28, 139.

44. "Selfishness and Self-Love," p. 523.

45. *The Art of Loving,* p. 31.

46. *Ibid.,* p. 18; *Psychoanalysis and Religion,* pp. 86–87. For Freud's somewhat different opinion of the love-thy-neighbor maxim see *Civilization and Its Discontents,* pp. 81ff.

47. *Escape from Freedom,* pp. 261, 114; *Man for Himself,* p. 101; *The Sane Society,* p. 31. Harry Stack Sullivan's more modest definition has love as a condition wherein another person's security or satisfaction is as significant as one's own. See *Conceptions of Modern Psychiatry,* p. 20.

48. *The Art of Loving,* p. 51; *The Sane Society,* pp. 36–37, 68; *Escape from Freedom,* p. 261. Kingsley Davis criticizes this idea in "Mental Hygiene and the Class Structure," p. 376n.

49. *The Sane Society,* pp. 299, 290–93, 181.

50. *Ibid.,* pp. 283–84, 321–22, 323 (emphasis removed), 326, 334–35.

51. *Ibid.,* pp. 306–21; the quotation is from p. 319. As some examples, the Spiritual Section comprehends the Catholic team, the Humanist team, the Materialist team, and the Protestant team; the Artistic Section is composed of the Theater team, the Singing team, the Interior Decorating team, and the Photo team; the Family Section includes the Child Care team, the Education team, and the Social Life team (p. 314).

52. *Ibid.,* pp. 350, 341.

53. *Ibid.,* p. 276. On collective art and rituals see *ibid.,* pp. 347–50.

54. *Ibid.,* p. 282.

55. Aristotle, *Pols.* 1325b, 1332b. One may also ponder the wisdom of Socrates' bitter renunciation of interpersonal beatitude. "The true champion of justice, if he intends to survive even for a short time, must necessarily confine himself to private life and leave politics alone." Plato, *Apol.* 31E–32A (*The Apology,* tr. Tredennick, p. 38).

56. See *Pols.* 1280b–1281a. One is reminded of Burke's contempt for construing society as a mere partnership in trade.

57. *The Forgotten Language*, pp. 207–8. In matriarchy, "what matters . . . is man himself, *the natural law,* and love" (*ibid.,* p. 213; emphasis supplied). Fromm suggests that in historical times the Middle Ages were matriarchal, while the Reformation ushered in patriarchal society. See *Escape from Freedom*, pp. 62, 73, 101–2, 103. The civilizations of antiquity are unfortunately not accounted for by this theory.

58. Alexander and Healy, *Roots of Crime,* p. 280; Kardiner, *The Individual and His Society,* p. 472.

59. Aside from *The Forgotten Language,* Fromm's writings give small notice to the phenomenon.

60. Abstract of Horney's contribution to Harold Kelman, ed., "Psychoanalysis and Moral Values," p. 65. Horney's difference from Fromm emerges most clearly in *Neurosis and Human Growth,* pp. 366–69.

61. *Self-Analysis,* p. 10.

CHAPTER 9

1. The Biographical Sketches, on pp. 233–37, for instance, reveal the Neo-Freudians to have founded or guided five institutes for the training of psychoanalysts.

2. A discussion of the scientific standing of psychoanalysis can be found in Pumpian-Mindlin, pp. 125–58. Since that has primary reference to Freudian theory and method, see also Alexander, "Psychoanalysis and Medicine," esp. pp. 74–83, which is more to the point of the Neo-Freudian approach.

3. *A General Introduction to Psycho-Analysis,* p. 359.

4. *Escape from Freedom,* p. 258, emphasis removed.

5. Plato, *Rep.* 423D–425E, 544D–E; Aristotle, *Pols.* 1310a, 1337a. Plato's teaching on this point emerges even more clearly in Books I, II, and VII of the *Laws.*

6. Intermittent revivals can be found in such works as Montesquieu, *The Spirit of the Laws,* XIV 2, XVIII 27, XXI 3, XXIV 5; Mill, *A System of Logic Ratiocinative and Inductive,* VI, v (esp. paragraphs 5–6); and Marx, *The Communist Manifesto,* I. Montesquieu's effort would today be regarded as a rather crude attempt to correlate soil and climate with character, lacking the binding link of a systematic psychology. Mill's proposal for a science of ethology, the study of the formation of character by circumstances subject to empirical laws, appears to have been unfulfilled in his own work. On Marx, see the discussion in Chap. 2, *supra.*

7. For a review of American experience since the 1920's see Lasswell, "Impact of Psychoanalytic Thinking," esp. pp. 84–90. See also Alexander, *The Western Mind in Transition,* pp. 101–9, for another account of the tribulations involved in introducing psychoanalysis to American social and scientific thought.

8. "Psychology and Political Science in the U.S.A.," p. 536. Lasswell's survey of the endeavors of his colleagues to utilize psychology here (*passim*) is unnecessarily generous.

9. The posthumous publication of Harry Stack Sullivan's writings, which took place during the 1950's, largely comprises editions of the lecture and discussion notes he used in the preceding decade.

10. *Sex and Morality,* pp. 195–98.

BIBLIOGRAPHY

PRIMARY SOURCES

This listing is not intended to be exhaustive;
only works cited in the text are included.

Alexander, Franz. "Adventure and Security in a Changing World,"
in Iago Galdston, ed., *Medicine in a Changing Society*. New York:
International Universities Press, Inc., 1956, pp. 3–19.

———. "Aggressiveness—Individual and Collective," in *The March of
Medicine*. New York: Columbia University Press, 1943, pp. 83–99.

———. "Analysis of the Therapeutic Factors in Psychoanalytic Treatment," in Clara Thompson, Milton Mazer, and Earl Witenberg, eds.,
An Outline of Psychoanalysis. New York: Random House, Inc., 1955,
pp. 436–54.

———. "Contribution to Psychological Factors in Anti-Social Behavior,"
Family, XIII (1932), 142–47.

———. "Development of the Fundamental Concepts of Psychoanalysis," in Franz Alexander and Helen Ross, eds., *Dynamic Psychiatry*.
Chicago: The University of Chicago Press, 1952, pp. 3–34.

———. "The Dynamics of Personality Development," *Social Casework*,
XXXII (1951), 139–43.

———. "Educative Influence of Personality Factors in the Environment," in Ernest W. Burgess *et al.*, *Environment and Education*.
Chicago: The University of Chicago, 1942, pp. 29–47, 62–66.

———. "Fundamental Concepts of Psychosomatic Research," *Psychosomatic Medicine*, III (1943), 205–10.

———. *Fundamentals of Psychoanalysis*. New York: W. W. Norton &
Company, Inc., 1948.

———. "Hostility and Fear in Social Life," *Social Forces*, XVII (1938),
27–29.

———. "Mental Hygiene and Criminology," tr. by E. F. Dexter, *Mental
Hygiene*, XIV (1930), 853–82.

———. "Neurosis and the Whole Personality," *International Journal
of Psychoanalysis*, VII (1926), 340–52.

———. "The Neurotic Character," *International Journal of Psychoanalysis*, XI (1930), 292–311.

———. *Our Age of Unreason*. New York: J. B. Lippincott Company,
1942; 2d ed., 1951.

———. "Psychoanalysis and Medicine," *Mental Hygiene*, XVI (1932),
63–84.

———. *Psychoanalysis and Psychotherapy*. New York: W. W. Norton
& Company, Inc., 1956.

268 BIBLIOGRAPHY

————. "Psychoanalysis Revised," *Psychoanalytic Quarterly*, XI (1940), 1–36.

————. "Psychoanalysis and Social Disorganization," *American Journal of Sociology*, XLII (1937), 781–813.

————. *The Psychoanalysis of the Total Personality*, tr. by Bernard Glueck and Bertram D. Lewin. New York: Nervous and Mental Disease Publishing Co., 1935.

————. "The Psychoanalyst Looks at Contemporary Art," in Robert Lindner, ed., *Explorations in Psychoanalysis*. New York: Julian Press, Inc. 1953, pp. 139–54.

————. "Psychoanalytic Aspect of Mental Hygiene and the Environment," *Mental Hygiene*, XXI (1937), 187–97.

————. *Psychosomatic Medicine*. New York: W. W. Norton & Company, Inc. 1950.

————. "A Review of Two Decades," in Franz Alexander and Helen Ross, eds., *Twenty Years of Psychoanalysis*. New York: W. W. Norton & Company, Inc., 1953, pp. 13–27.

————. "Sigmund Freud 1856–1939," *Archives of Neurology and Psychiatry*, XLIII (1940), 575–80.

————. "The Sociological and Biological Orientation of Psychoanalysis," *Mental Hygiene*, XX (1936), 232–48.

————. "A Tentative Analysis of the Variables in Personality Development," *American Journal of Orthopsychiatry*, VIII (1938), 587–91.

————. *The Western Mind in Transition*. New York: Random House, 1960.

Alexander, Franz, and William Healy, *Roots of Crime*. New York: Alfred A. Knopf, 1935.

Alexander, Franz, and Hugo Staub, *The Criminal, the Judge, and the Public*, tr. by Gregory Zilboorg. Glencoe, Ill.: The Free Press, 1956.

Freud, Sigmund. *Beyond the Pleasure Principle*, tr. by James Strachey. New York: Liveright Publishing Corporation, 1950.

————. "Character and Anal Erotism," tr. by R. C. McWatters, in *Collected Papers*. New York: Basic Books, Inc., 1959, II, 45-50.

————. *Civilization and Its Discontents*, tr. by Joan Riviere. London: The Hogarth Press Ltd., 1955.

————. " 'Civilized' Sexual Morality and Modern Nervousness," tr. by E. B. Herford and E. Colburn Mayne, in *Collected Papers*. New York: Basic Books, Inc., 1959, II, 76–99.

————. *The Ego and the Id*, tr. by Joan Riviere. London: The Hogarth Press Ltd., 1949.

————. *The Future of an Illusion*, tr. by W. D. Robson-Scott. Garden City, N.Y.: Doubleday & Company, Inc., 1957.

————. *A General Introduction to Psycho-Analysis*, tr. by Joan Riviere. New York: Liveright Publishing Corporation, 1935.

————. *Group Psychology and the Analysis of the Ego*, tr. by James Strachey. New York: Liveright Publishing Corporation, 1951.

————. *The History of the Psychoanalytic Movement*, in A. A. Brill, ed., *The Basic Writings of Sigmund Freud*. New York: Random House, Inc., 1938, pp. 933–77.

————. *The Interpretation of Dreams*, in A. A. Brill, ed., *The Basic*

Writings of Sigmund Freud. New York: Random House, Inc., 1938, pp. 181–549.

———. "The Libido Theory," tr. by James Strachey, in *Collected Papers.* New York: Basic Books, Inc., 1959, V, 131–35.

———. "The Moses of Michelangelo," tr. by Alix Strachey, in *Collected Papers.* New York: Basic Books, Inc., 1959, IV, 257–87.

———. *Moses and Monotheism,* tr. by Katherine Jones. New York: Alfred A. Knopf, 1939.

———. *New Introductory Lectures on Psycho-Analysis,* tr. by W. J. H. Sprott. New York: W. W. Norton & Company, Inc., 1933.

———. *An Outline of Psychoanalysis,* tr. by James Strachey. New York: W. W. Norton & Company, Inc., 1949.

———. *The Problem of Anxiety,* tr. by Henry Alden Bunker. New York: W. W. Norton & Company, Inc., 1936.

———. "Psycho-Analysis" [anon. tr.], *International Journal of Psycho-analysis,* XXIII (1942), 97–105.

———. "Some Character-Types Met with in Psycho-Analytic Work," tr. by E. Colburn Mayne, in *Collected Papers.* New York: Basic Books, Inc., 1959, IV, 318–41.

———. *Three Contributions to the Theory of Sex,* in A. A. Brill, ed., *The Basic Writings of Sigmund Freud.* New York: Random House, Inc., 1938, pp. 553–629.

———. *Totem and Taboo,* in A. A. Brill, ed., *The Basic Writings of Sigmund Freud.* New York: Random House, Inc., 1938, pp. 807–930.

———. "Why War?" tr. by James Strachey, in *Collected Papers.* New York: Basic Books, Inc., 1959, V, 273–87.

———. *Wit and Its Relation to the Unconscious,* in A. A. Brill, ed., *The Basic Writings of Sigmund Freud.* New York: Random House, Inc., 1938, pp. 633–803.

Fromm, Erich. *The Art of Loving.* New York: Harper & Brothers Publishers, 1956.

———. "The Contribution of the Social Sciences to Mental Hygiene," in Alfonso Millan, ed., *Proceedings of the Fourth International Congress on Mental Health.* Mexico [City]: La Prensa Médica Mexicana [1952], pp. 38–42.

———. "Die Entwicklung des Christusdogmas," *Imago,* XVI (1930), 305–73.

———. *Escape from Freedom.* New York: Rinehart & Company, Inc., 1941.

———. "Faith as a Character Trait," *Psychiatry,* V (1942), 307–19.

———. *The Forgotten Language.* New York: Holt, Rinehart & Winston, Inc., 1951.

———. "The Humanistic Implications of Instinctivistic 'Radicalism,'" *Dissent,* II (1955), 342–49.

———. "Individual and Social Origins of Neurosis," *American Sociological Review,* IX (1944), 380–84.

———. *Man for Himself.* New York: Rinehart and Company, Inc., 1947.

———. "Man Is Not a Thing," *Saturday Review,* XL (16 Mar. 1957), 9–11.

————. "Politik und Psychoanalyse," *Psychoanalytische Bewegung*, III (1931), 440–47.

————. *Psychoanalysis and Religion*. New Haven: Yale University Press, 1955.

————. "Psychoanalytic Characterology and Its Application to the Understanding of Culture," in S. Stansfeld Sargent and Marian W. Smith, eds., *Culture and Personality*. New York: The Viking Fund, Inc., 1949, pp. 1–12.

————. "Die psychoanalytische Charakterologie und ihre Bedeutung für die Sozialpsychologie," *Zeitschrift für Sozialforschung*, I (1932), 253–77.

————. "Remarks on the Problem of Free Association," *Psychiatric Research Reports 2*. Washington, D.C.: American Psychiatric Association, 1956, pp. 1–6.

————. *The Sane Society*. New York: Rinehart & Company, Inc., 1955.

————. "Selfishness and Self-Love," *Psychiatry*, II (1939), 507–23.

————. "Sex and Character," in Ruth Nanda Anshen, ed., *The Family: Its Function and Destiny*. New York: Harper & Brothers Publishers, 1949, pp. 375–92.

————. "Sex and Character: The Kinsey Report Viewed from the Standpoint of Psychoanalysis," in Jerome Himelhoch and Sylvia Fleis Fava, eds., *Sexual Behavior in American Society*. New York: W. W. Norton & Company, Inc., 1955, pp. 301–11.

————. *Sigmund Freud's Mission*. New York: Harper & Brothers Publishers, 1959.

————. "The Social Philosophy of 'Will Therapy,'" *Psychiatry*, II (1939), 229–37.

————. "Über Methode und Aufgabe einer analytischen Sozialpsychologie," *Zeitschrift für Sozialforschung*, I (1932), 28–54.

————. "What Shall We Do with Germany?," *Saturday Review of Literature*, XXVI (29 May 1943), 10.

Horney, Karen. "Can You Take a Stand?," *Journal of Adult Education*, XI (1939), 129–32.

————. "Culture and Neurosis," *American Sociological Review*, I (1936), 221–35.

————. "The Flight from Womanhood," *International Journal of Psychoanalysis*, VII (1926), 324–39.

————. "Der Kampf in der Kultur," *Vorträge des Institüts für Geschichte der Medizin an der Universität Leipzig*, IV (1931), 105–18.

————. "Maturity and the Individual," *American Journal of Psychoanalysis*, VII (1947), 85–87.

————. *Neurosis and Human Growth*. New York: W. W. Norton & Company, Inc., 1950.

————. *The Neurotic Personality of Our Time*. New York: W. W. Norton & Company, Inc., 1937.

————. *New Ways in Psychoanalysis*. New York: W. W. Norton & Company, Inc., 1939.

————. "On Difficulties in Dealing with the Transference," *News-Letter of the American Association of Psychiatric Social Workers*, V (1935), 1–5.

———. *Our Inner Conflicts.* New York: W. W. Norton & Company, Inc., 1945.

———. "The Problem of Feminine Masochism," *Psychoanalytic Review,* XXII (1935), 241–57.

———. *Self-Analysis.* New York: W. W. Norton & Company, Inc., 1942.

———. "Tenth Anniversary," *American Journal of Psychoanalysis,* XI (1951), 3–4.

———. "What Does the Analyst Do?," in Karen Horney, ed., *Are You Considering Psychoanalysis?* New York: W. W. Norton & Company, Inc., 1946.

———. "What Is a Neurosis?" *American Journal of Sociology,* XLV (1939), 426–32.

———, in Harold Kelman, ed., "Human Nature Can Change," *American Journal of Psychoanalysis,* XII (1952), 68.

———, in Harold Kelman, ed., "Psychoanalysis and Moral Values," *American Journal of Psychoanalysis,* X (1950), 64–65.

Kardiner, Abram. "Adaptational Theory: The Cross Cultural Point of View," in Sandor Rado and George E. Daniels, eds., *Changing Concepts of Psychoanalytic Medicine.* New York: Grune & Stratton, Inc., 1956, pp. 59–68.

———. "Cultural Factors in Prophylaxis," *American Journal of Orthopsychiatry,* XXVII (1957), 231–38.

———. *The Individual and His Society.* New York: Columbia University Press, 1946.

———. "New Attitudes Toward Sex," in Johnson E. Fairchild, ed., *Personal Problems & Psychological Frontiers.* New York: Sheridan House, 1957, pp. 121–36.

———. "Psychoanalysis and Psychology," *Philosophy of Science,* VIII (1941), 233–54.

———. "Psychodynamics and the Social Sciences," *Dialectica,* III (1949), 314–23.

———. *The Psychological Frontiers of Society.* New York: Columbia University Press, 1946.

———. "The Relation of Culture to Mental Disorder," in Paul H. Hoch and Joseph Zubin, eds., *Current Problems in Psychiatric Diagnosis.* New York: Grune & Stratton, 1953, pp. 157–79.

———. "Security, Cultural Restraints, Intrasocial Dependencies, and Hostilities," *Family,* XVIII (1937), 183–96.

———. *Sex and Morality.* New York: The Bobbs-Merrill Company, Inc., 1954.

Kardiner, Abram, and Lionel Ovesey, *The Mark of Oppression.* New York: W. W. Norton & Company, Inc., 1951.

Lasswell, Harold D. "Afterthoughts," see below: *Psychopathology and Politics.*

———. "Agitation," in *Encyclopedia of the Social Sciences.* New York: The Macmillan Company, 1930, I, 487–88.

———. "Bribery," in *Encyclopedia of the Social Sciences.* New York: The Macmillan Company, 1930, II, 690–92.

———. "Chauvinism," in *Encyclopedia of the Social Sciences.* New York: The Macmillan Company, 1930, III, 361.

————. "Compromise," in *Encyclopedia of the Social Sciences*. New York: The Macmillan Company, 1931, IV, 147–49.

————. "Current Studies of the Decision Process: Automation Versus Creativity," *Western Political Quarterly*, VIII (1955), 381–99.

————. "The Data of Psychoanalysis and the Social Sciences," *American Journal of Psychoanalysis*, VII (1947), 26–35.

————. *Democracy Through Public Opinion*. [Menasha, Wis.:] George Banta Publishing Company, 1941.

————. *Democratic Character*, in *The Political Writings of Harold D. Lasswell*. Glencoe, Ill.: The Free Press, 1951, pp. 465–525.

————. "The Developing Science of Democracy," in Leonard D. White, ed., *The Future of Government in the United States*. Chicago: The University of Chicago Press, 1942, pp. 25–48.

————. "The Elite Concept," in Harold D. Lasswell, Daniel Lerner, and C. Easton Rothwell, *The Comparative Study of Elites*. Stanford, Calif.: Stanford University Press, 1952, pp. 6–21.

————. "Faction," in *Encyclopedia of the Social Sciences*. New York: The Macmillan Company, 1931, VI, 49–51.

————. "Feuds," in *Encyclopedia of the Social Sciences*. New York: The Macmillan Company, 1931, VI, 220–21.

————. "Fraternizing," in *Encyclopedia of the Social Sciences*. New York: The Macmillan Company, 1931, VI, 425–27.

————. "A Hypothesis Rooted in the Preconceptions of a Single Civilization Tested by Bronislaw Malinowski," in Stuart A. Rice, ed., *Methods in Social Science*. Chicago: The University of Chicago Press, 1931, pp. 480–88.

————. "Impact of Psychoanalytic Thinking on the Social Sciences," in Leonard D. White, ed., *The State of the Social Sciences*. Chicago: The University of Chicago Press, 1957, pp. 84–115.

————. "The Moral Vocation of the Middle-Income Skill Group," *International Journal of Ethics*, XLV (1935), 127–37.

————. "Morale," in *Encyclopedia of the Social Sciences*. New York: The Macmillan Company, 1933, X, 640–42.

————. *National Security and Individual Freedom*. New York: McGraw-Hill Book Company, Inc., 1950.

————. "The Normative Impact of the Behavioral Sciences," *Ethics*, LXVII (1957) (Part II), 1–42.

————. "The Person: Subject and Object of Propaganda," *Annals*, CLXXIX (1935), 187–93.

————. "Political Power and Democratic Values," in Arthur Kornhauser, ed., *Problems of Power in American Democracy*. Detroit: Wayne State University Press, 1957, pp. 57–91.

————. "The Political Science of Science," *American Political Science Review*, L (1956), 961–79.

————. *Politics: Who Gets What, When, How*. New York: McGraw-Hill Book Company, Inc., 1936.

————. *Power and Personality*. New York: W. W. Norton & Company, Inc., 1948.

————. "Propaganda," in *Encyclopedia of the Social Sciences*. New York: The Macmillan Company, 1934, XII, 521–27.

————. "Propaganda and Mass Insecurity," in Alfred H. Stanton and

Stewart E. Perry, eds., *Personality and Political Crisis*. Glencoe, Ill.: The Free Press, 1951, pp. 15–43.

———. *Propaganda Technique in the World War*. New York: Alfred A. Knopf, 1927.

———. "A Provisional Classification of Symbol Data," *Psychiatry*, I (1938), 197–204.

———. "The Psychology of Hitlerism as a Response of the Lower Middle Classes to Continuing Insecurity," in *The Analysis of Political Behaviour*. London: Oxford University Press, 1947, pp. 235–45.

———. "Psychology Looks at Morals and Politics," *Ethics*, LI (1941), 325–36.

———. "Psychology and Political Science in the U.S.A.," in *Contemporary Political Science*. Paris: UNESCO, 1950, pp. 526–37.

———. *Psychopathology and Politics*. Chicago: The University of Chicago Press, 1931; reissued 1960, with "Afterthoughts" appended, by The Viking Press, New York.

———. "The Strategy of Revolutionary and War Propaganda," in Quincy Wright, ed., *Public Opinion and World-Politics*. Chicago: The University of Chicago Press, 1933, pp. 187–221.

———. "The Study of the Ill as a Method of Research into Political Personalities," *American Political Science Review*. XXIII (1929), 996–1001.

———. "The Study and Practice of Propaganda," in Harold D. Lasswell, Ralph D. Casey, and Bruce Lannes Smith, eds., *Propaganda and Promotional Activities*. Minneapolis: The University of Minnesota Press, 1935, pp. 3–27.

———. "The Theory of Political Propaganda," *American Political Science Review*, XXI (1927), 627–31.

———. "The Triple-Appeal Principle: A Contribution of Psychoanalysis to Political and Social Science," *American Journal of Sociology*, XXXVII (1932), 523–38.

———. "Types of Political Personalities," in *The Relation of the Individual to the Group*. Chicago: University of Chicago Press, 1928, pp. 159–68.

———. "Veränderungen an einer Versuchperson während einer kurzen Folge von psychoanalytischen Interviews," *Imago*, XXIII (1937), 375–80.

———. "What Psychiatrists and Social Scientists Can Learn from One Another," *Psychiatry*, I (1938), 33–39.

———. *World Politics Faces Economics*. New York: McGraw-Hill Book Company, Inc., 1945.

———. *World Politics and Personal Insecurity*. New York: McGraw-Hill Book Company, Inc., 1935.

———. *The World Revolution of Our Time*. Stanford, Calif.: Stanford University Press, 1951.

———. "The World Revolutionary Situation," in Carl J. Friedrich, ed., *Totalitarianism*. Cambridge: Harvard University Press, 1954, pp. 360–72.

Lasswell, Harold D., and Dorothy Blumenstock, *World Revolutionary Propaganda*. New York: Alfred A. Knopf, 1939.

Lasswell, Harold D., and Abraham Kaplan, *Power and Society*. New Haven: Yale University Press, 1950.

Lasswell, Harold D., Nathan Leites, *et al.*, *Language of Politics*. New York: George W. Stewart, Publisher, Inc., 1949.

Lasswell, Harold D., and Myres S. McDougal, "Legal Education and Public Policy: Professional Training in the Public Interest," in *The Analysis of Political Behaviour*. London: Oxford University Press, 1947, pp. 21–119.

Sullivan, Harry Stack. *Clinical Studies in Psychiatry*. New York: W. W. Norton & Company, Inc., 1956.

———. *Conceptions of Modern Psychiatry*. Washington, D.C.: The William Alanson White Psychiatric Foundation, 1947.

———. "The Cultural Revolution to End War," *Psychiatry*, IX (1946), 81–87.

———. "Environmental Factors in Etiology and Course Under Treatment of Schizophrenia," *Medical Journal and Record*, CXXXIII (1931), 19–22.

———. "The Illusion of Personal Individuality," *Psychiatry*, XIII (1950), 317–32.

———. *The Interpersonal Theory of Psychiatry*. New York: W. W. Norton & Company, Inc., 1953.

———. "The Meaning of Anxiety in Psychiatry and in Life," *Psychiatry*, XI (1948), 1–13.

———. "Mental Disorders," in *Encyclopedia of the Social Sciences*. New York: The Macmillan Company, 1933, X, 313–19.

———. "Mental-Health Potentialities of the World Health Organization," *Mental Hygiene*, XXXII (1948), 27–36.

———. "A Note on Formulating the Relationship of the Individual and the Group," *American Journal of Sociology*, XLIV (1939), 932–37.

———. "A Note on the Implications of Psychiatry, the Study of Interpersonal Relations, for Investigations in the Social Sciences," *American Journal of Sociology*, XLII (1937), 848–61.

———. "Notes on Investigation, Therapy, and Education in Psychiatry and Their Relations to Schizophrenia," *Psychiatry*, X (1947), 271–80.

———. *The Psychiatric Interview*. New York: W. W. Norton & Company, Inc., 1954.

———. "Psychiatry," in *Encyclopedia of the Social Sciences*. New York: The Macmillan Company, 1934, XII, 578–80.

———. "Psychiatry: Introduction to the Study of Interpersonal Relations," *Psychiatry*, I (1938), 121–34.

———. "Socio-Psychiatric Research. Its Implications for the Schizophrenia Problem and for Mental Hygiene," *American Journal of Psychiatry*, X (New Series) (1931), 977–91.

———. "Tensions Interpersonal and International: A Psychiatrist's View," in Hadley Cantril, ed., *Tensions That Cause Wars*. Urbana, Ill.: University of Illinois Press, 1950, pp. 79–138.

———. "Towards a Psychiatry of Peoples," *Psychiatry*, XI (1948), 105–16.

———. "Training of the General Medical Student in Psychiatry," *American Journal of Orthopsychiatry*, I (1931), 371–79.

SECONDARY SOURCES

Abraham, Karl. *Selected Papers of Karl Abraham*, tr. by Douglas Bryan and Alix Strachey. London: The Hogarth Press Ltd., 1949.
Anonymous. Review of Harry Stack Sullivan, *Conceptions of Modern Psychiatry. Psychiatric Quarterly*, XXI (1947), 494–99.
Aristotle. *Nicomachean Ethics. (The Ethics of Aristotle*, tr. by D. P. Chase. New York: E. P. Dutton and Company, Inc., 1950.)
———. *Politics. (The Politics of Aristotle*, tr. by Ernest Barker. London: Oxford University Press, 1950.)
Ascoli, Max. Review of Harold D. Lasswell, *Politics: Who Gets What, When, How. Nation*, CXLII (1936), 425–26.
Bain, Read. Review of Abram Kardiner, *The Individual and His Society. American Sociological Review*, V (1940), 254–57.
Bentham, Jeremy. *Introduction to the Principles of Morals and Legislation.* Oxford: Basil Blackwell, 1948.
Blitsten, Dorothy R. "The Significance of Harry Stack Sullivan's Theories for Social Science." New York: unpublished dissertation for Columbia University, 1952.
Bok, Curtis. *Star Wormwood.* New York: Alfred A. Knopf, 1959.
Briggs, Asa. Review of Erich Fromm, *The Sane Society. New Statesman and Nation*, LI (1956), 739.
Brill, A. A. "Introduction" to *The Basic Writings of Sigmund Freud.* New York: Random House, Inc., 1938, pp. 3–32.
———. "Reminiscences of Freud," *Psychoanalytic Quarterly*, IX (1940), 177–83.
Carr, E. H. *The Twenty Years' Crisis.* London: Macmillan & Co. Ltd., 1948.
Cervantes de Saavedra, Miguel. *The Adventures of Don Quixote*, tr. by J. M. Cohen. London: Penguin Books, 1954.
Commager, Henry Steele. *The American Mind.* London: Oxford University Press, 1950.
Current Biography. New York: The H. W. Wilson Company, 1942.
Davis, Kingsley. "Mental Hygiene and the Class Structure," in Patrick Mullahy, ed., *A Study of Interpersonal Relations.* New York: Hermitage Press, Inc., 1950, pp. 364–85.
Devereux, George, ed., *Culture and Mental Disorders*, by Ralph Linton. Springfield, Ill.: Charles C Thomas, Publisher, 1956.
Easton, David. "Harold Lasswell: Policy Scientist for a Democratic Society," *Journal of Politics*, XII (1950), 450–77.
Esfandiary, Fereidoun. "Is It the Mysterious—or Neurotic—East?" in *The New York Times Magazine*, March 24, 1957; pp. 13, 70–72.
Fenichel, Otto. Review of Karen Horney, *New Ways in Psychoanalysis. Psychoanalytic Quarterly*, IX (1940), 114–21.
Frank, Lawrence K. "Society as the Patient," *American Journal of Sociology*, XLII (1936), 335–44.
Freeman, Nathan. "Concepts of Adler and Horney," *American Journal of Psychoanalysis*, X (1950), 18–26.
Gervais, Terence White. "Freud and the Culture-Psychologists," *British Journal of Psychology*, XLVI (1955), 293–305.

Gewirth, Alan. Review of Erich Fromm, *The Sane Society. Ethics,* LXVI (1956), 289–92.
Goldman, Eric F. *Rendezvous with Destiny.* New York: Alfred A. Knopf, 1952.
Green, Arnold W. "Sociological Analysis of Horney and Fromm," *American Journal of Sociology,* LI (1946), 533–40.
Green, T. H. *Lectures on the Principles of Political Obligation.* London: Longmans, Green and Co., 1950.
Hadley, Ernest E., ed., "Escape from Freedom: a Synoptic Series of Reviews," *Psychiatry,* V (1942), 109–34.
Hall, Jerome. "Psychiatry and Criminal Responsibility," *Yale Law Journal,* LXV (1956), 761–85.
Harris, A. D. "Let Your Soul Alone," *New Statesman and Nation,* XLII (1951), 288.
Harris, Catherine. "Sullivan's Concept of Scientific Method as Applied to Psychiatry," *Philosophy of Science,* XXI (1954), 33–43.
"Insanity and the Criminal Law," *University of Chicago Law Review,* XXII (1955), 317–404.
Jacobson, Edith. Review of Harry Stack Sullivan, *Conceptions of Modern Psychiatry. Psychoanalytic Quarterly,* XVII (1948), 393–95.
James, Walter T. "Karen Horney and Erich Fromm in Relation to Alfred Adler," *Individual Psychology Bulletin,* VI (1947), 105–16.
Jászi, Oscar. Review of Harold D. Lasswell, *World Politics and Personal Insecurity. International Journal of Ethics,* XLV (1935), 440–48.
Jones, Ernest. *The Life and Work of Sigmund Freud.* New York: Basic Books, Inc., 3 vols., 1953, 1955, 1957.
———. Review of Karen Horney, *The Neurotic Personality of Our Time. International Journal of Psychoanalysis,* XXI (1940), 240–41.
Juvenile Delinquency. Washington, D.C.: United States Senate, 1957. (Senate Report No. 130, 85th Congress, 1st Session.)
Kariel, Henry S. "The Normative Pattern of Erich Fromm's Escape from Freedom," *Journal of Politics,* XIX (1957), 640–54.
Kroeber, A. L. "Totem and Taboo: An Ethnologic Psychoanalysis," *American Anthropologist,* XXII (New Series) (1920), 48–55.
Laski, Harold J. *A Grammar of Politics.* London: George Allen & Unwin Ltd., 1950.
———. *The State in Theory and Practice.* New York: The Viking Press, 1938.
Linton, Ralph. "The Concept of National Character," in Alfred H. Stanton and Stewart E. Perry, eds., *Personality and Political Crisis.* Glencoe, Ill.: The Free Press, 1951, pp. 133–50.
Malinowski, Bronislaw. *Sex and Repression in Savage Society.* New York: Harcourt, Brace & Company, Inc., 1927.
Mandelstam, Paul. "The Freudian Impact Upon Contemporary Political Thinking." Cambridge, Mass.: unpublished dissertation for Harvard University, 1952.
Marx, Karl. *The Communist Manifesto,* in Harold J. Laski, ed., *Communist Manifesto Socialist Landmark.* London: George Allen & Unwin Ltd., 1954.
McLean, Helen V. "A Few Comments on 'Moses and Monotheism,'" *Psychoanalytic Quarterly,* IX (1940), 207–13.

Menninger, Karl. "Loneliness in the Modern World," *Nation,* CLIV (1942), 317.

Mill, John Stuart. *Autobiography.* New York: Columbia University Press, 1948.

———. *A System of Logic Ratiocinative and Inductive.* 8th ed. London: Longmans, Green and Co., 1941.

Montesquieu, Baron de. *The Spirit of the Laws,* tr. by Thomas Nugent. New York: Hafner Publishing Company, 1949.

Mullahy, Patrick. "Introduction" to *A Study of Interpersonal Relations.* New York: Hermitage Press, Inc., 1950, pp. xv–xxxi.

———. "Philosophical Anthropology Versus Empirical Science," *Psychiatry,* XVIII (1955), 399–409.

———. "The Theories of H. S. Sullivan," in *The Contributions of Harry Stack Sullivan.* New York: Hermitage House, 1952, pp. 13–59.

Murphy, Gardner, and Elizabeth Cattell. "Sullivan and Field Theory," in Patrick Mullahy, ed., *The Contributions of Harry Stack Sullivan.* New York: Hermitage House, 1952, pp. 161–79.

Murphy, William F. Review of Harry Stack Sullivan, *The Interpersonal Theory of Psychiatry. Psychoanalytic Quarterly,* XXII (1954), 446–50. *The New York Times.*

Oberndorf, C. P. *A History of Psychoanalysis in America.* New York: Grune & Stratton, 1953.

Orwell, George. *Nineteen Eighty-Four.* London: Penguin Books, 1954.

Plato. *Apology,* in *The Last Days of Socrates,* tr. by Hugh Tredennick. London: Penguin Books, 1955, pp. 19–50.

———. *Republic. (The Republic of Plato,* tr. by Francis Macdonald Cornford. New York: Oxford University Press, 1947.)

Portnoy, Isidore. Review of Karen Horney, *Neurosis and Human Growth. American Journal of Psychoanalysis,* XI (1951), 63–71.

Pumpian-Mindlin, E. "The Position of Psychoanalysis in Relation to the Biological and Social Sciences," in E. Pumpian-Mindlin, ed., *Psychoanalysis as Science.* Stanford, Calif.: Stanford University Press, 1952, pp. 125–58.

Riesman, David. "The Themes of Work and Play in the Structure of Freud's Thought," in *Individualism Reconsidered.* Glencoe, Ill.: The Free Press, 1954, pp. 310–33.

Rioch, Janet MacKenzie. "The Transference Phenomenon in Psychoanalytic Therapy," in Patrick Mullahy, ed., *A Study of Interpersonal Relations.* New York: Hermitage Press, Inc., 1950, pp. 80–97.

Roche, Philip Q. "Criminal Responsibility," in Paul H. Hoch and Joseph Zubin, eds., *Psychiatry and the Law.* New York: Grune & Stratton, 1955, pp. 107–15.

Róheim, Géza. "Society and the Individual," *Psychoanalytic Quarterly,* IX (1940), 526–45.

Sapir, Edward. "Why Cultural Anthropology Needs the Psychiatrist," in Patrick Mullahy, ed., *A Study of Interpersonal Relations.* New York: Hermitage Press, Inc., 1950, pp. 239–49.

Scheidlinger, Saul. *Psychoanalysis and Group Behavior.* New York: W. W. Norton & Company, Inc., 1952.

Schoenwald, Richard L. *Freud: The Man and His Mind 1856–1956.* New York: Alfred A. Knopf, 1956.

Schwartz, Delmore. "The Sick City and the Family Romance," *Nation*, CLXII (1946), 46–48.

Sobeloff, Simon E. "Insanity and the Criminal Law: From McNaghten to Durham, and Beyond," *American Bar Association Journal*, XLI (1955), 783–86, 877–79.

Stamps, Norman L. *Why Democracies Fail*. Notre Dame, Ind.: University of Notre Dame Press, 1957.

Stanton, Alfred H. "Sullivan's Conceptions," in Patrick Mullahy, ed., *The Contributions of Harry Stack Sullivan*. New York: Hermitage House, 1952, pp. 61–86.

Stern, Adolph. Review of Karen Horney, *New Ways in Psychoanalysis*. *International Journal of Psychoanalysis*, XXI (1940), 360–63.

Strupp, Hans H. "Infantile Sexuality in the Theories of Freud & Sullivan," *Complex*, VII (1952), 51–62.

Thompson, Clara. *Psychoanalysis: Evolution and Development*. New York: Hermitage House, Inc., 1950.

Weber, Max. *The Protestant Ethic and the Spirit of Capitalism*, tr. by Talcott Parsons. London: George Allen & Unwin Ltd., 1948.

Weiss, Frederick A. "Karen Horney—Her Early Papers," *American Journal of Psychoanalysis*, XIV (1954), 55–64.

Westermarck, Edward. *Three Essays on Sex and Marriage*. London: Macmillan & Co. Ltd., 1934.

Winner, Percy. Review of Harold D. Lasswell, *Power and Personality*. *Psychoanalytic Quarterly*, XVIII (1949), 240–42.

Zilboorg, Gregory. "The Contribution of Psycho-Analysis to Forensic Psychiatry," *International Journal of Psycho-Analysis*, XXXVII (1956), 318–24.

———. *Sigmund Freud*. New York: Charles Scribner's Sons, 1951.

Zuger, Bernard. Review of Erich Fromm, *Man for Himself*. *American Journal of Psychoanalysis*, VIII (1948), 63–65.

INDEX

75, 184; skills, 170–71, 172; preventive politics, 179–84, 206, 230
LeBon, Gustave, 28
Lenin, Vladimir, 2
Libido: Freud on, 15–17, 22, 26, 28, 40, 41, 53, 99; Neo-Freudians on, 49–50, 53–54, 214, 216; Horney on, 53–54; Sullivan on, 54, 100, 101, 245; Fromm on, 78–80, 150; Lasswell on, 158, 159–61, 163
Linton, Ralph, 74
Locke, John, 2, 37–39
Love: Freud on, 11, 15–16, 240; Horney on, 45–46, 91, 92, 110; Kardiner on, 48, 126, 145–46; Alexander on, 141; Fromm on, 152, 195–97, 216; Neo-Freudians on, 216–17
Luther, Martin, 2

Machiavelli, Niccolo, 35, 36, 156, 183
M'Naghten rule, 136
Malinowski, Bronislaw, 24
Marx, Karl, 2, 37, 40–42, 78, 96, 187
Matriarchy, 47–48, 87–89, 202
Mental health, 64, 95–96, 98, 210–12, 214
Mental illness: Freud on, 4, 5, 6–7, 40; Lasswell on, 7; Sullivan on, 58, 61, 99, 109; Fromm on, 86–88, 151; Horney on, 109; Alexander on, 114–18, 129–34 passim, 140. See also Neurosis
Metapsychology, 17–19, 22, 56
Michelangelo, 31
Middle class, 124–27, 152, 170, 172, 189–90, 218
Mill, James, 33
Mill, John Stuart, 33, 34, 266
Montesquieu, 2, 266
Morale, 164–65
Moses, 26, 28, 31–32

National character, 72, 222
Nationalism, 189
Natural law, 84–85, 86–87, 89, 190–91, 202, 205–6
Negro, American, 142–47, 223
Neo-Freudians on: Oedipus complex, 45, 49–50, 68, 231; instincts, 49–50, 68; libido, 49–50, 53–54, 214, 216; social institutions, 49–50, 210, 211–12, 221–23; environment, 49–50, 64–65, 68, 215; ego, 55–56, 69, 216; interpersonal relations, 62–64, 68, 215, 220–21, 224–26; transference, 64; adaptation, 68, 214, 215; childhood and family, 69, 230–31; politics, 106–7, 169, 184–85; human nature, 212–18,

219; psychic growth, 213–15, 218; love, 216–17
Neurosis: Freud on, 6–7, 10, 11, 18, 19, 21, 29, 213; Horney on, 55, 90–95, 107, 109; Kardiner on, 56; Alexander on, 114–18, 130–31. See also Mental illness

Oedipus complex: Freud on, 18, 19–23, 25, 27, 40, 41, 88–89; Neo-Freudians on, 45, 49–50, 68, 231; Horney on, 45–46; Fromm on, 46–48, 88–89, 204; Kardiner on, 48–49, 73, 122–23; Sullivan on, 100; Lasswell on, 158, 159–61, 164
Ogburn, William F., 117
Ontogeny, 19, 20–21, 29, 31, 34, 35, 37, 38, 47, 48–49, 55, 68–69, 87, 131–32
Ovesey, Lionel, 223

Paine, Thomas, 84
Parapraxes, 8
Parataxic distortion, 64, 106, 179, 230, 252
Patriarchy, 47–48, 78–89, 202
Phylogeny, 19, 20–21, 29, 31, 34, 35, 37, 38, 41, 42, 47, 48–49, 55, 68–69, 87, 131–32
Plato, 2, 34, 35, 36, 67, 167, 171, 219, 222, 230, 240
Pleasure, 9, 10, 32, 35, 99–100
Pleasure principle, 9, 17, 35, 64, 92, 103, 133, 139, 141, 158
Policy sciences, 175, 184
Political formula, 159, 170
Political personality, 159–61, 169–70
Politics: Freud on, 23, 28, 38; Sullivan on, 106; Neo-Freudians on, 106–7, 169, 184–85; Alexander on, 119–21; Fromm on, 152, 154–55, 199, 200; of psychopathology, 157–70, 177, 183–84; of democracy, 168, 170–75, 181–82, 184; of power, 169–70, 184; of prevention, 179–84, 206, 230
Power, 118, 125, 169–70, 173–75, 184
Primal horde, 22–23, 26, 28, 37
Primary institutions, 49, 55, 71, 72–73, 122, 123
Projective systems, see Secondary institutions
Psychoanalysis, use of, by: Freud, 4, 5, 6–7, 12, 42, 189–90; Sullivan, 57, 58, 97, 105; Alexander, 65–68, 110–11, 121, 130, 132, 134, 250; Kardiner, 72, 75, 127, 142–43, 144–45, 223–24; Fromm, 78–80, 85–86, 102, 187, 203–5, 264; Horney, 89–90, 92, 96, 109,